Fairy Mythology

Fairy Mythology
Romance and Superstition of Various Countries 1
Author: Thomas Keightley

Original publication: The Fairy Mythology, Illustrative of the Romance and Superstition of
                          Various Countries (1870)
Cover image: *Femme Papillon* (1888), Luis Ricardo Falero (1851 – 1896)
Lay-out: www.burokd.nl

ISBN 978-94-92355-09-6

VAMzzz Publishing
P.O. Box 3340
1001 AC Amsterdam
The Netherlands
www.vamzzz.com
contactvamzzz@gmail.com

FAIRY
MYTHOLOGY
Romance and Superstition
of Various Countries 1

Thomas Keightley

VAMzzz PUBLISHING

contents

To
the Right Honourable
Francis Earl of Ellesmere,
in Testimony of
Esteem and Respect for Public and Private Virtue,
Literary Taste, Talent, and Acquirements,
and Patronage of Literature and the Arts.

Preface

A PREFACE is to a book what a prologue is to a play—a usual, often agreeable, but by no means necessary precursor. It may therefore be altered or omitted at pleasure. I have at times exercised this right, and this is the third I have written for the present work.

In the first, after briefly stating what had given occasion to it, I gave the germs of the theory which I afterwards developed in the *Tales and Popular Fictions*. The second contained the following paragraph:

"I never heard of any one who read it that was not pleased with it. It was translated into German as soon as it appeared, and was very favourably received. Goethe thought well of it. Dr. Jacob Grimm— perhaps the first authority on these matters in Europe—wrote me a letter commending it, and assuring me that even to *him* it offered something new; and I was one Christmas most agreeably surprised by the receipt of a letter from Vienna, from the celebrated orientalist, Jos Von Hammer, informing me that it had been the companion of a journey he had lately made to his native province of Styria, and had afforded much pleasure and information to himself and to some ladies of high rank and cultivated minds in that country. The initials at the end of the preface, he said, led him to suppose it was a work of mine. So far for the Continent. In this country, when I mention the name of Robert Southey as that of one who has more than once expressed his decided approbation of this performance, I am sure I shall have said quite enough to satisfy any one that the work is not devoid of merit."

I could now add many names of distinguished persons who have been pleased with this work and its pendant, the *Tales and Popular Fictions*. I shall only mention that of the late Mr. Douce, who, very shortly before his death, on the occasion of the publication of this last work, called on me to assure me that "it was many, many years indeed, since he had read a book which had yielded him so much delight."

The contents of the work which gave such pleasure to this learned antiquary are as follows:—

I. Introduction—Similarity of Arts and Customs—Similarity of Names—Origin of the Work—Imitation—Casual Coincidence—Milton—Dante.

II. The Thousand and One Nights—Bedoween Audience around a Story-teller—Cleomades and Claremond—Enchanted Horses—Peter of Provence and the fair Maguelone.

III. The Pleasant Nights—The Dancing Water, the Singing Apple, and the Beautiful Green Bird—The Three Little Birds—Lactantius—Ulysses and Sindbad.

IV. The Shah-Nameh—Roostem and Soohrab—Conloch and Cuchullin—Macpherson's Ossian—Irish Antiquities.

V. The Pentamerone—Tale of the Serpent—Hindoo Legend.

VI. Jack the Giant-killer—The Brave Tailoring—Thor's Journey to Utgard—Ameen of Isfshan and the Ghool—The Lion and the

Never, I am convinced, did any one enter on a literary career with more reluctance than I did when I found it to be my only resource—fortune being gone, ill health and delicacy of constitution excluding me from the learned professions, want of interest from every thing else. As I journeyed to the metropolis, I might have sung with the page whom Don Quixote met going a-soldiering:

A la guerra me lieva—mi necesidad,
Si tuviera dineros—no fuera en verdad:

For of all arts and professions in this country, that of literature is the least respected and the worst remunerated. There is something actually degrading in the expression "an author by trade," which I have seen used even of Southey, and that by one who did not mean to disparage him in the slightest degree. My advice to those who may read these pages is to shun literature, if not already blest with competence.

One of my earliest literary friends in London was T. Crofton Croker, who was then engaged in collecting materials for the *Fairy Legends of the South of Ireland*. He of course applied to his friends for aid and information; and I, having most leisure, and, I may add, most knowledge, was able to give him the greatest amount of assistance. My inquiries on the subject led, to the writing of the present work, which was succeeded by the *Mythology of Ancient Greece and Italy*, and the *Tales and Popular Fictions*; so that, in effect, if Mr. Croker had not planned the *Fairy Legends*, these works, be their value what it may, would in all probability never have been written.

Writing and reading about Fairies some may deem to be the mark of a trilling turn of mind. On this subject I have given my ideas in the Conclusion; here I will only remind such critics, that as soon as this work was completed, I commenced, and wrote in the space of a few weeks, my *Outlines of History*; and whatever the faults of that work may be, no one has ever reckoned among them want of vigour in either thought or expression.. It was also necessary, in order to write this work and its pendent, to be able to read, perhaps, as many as eighteen or twenty different languages, dialects, and modes of orthography, and to employ different styles both in prose and verse. At all events, even if it were trifling, *dulce est despere in loco;* and I shall never forget the happy hours it caused me, especially those spent over the black-letter pages of the French romances of chivalry, in the old reading-room of the British Museum.

Many years have elapsed since this work was first published. In that period much new matter has appeared in various works, especially in the valuable Deutsche Mythologie of Dr. Grimm. Hence it will be found to be greatly enlarged, particularly in the sections of England and Prance. I have also inserted much which want of space obliged me to omit in the former edition. In its present form, I am presumptuous enough to expect that it may live for many years, and be an authority on the subject of popular lore. The active industry of the Grimms, of Thiele, and others, had collected the popular traditions of various countries. I came then and gathered in the harvest, leaving little, I apprehend, but gleanings for future writers on this subject. The legends will probably fade fast away from the popular memory; it is not likely that any one will relate those which I have given over again; and it therefore seems more probable that this volume may in future be reprinted, with notes and additions. For human nature will ever remain unchanged; the love of gain and of material enjoyments, omnipotent as it appears to be at present, will never totally extinguish the higher and purer aspirations of mind; and there will always be those, however limited in number, who will desire to know how the former dwellers of earth thought, felt, and acted. For these mythology, as connected with religion and history, will always have attractions.

–Thomas Keightley, *England*

Introduction

In olde days of the King Artour,
Of which that Bretons spoken gret honour,
All was this lond fulfilled of faërie;
The elf-qrene with hir jolts companie
Danced full oft in many a grene mede.
CHAUCER.

Origin of the belief in Fairies

ACCORDING to a well-known law of our nature, effects suggest causes; and another law, perhaps equally general, impels us to ascribe to the actual and efficient cause the attribute of intelligence. The mind of the deepest philosopher is thus acted upon equally with that of the peasant or the savage; the only difference lies in the nature of the intelligent cause at which they respectively stop. The one pursues the chain of cause and effect, and traces out its various links till he arrives at the great intelligent cause of all, however he may designate him; the other, when unusual phenomena excite his attention, ascribes their production to the immediate agency of some of the inferior beings recognised by his legendary creed.

The action of this latter principle must forcibly strike the minds of those who disdain not to bestow a portion of their attention on the popular legends and traditions of different countries. Every extraordinary appearance is found to have its extraordinary cause assigned; a cause always connected with the history or religion, ancient or modern, of the country, and not unfrequently varying with a change of faith. [a]

The noises and eruptions of Aetna and Stromboli were, in ancient times, ascribed to Typhon or Vulcan, and at this day the popular belief connects them with the infernal regions. The sounds resembling the clanking of chains, hammering of iron, and blowing of bellows, once to be heard in the island of Barrie, were made by the fiends whom Merlin had set to work to frame the wail of brass to surround Caermarthen. [b] The marks which natural causes have impressed on the solid and unyielding granite rock were produced, according to the popular creed, by the contact of the hero, the saint, or the god: masses of stone, resembling domestic implements in form, were the toys, or the corresponding implements of the heroes and giants of old. Grecian imagination ascribed to the galaxy or milky way an origin in the teeming breast of the queen of heaven: marks appeared in the petals of flowers on the occasion of a youth's or a hero's untimely death: the rose derived its present hue from the blood of Venus, as she hurried barefoot through the woods and lawns; while the professors of Islam, less fancifully, refer the origin of this flower to the moisture that exuded from the sacred person of their prophet. Under a purer form of religion, the cruciform stripes which mark the back and shoulders of the patient ass first appeared, according to the popular tradition, when the Son of God condescended to enter the Holy City, mounted on that animal; and a fish only to be found in the sea [the Haddock] stills bears the impress of the finger and thumb of the apostle, who drew him out of the waters of Lake Tiberias to take the tribute-money that lay in his mouth. The repetition of the voice among the hills is, in Norway and Sweden, ascribed to the Dwarfs mocking the human speaker, while the more elegant fancy of Greece gave birth to Echo, a nymph who pined for love, and who still fondly repeats the accents that she hears. The magic scenery occasionally presented on the waters of the Straits of Messina is produced by the power of the Fata Morgana; the gossamers that float through the haze of an autumnal morning, are woven, by the ingenious dwarfs; the verdant circlets in the mead are traced beneath the light steps of the dancing elves; and St. Cuthbert forges and fashions the beads that bear his name, and lie scattered along the shore of Lindisfarne. [c]

In accordance with these laws, we find in most countries a popular belief in different classes of beings distinct from men, and from the higher orders of divinities. These beings are usually believed to inhabit, in the caverns of earth, or the depths of the waters, a region of their own. They generally excel mankind in power and in knowledge, and like them are subject to the inevitable laws of death, though after a more prolonged period of existence.

How these classes were first called into existence it is not easy to say; but if as some assert, all the ancient systems of heathen religion were devised by philosophers for the instruction of rude tribes by appeals to their senses, we might suppose that the minds which peopled the skies with their thousands and tens of thousands of divinities gave birth also to the inhabitants of the field and flood, and that the numerous tales of their exploits and adventures are the production of poetic fiction or rude invention. It may further be observed, that not unfrequently a change of religious faith has invested with dark and malignant attributes beings once the objects of love, confidence, and veneration. [d]

It is not our intention in the following pages to treat of the awful or lovely deities of Olympus, Valhalla, or Meru. Our subject is less aspiring; and we confine ourselves to those beings who are our fellow-inhabitants of earth, whose manners we aim to describe, and whose deeds we propose to record. We write of FAIRIES, FAYS, ELVES, *aut alio quo nomine gaudent.*

Origin of the word Fairy

Like every other word in extensive use, whose derivation is not historically certain, the word Fairy has obtained various and opposite etymons. Meyric Casaubon, and those who like him deduce everything from a classic source, however unlikely, derive Fairy from Φήρ, a Homeric name of the Centaurs; [e] or think that *fée,* whence Fairy, is the last syllable of *nympha.* Sir W. Ouseley derives it from the Hebrew פאר (*peer*), *to adorn;* Skinner, from the Anglo-Saxon *ranan, to fare, to go;* others from Feres, companions, or think that Fairy-folk is *quasi* Fair-folk. Finally, it has been queried if it be not Celtic. [f]

But no theory is so plausible, or is supported by such names, as that which deduces the English Fairy from the Persian Peri. It is said that the Paynim foe, whom the warriors of the Cross encountered in Palestine, spoke only Arabic; the alphabet of which language, it is well known, possesses no *p,* and therefore organically substitutes an *f* in such foreign words as contain the former letter; consequently Peri became, in the mouth of an Arab, Feri, whence the crusaders and pilgrims, who carried back to Europe the marvellous tales of Asia, introduced into the West the Arabo-Persian word *Fairy.* It is further added, that the Morgain or Morgana, so celebrated in old romance, is Merjan Peri, equally celebrated all over the East.

All that is wanting to this so very plausible theory is something like proof, and some slight agreement with the ordinary rules of etymology. Had Feërie, or Fairy, originally signified the individual in the French and English, the only languages in which the word occurs, we might feel disposed to acquiesce in it. But they do not: and even if they did, how should we deduce from them the Italian Fata, and the Spanish Fads or Hada, (words which unquestionably stand for the same imaginary being,) unless on the principle by which Menage must have deduced Lutin from Lemur—the first letter being the same in both? As to the fair Merjan Peri (D'Herbelot calls her Merjan Banou—D'Herbelot *titre* Mergian says, "C'est du nom de cette Fée quo nos anciens romans ont formé celui de *Morgante la Déconnue.*" He here confounds Morgana with Urganda, and he has been followed in his mistake. D'Herbelot also thinks it possible that*Féerie* may come from *Peri;* but he regards the common derivation from *Fata* as much more probable. Cambrian etymologists, by the way, *say* that Morgain is Mor Gwynn, the *White Maid.*), we fancy a little too much importance has been attached to her. Her name, as far as we can leant, only occurs in the Cahermân Nâmeh, a Turkish romance, though perhaps translated from the Persian.

The foregoing etymologies, it is to be observed, are all the conjectures of English scholars; for the English is the only language in which the name of the individual, Fairy, has the canine letter to afford any foundation for them.

Leaving, then, these sports of fancy, we will discuss the true origin of the words used in the Romanic languages to express the being which we name Fairy of Romance. These are *Faée, Fée,*French; *Fada,* Provençal (whence *Hada,* Spanish); and *Fata,* Italian.

The root is evidently, we think, the Latin *fatum.* In the fourth century of our aera we find this word made plural, and even feminine, and used as the equivalent of Parcae. On the reverse of a gold medal of the Emperor Diocletian are three female figures, with the legend *Fatis victricibus;* a *cippus,* found at Valencia in Spain, has on one of its sides *Fat. Q. Fabius ex voto,* and on the other, three female figures, with the attributes of the Moerae or Parcae. [these two instances are given by Mdlle. Amélie Bosquet (La Normandie Romanesque, etc. p. 91.) from Dom Martin, *Rel. des Gautois,* ii. ch. 23 and 24.] In this last place the gender is uncertain, but the figures would lead us to suppose it feminine. On the other hand, Ausonius [Gryphus ternaril numeri] has *tres Charites,, tria Fata;* and Procopius [Do Bell. Got. i. 25] names a building at the Roman Forum τά τρία, adding οὗτω γάρ 'Ρωμας τάς μοίρας νενομίκαδι καλείν. The Fate or Fata, then, being persons, and their name coinciding so exactly with the modem terms, and. it being observed that the Moerae were, at the birth of Meleager, just as the Fees were at that of Ogier le Danois, and. other heroes of romance and tale, their identity has been at once asserted, and this is now, we believe, the most prevalent theory. To this it may be added, that in Gervase of Tilbury, and other writers of the thirteenth century, the Fada or Fée seems to be regarded as a being different from human kind. [8]

On the other hand, in a passage presently to be quoted from a celebrated old romance, we shall meet a definition of the word *Fée,* which expressly asserts that such a being was nothing more than a woman skilled in magic; and such, on examination, we shall find to have been all the Fées of the romances of chivalry and of the popular tales; in effect, that *fée* is a participle, and the words *dame* or *femme* is—to be understood.

In the middle ages there was in use a Latin verb, *fatare,* [h] derived from *fatum* or *fata,* and signifying to enchant. This verb was adopted *by* the Italian, Provençal [1] and Spanish languages; in French it became, according to the analogy of that tongue, *faer, féer.* Of this verb the past participle is *faé, fé;* hence in the romances we continually meet with *les chevalier, faés, les dames faées, Oberon la faé, le cheval étoit faé, la clef était fée,* and such like. We have further, we think, demonstrated [see our Virgil, Excurs. ix.] that it was the practice of the Latin language to elide accented syllables, especially in the past participle of verbs of the first conjugation, and. that this practice had been transmitted to the Italian, whence *fatato-a* would *form fato-a,* and *una donna fatata* might thus become *una fata.* Whether the same was the case in the Provençal we cannot affirm, as our knowledge of that dialect is very slight; but, judging from analogy, we would. say it was, for in Spanish *Hadada* and *Hada* are synonymous. In the Neapolitan Pentamerone *Fata* and *Maga* are the same, and a Fata sends the heroine of it to a sister of hers, *pure fatata.* Ariosto says of Medea—

E perchè per virtu d' erbe e d'incanti
Delle Fate una ed immortal fatta era.
—*I Cinque Canti,* ii. 106.

The same poet, however, elsewhere says—

Queste che or Fate e dagli antichi foro
Gia dette Ninfe e Dee con piu bel nome.
—Ibid. i. 9.

and,

Nascemmo ad un punto che d'ogni altro male
Siamo capaci fuorchè della morto.
—Orl. *Fur.* xliii. 48.

which last, however, is not decisive. Bojardo also calls the water-nymphs Fate; and our old translators of the Classics named them *fairies*. From all this can only, we apprehend, be collected, that the ideas *of* the Italian poets, and others, were somewhat vague on the subject.

From the verb *faer, féer,* to enchant, illude, the French made a substantive *faerie, féerie,* [i] illusion, enchantment, the meaning of which was afterwards extended, particularly after it had been adopted into the English language.

We find the word Faerie, in fact, to be employed in four different senses, which we will now arrange and exemplify.

1. Illusion, enchantment.

Plusieurs parlent de Guenart,
Du Loup, de l'Asne, de Renart,
De *faeries* et de songes,
De phantosmes et do mensonges.
Gul. Giar. ap. Ducange

Where we must observe, as Sir Walter Scott seems not to have been aware of it, that the four last substantives bear the same relation to each other as those in the two first verses do.

Me bifel a ferly
Of *faerie,* me thought
Vision of Piers Plowman, v. 11.

Maius that sit with so benigne a chere,
Hire to behold it seemed faerie.
Chaucer, Marchante's Tale.

It *(the horse of brass)* was of *fairie* as the pople semed,

Diversè folk diversely han demed.
—*Squier's Tale.*

The Emperor said on high,
Certes it is a *faerie,*
Or elles a vanité
—Emare.

With phantasme and *faerie,*
Thus she bleredè his eye.
—Libeaus *Disconus.*

The God of her has made an end,
And fro this worldes *faerie*
Hath taken her into companie.
—Gower, *Constance.*

Mr. Ritson professes not to understand the meaning of *faerie* in this last passage. Mr. Ritson should, as Sir Hugh Evans says, have 'prayed his pible petter;' where, among other things that might have been of service to him, he would have learned that 'man walketh in a *vain* shew,' that 'all is *vanity*,' and that 'the fashion of this world passeth away;' and then he would have found no difficulty in comprehending the pious language of 'moral Gower,' in his allusion to the transitory and deceptive vanities of the world.

2. From the sense of illusion simply, the transition was easy to that of the land of illusions, the abode of the Faés, who produced them; and Faerie next came to signify the country of the Fays. Analogy also was here aiding; for as a Nonnerie was a place inhabited by Nonnes, a Jewerie a place inhabited by Jews, so a Faerie was naturally

a place inhabited by Fays. Its termination, too, corresponded with a usual one in the names of countries: Tartarie, for instance, and 'the regne of Feminie.'

> Here beside an elfish knight
> Hath taken my lord in fight,
> And hath him led with him away
>
> Into the *Faerie*, sir, parmafay.
> —*Sir Guy.*
>
> La puissance qu'il avoit aur toutes *faeries* du monde.
> —*Huon de Bordeaux.*
>
> En effect, s'il me falloit retourner en *faerie*, je ne sçauroye ou prendre mon chemin.
> —*Ogier le Dannoys.*
>
> That Gawain with his oldè curtesie,
> Though he were come agen out of *faerie*.
> —*Squier's Tale.*
>
> He (Arthur) is a king y-crowned in *Faerie*,
> With sceptre and pall, and with his regalty
> Shailè resort, as lord and sovereigne,
>
> Out of *Faerie* and reignè in Bretaine,
> And repair again the ouldè Roundè Table.
> —*Lydgate, Fall* of *Princes*, bk. viii. c. 24.

3. From the country the appellation passed to the inhabitants in their collective capacity, and the Faerie now signified the people of Fairy-land. [k]

> Of the fourth kind of Spritis called the Phairie.
> —*K. James, Demonologie*, 1.3.

Full often time he, Pluto, and his quene
Proserpina, and alle hir *faerie,*
Disporten hem, and maken melodie
About that well
—*Marchante's Tale*

The feasts that underground the *Faerie* did him make,
And there how he enjoyed the Lady of the Lake.
—*Drayton, Poly-Olb., Song* IV.

4. Lastly, the word came to signify the individual denizen of Fairy-land, and was equally applied to the full-sized fairy knights and ladies of romance, and to the pygmy elves that haunt the woods and dells. At what precise period it got this its last, and subsequently most usual sense, we are unable to say positively; but it was probably posterior to Chaucer, in whom it never occurs, and certainly anterior to Spenser, to whom, however, it seems chiefly indebted for its future general currency. [l] It was employed during the sixteenth century [m] for the Fays of romance, and also, especially by translators, for the Elves, as corresponding to the Latin Nympha.

They believed that king Arthur was not dead, but carried awaie by the *Fairies* into some pleasant place, where he should remaine for a time, and then returne again and reign in as great authority as ever.

Hollingshed, bk. v. c. 14. Printed 1577.
Semicaper Pan
Nunc tenet, at quodam tenuerunt tempore nymphae,
—*Ovid, Met.* xiv. 520.

The halfe-goate Pan that howre
Possessed it, but heretofore it was the *Faries'* bower.
—*Golding,* 1567.

Haec nemora indigenae fauni nymphaeque tenebant,
Gensque virum truncis et duro robore nata.
—*Virgil, Aeneis,* viii. 314.

With nymphis and faunis apoun every side,
Qwhilk *Farefolkis* or than *Elfis* clepen we.
—*Gawin Dowglas.*
The weeds (quoth he) sometime both farms and nymphs,
and gods of ground,
And *Fairy-queens* did keep, and under them a nation rough.
—*Phaer,* 1562.

Inter Hamadryadsa celeberrima Nonacrinas
Naias una fuit.
—*Ovid, Met.* l. i. 690.

Of all the nymphes of Nonacris and *Fairie* ferre and neere,
In beautie and in personage this ladie had no peere.
—*Golding.*

Pan ibi dum teneris jactat sua carmina nymphis.
—*Ov. lb* .xi. 153.

There Pan among the *Faire-elves,* that daunced round togither.
—*Golding.*

Solaque Naiadum celeri non nota Dianae
—*Ov. lb.* iv. 304.

Of all the *water-fayries,* she alonely was unknowne.
To swift Diana.
—*Golding.*

Nymphis latura coronas
—*Ov. lb.* ix. 337

Was to the *fairies* of the lake fresh garlands for to bear.
—*Golding.*

Thus we have endeavoured to trace out the origin, and mark the progress of the word Fairy, through its varying significations, and trust that the subject will now appear placed in a clear and intelligible light.

After the appearance of the Faerie Queene, all distinctions were confounded, the name and attributes of the real Fays or Fairies of romance were completely transferred to the little beings who, according to the popular belief, made 'the green sour ringlets whereof the ewe not bites.' The change thus operated by the poets established itself firmly among the people; a strong proof, if this idea be correct, of the power of the poetry of a nation in altering the phraseology of even the lowest classes [n] of its society.

Shakspeare must be regarded as a principal agent in the revolution; yet even he uses Fairy once in the proper sense of Fay; a sense it seems to have nearly lost, till it was again brought into use by the translators of the French Contes des Fées in the last century.

> To this great Fairy I'll commend thy acts.
> *Anthony and Cleopatra,* act iv. sc. 8.

And Milton speaks

> Of Faery damsels met in forests wide
> By knights of Logres or of Lyones,
> Lancelot, or Pelleas, or Pellinore.
> Yet he elsewhere mentions the
> Faery elves,
> Whose midnight revels by a forest side
> Or fountain some belated peasant sees.

Finally, Randolph, in his Amyntas, employs it, for perhaps the last time, in its second sense, Fairy-land:

> I do think
> There will be of Jocastus' brood in Fairy.
> Act i. sc. 3.

We must not here omit to mention that the Germans, along with the French romances, early adopted the name of the Fees. They called them Feen and Feinen. [o] In the Tristram of Gottfried von Strazburg we are told that Duke Gylan had a syren-like little dog,

> Dez sie dem Herzoge gesandt'
>   Twas sent unto the duke, pardé,
> Uz Avalun, der .*Feinen* land,
>   From Avalun, the Fays' countrie,
> Von omen Gottinne.—V. 1673.
> By a gentle goddess.

In the old German romance of Isotte and Blanscheflur, the hunter who sees Isotte asleep says, I doubt

> Des the menachlich sei,
>   If she human be,
> Sic ist schoner denn eine *Feine*.
>   She is fairer than a Pay.
> Von Fleische noch von Beine
>   Of flesh or bone, I say,
> Kunte nit gewerden
>   Never could have birth
> So schones auf den erden.
>   A thing so fair on earth.

Our subject naturally divides itself into two principal branch-es, corresponding to the different classes of beings to which the name Fairy has been applied. The first, beings of the human race, but endowed with powers beyond those usually allotted to men, whom we shall term FAYs, or FAIRIES OF ROMANCE. The second, those little beings of the popular creeds, whose descent we propose to trace from the cunning and ingenious Duergar or dwarfs of northern mythology, and whom we shall denominate ELVES or POPULAR FAIRIES.

It cannot be expected that our classifications should vie in accuracy and determinateness with those of natural science. The human imagination, of which these beings are the offspring, works not, at least that we can discover, like nature, by fixed and invariable laws; and it would be hard indeed to exact from the Fairy historian the rigid distinction of classes and orders which we expect from the botanist or chemist. The various species so run into and are confounded with one another; the actions and attributes of one kind are so frequently ascribed to another, that scarcely have we begun to erect our system, when we find the foundation crumbling under our feet. Indeed it could not well be otherwise, when we recollect that all these beings once formed parts of ancient and exploded systems of religion, and that it is chiefly in the traditions of the peasantry that their memorial has been preserved.

We will now proceed to consider the Fairies of romance; and as they are indebted, though not for their name, yet perhaps for some of their attributes, to the Peries of Persia, we will commence with that country. We will thence pursue our course through Arabia, till we arrive at the middle-age romance of Europe, and the gorgeous realms of Fairy-land; and thence, casting a glance at the Faerie Queene, advance to the mountains and forests of the North, there to trace the origin of the light-hearted, night-tripping elves.

NOTES

[a] the mark on Adam's Peak in Ceylon is, by the Buddhists, ascribed to Buddha; by the Mohammedans, to Adam. It reminds one of the story of the lady and the vicar, viewing the moon through a telescope; they saw in it, as they thought, two figures inclined toward each other: "Methinks," says the lady," they are two fond lovers, meeting to pour forth their vows by earth-light." "Not at all," says the vicar, taking his turn at the glass; "they are the steeples of two neighbouring churches"

[b] Faerie Queene, III. c. iii. st. 8, 9, 10, 11. Drayton, Poly-Olbion, Song VI. We fear, however, that there is only poetic authority for this belief. Mr. Todd merely quotes Warton, who says that Spenser borrowed it from Giraldus Cambrensis, who picked it up among the romantic traditions propagated by the Welsh bards. The reader will be, perhaps, surprised to hear that Giraldus says nothing of the demons. He mentions the sounds, and endeavours to explain them by natural causes. Hollingshed indeed (l. i. c. 24.) says, "whereof the superstitious sort do gather many toys."

[c] for a well-chosen collection of examples, see the very learned and philosophical preface of the late Mr. Price to his edition of Warton's History of English Poetry, p.28 *et seq.*

[d] in the Middle Ages the gods of the heathens were all held to be devils.

[e] Φήρ is the Ionic form of θήρ, and is nearly related to the German *thier,* beast, animal. The Scandinavian *dyr,* and the Anglo-Saxon *deon,* have the same signification; and it is curious to observe the restricted sense which this last has gotten in the English *deer.*

[f] preface to Warton, p. 44; and Breton philologists furnish us with an etymon; not, indeed, of Fairy, but of Fada. "Fada, fata, etc.," says M. de Cambry (Monumens Celtiques), "come from the Breton *mat* or *mad,* in construction *fat,* good; whence the English, maid."

[g] see below, *France.* It is also remarked that in some of the tales of the Pentamerone, the number of the *Fate* is three; but to this it may be replied, that in Italy every thing took a classic tinge, and that the Fate of those tales are only Maghe; so in the Amadigi of Bernardo Tasso we meet with La *Fata* Urganda. In Spain and France the number would rather seem to have been seven. Cervantes speaks of "los siete castillos do las *siete* fadas;" in the Rom. de la Infantina it is said, *"siete* fadas me *fadaron,* en brazos de una ama mia," and the *Fées* are *seven* in La Belle au Bois dormant. In the romance, however, of Guillaume au Court-nez, the *Fées* who carry the sleeping Renoart out of the boat are *three* in number—See Grimm Deutsche Mythologie, p. 383.

[h] a MS. Of the 13th century, quoted by Grimm (*ut sup.* p. 405), thus relates the origin of Aquisgrani (Aix la Chapelle): Aquisgrani dicitur Ays, et dicitur eo, quod Karolus tenebrat ibi quandum *mulierem fatatam,* sive quandum *fatum.* Quae alio nominee *nimpha* vel *dea* vel *adriades* (l. *dryas*) appellatur, et ad hanc consuetudinem habetat et eam cognoscebat; et ita erat, quod ipso accedente ad eam vivebat ipsa, ipso Karola recedente moriebatur. Contigit dum quadam vice ad ipsam accessisset ut cum ea delectaretur, radius solis intravit os ejus, et tune Karolus vidit *granum auri* lingue ejus affixum, quod facit abscindi et contingenti (l. in continenti) mortua est, nec postea revixit.

[i] "Aissim *fadaro* tres serors / En aquella ora qu' ieu sui natz / Que totz temps fos enamoratz."—*Folquet de Romans.* (Thus three sisters *fated* in the hour that I was born, that I should be at all times in love.): "Aissi fuy de nueitz *fadatz* sobr' un puegau."—*Guilh. De Poitou.* (Thus was I *fated* by night on a hill.)—Grimm, *ut sup.* p. 383

[j] following the analogy of the Gotho-German tongues, *zauberei,* Germ. *trylleri,* Dan. *trolleri,* Swed. illusion, enchantment. The Italian word is *fattucchiera.*

[k] here too there *is perhaps* an analogy with *cavalry, infantry, squierie,* and similar collective terms.

[l] the Faerie Queene was published some years before the Midsummer Night's Dream. Warton,(Obs. on the Faerie Queene) observes: "It appears from Marston's Satires, printed 1598, that the Faerie Queene occasioned many publications in which Faeries were the principal actors. Go buy some ballad of the FAERY KING.—*Ad Lectorem.*:
Out steps some Faery with quick motion, / And tells him wonders of some flowerie vale—/ Awakes, straight rubs his eyes, and prints his tale.—B. III. Sat. 6."

[m] it is in this century that we first meet with *Faery* as a dissyllable, and with a plural. It is then used in its fourth and last sense.

[n] the Fata Morgana of the Straits of Messina is an example; for the name of Morgana, whencesoever derived, was probably brought into Italy by the poets.

[o] Dobenek, des deutschen Mittelalters und Volksglauben. Berlin, 1816.

ORIENTAL ROMANCE [a]

Persian Romance

THE PURE and simple religion of ancient Persia, onginating, it is said, with a pastoral and hunting race among the lofty bills of Aderbijan, or, as others think, in the elevated plains of Bactria, in a region where light appears in all its splendour, took as its fundamental principle the opposition between light and darkness, and viewed that opposition as a conflict. Light was happiness; and the people of lran, the land of light, were the favourites of Heaven; while those of Turan, the gloomy region beyond the mountains to the north, were its enemies. ln the realms of supernal light sits enthroned Ormuzd, the first-born of beings; around him are the six Amshaspands, the twenty-eight lzeds, and the countless myriads of Ferohers. [b] ln the opposite kingdom of darkness.

Aherman is supreme, and his throne is encompassed by the six Arch-Deevs, and the numerous hosts of inferior Deevs. Between these rival powers ceaseless warfare prevails; but at the end the prince of darkness will be subdued, and peace and happiness prevail beneath the righteous sway of Ormuzd.

From this sublime system of religion probably arose the Peri- [c] or Fairy-system of modern Persia; and thus what was once taught by sages, and believed by monarchs, has shared the fate of everything human, and has sunk from its pristine rank to become the material and the machinery of poets and romancers. The wars waged by the fanatical successors of the Prophet, in which literature was confounded with idolatry, have deprived us of the means of judging of this system in its perfect form; and in what has been written respecting the Peries and their country since Persia has received the law of Mohammed, the admixture of the tenets and ideas of Islam is evidently perceptible. If, however, Orientalists be right in their interpretation of the name of Artaxerxes' queen, Parisatis, as Pari-zadeh [d] *(Peri-born),* the Peri must be coeval with the religion of Zoroaster.

The Peries and Deevs of the modern Persians answer to the good and evil Jinn of the Arabs, of whose origin and nature we shall presently give an account. The same Suleymans ruled over them as over the Jinn, and both alike were punished for disobedience. It is difficult to say which is the original; but when we recollect in how much higher. a state of culture the Persians were than the Arabs, and how well this view accords with their ancient system of religion, we shall feel inclined to believe that the Arabs were the borrowers, and that by mingling with the Persian system ideas derived from the Jews, that one was formed by them which is now the common property of all Moslems.

In like manner we regard the mountains of Kaf, the abode alike of Jinn and of Peries and Deevs, as having belonged originally to Persian geography. The fullest account of it appears in the Persian romance of Hatim Tai [e] the hero of which often visited its regions. From this it would seem that this mountain-range was regarded as, like that of the ancient Greek cosmology, surrounding the flat circular earth like a ring, or rather like the bulwarks of a ship, outside of which flowed the ocean; while some Arab authorities make it to lie beyond, and to enclose the ocean as well as the earth. [f] It is said to be composed of green chrysolite, the reflection of which gives its greenish tint to the sky. According to some, its height is two thousand English miles.

Jinnestan is the common appellation of the whole of this ideal region. Its respective empires were divided into many kingdoms, containing numerous provinces and cities. Thus in the Peri-realms we meet with the luxuriant province of Shad-u-kam *(Pleasure and Delight)*, with its magnificent capital Juherabad *(Jewel-city)*, whose two kings solicited the aid of Caherman against the Deevs [8] and also the stately Amberabad *(Amber-city)*, and others equally splendid. The metropolis of the Deev-empire is named Ahermanabad *(Aherman's* city); and imagination has lavished its stores in the description of the enchanted castle, palace, and gallery of the Deev monarch, Arzshenk.

The Deevs and Peries wage incessant war with each other. Like mankind, they are subject to death, but after a much longer period of existence; and, though far superior to man in power, they partake of his sentiments and passions.

We are told that when the Deevs in their wars make, prisoners of the Peries, they shut them up in iron cages, and hang them from the tops of the highest trees, exposed to every gaze and to every chilling blast. Here their companions visit them, and bring them the choicest odours to feed on; for the ethereal Peri lives on perfume, which has moreover the property of repelling the cruel Deevs, whose malignant nature is impatient of fragrance. [h]

When the Peries are unable to withstand their foes, they solicit the aid of some mortal hero. Enchanted arms and talismans enable him to cope with the gigantic Deevs, and he is conveyed to Jinnestan on the back of some strange and wonderful animal. His adventures in that country usually furnish a wide field for poetry and romance to expatiate in.

The most celebrated adventurer in Jinnestan was Tahmuras, surnamed Deev-bend *(Deev-binder),* [i] one of the ancient kings of Persia. The Peries sent him a splendid embassy, and the Deevs, who dreaded him, despatched another. Tahmuras, in doubt how to act, consults the wonderful bird Seemurgh, [j] who speaks all languages, and whose knowledge embraces futurity. She advises him to aid the Peries, warns him of the dangers he has to encounter, and discloses his proper line of action. She further offers to convey him to Jinnestan, and plucks some feathers from her breast, with which the Persian monarch adorns his helmet.

Mounted on the Seemurgh, and bracing on his arm the potent buckler of Jan-ibn-Jan. [k] Tahmuras crosses the abyss impassable to unaided mortality. The vizier Imlan, who had headed the Deev embassy, deserting his original friends, had gone over to Tahmuras, and through the magic arts of the Deev, and his own daring valour, the Persian hero defeats the Deev-king Arzshenk. He next vanquishes a Deev still more fierce, named Demrush, who dwelt in a gloomy cavern, surrounded by piles of wealth plundered from the neighbouring realms of Persia and India. Here Tahmuras finds a fair captive, the Peri Merjan, [l] whom Demrush had carried off, and whom her brothers, Dal Peri and Milan Shah Peri, had long sought in vain. He chains the Deev in the centre of the mountain, and at the suit of Merjan hastens to attack another powerful Deev named Houndkonz;

but here, alas! fortune deserts him, and, maugre his talismans and enchanted arms, the gallant Tahmuras falls beneath his foe.

The great Deev-bend, or conqueror of Deevs, of the Shah-Nameh [m] is the illustrious Roostem. In the third of his Seven Tables or adventures, on his way to relieve the Shah Ky-Caoos, whom the artifice of a Deev had led to Mazenderan, where he was in danger of perishing, he encounters in the dark of the night a Deev named Asdeev, who stole on him in a dragon's form as he slept. Twice the hero's steed, Reksh, awoke him, but each time the Deev vanished, and Roostem was near slaying his good steed for giving him a false alarm. The third time be saw the Deev and slew him after a fearful combat. He then pursued his way to the cleft in the mountain in which abode the great Deev Sefeed, or White Deev. The seventh Table brought him to where lay an army of the Deev Sefeed's Deevs, commanded by Arzshenk, whose head he struck off, and put his troops to flight. At length he reached the gloomy cavern of the Deev Sefeed himself whom be found asleep, and scorning the advantage he awoke him, and after a terrific combat deprived him also of life.

Many years after, when Ky-Khosroo sat on the throne, a wild ass of huge size, his skin like the sun, and a black stripe along his back, appeared among the royal herds and destroyed the horses. It was supposed to be the Deev Akvan,who was known to haunt an adjacent spring. Roostem went in quest of him; on the fourth day he found him and cast his noose at him, but the Deev vanished. He re-appeared; the hero shot at him, but he became again invisible. Roostem then let Reksh graze, and laid him to sleep by the fount. As he slept, Akvan came and flew up into the air with him; and when he awoke, he gave him his choice of being let fall on the mountains or the sea. Roostem secretly chose the latter, and to obtain it he pretended to have heard that he who was drowned never entered paradise. Akvan thereupon let him fall into the sea, from which he escaped, and returning to the fount, he there met and slew the Deev. Roostem's last encounter with Deeva was with Akvan's son, Berkhyas, and his army, when he went to deliver Peshen from the dry well in which he was confined by Afrasiab. He slew him and two-thirds of his troops. Berkhyas is described as being a mountain in size, his face black, his body covered with hair, his neck like that of a dragon, two boar's tusks from his mouth, his eyes wells of blood, his hair bristling like needles, his height 140 ells, his breadth 17, pigeons nestling in his snaky locks. Akvan had had a head like an elephant.

In the Hindoo-Persian Bahar Danush *(Garden of Knowledge)* of Ynyet-ullah, written in India A.D. 1650, [n] we find the following tale of the Peries, which has a surprising resemblance to European legends hereafter to be noticed. [o]

NOTES

[a] see D'Herhelot, Richardson's Dissertation, Ouseley's Persian Miscellanies, Wahl in the Mines de l'Orient, Lane, Thousand and One Nights, Forbes, Hathn Tai, etc., etc.

[b] Ormuzd employed himself for three thousand years in making the heavens and their celestial inhabitants, the Ferohers, which are the angels and the unembodied souls of all intelligent beings. All nature is filled with Ferohers, or guardian angels, who watch over its various departments, and are occupied in performing their various tasks for the benefit of mankind.—*Erskine on the Sacred* Books *and Religion* of *the Parsis, in the Transactions of the Literary Society of Bombay,* vol. ii. p. 318. The Feroher bears in fact a very strong resemblance to the Genius of the ancient Roman religion: see our Mythology of Greece and Italy.

[c] This word is pronounced *Perry* or rather *Parry*.

[d] † پَرِي Hence it follows that the very plausible idea of the Peri having been the same with the Feroher cannot be correct.

[e] translated by Mr. Duncan Forbes. It is to be regretted that he has employed the terms Fairies and Demons instead of Peries and Deevs.

[f] see Lane, Thousand and One Nights, i. p. 21, *seq.*

[g] the Caherman Nameh is a romance in Turkish. Caherman, was the father of Sam, the grandfather of the celebrated Roostem.

[h] it is in the Cahermtn Nameh that this circumstance occurs

[i] and

[j]

* دیو بند The Tahmuras Nâmeh is also in Turkish. It and the Cahermân Nâmeh are probably translations from the Persian. As far as we are aware, Richardson is the only orientalist who mentions these two romances.

† سیمرغ It signifies 'thirty birds,' and is thought to be the ʿve as the Arabs. The poet Sâdee, to express the bounty of the Almighty says

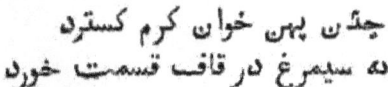

His liberal board he spreadeth out so wide,
On Kâf the Seemurgh is with food supplied.

The Seemurgh probably belongs to the original mythology of Persia. for she appears in the early part of the Shah Nameh. When Zal was born to Sam Neriman, his hair proved to be white. The father regarding this as a proof of Deev origin, resolved to expose him, and sent him for that purpose to Mount Elburz. Here the poor babe lay crying and sucking his finger. til he was found by the Seemurgh, who abode on the summit of Elburz, as one was looking for food for her young ones. But God put pity into her heart, and see took him to her nest and reared him with her young. As he grew up, the caravans that passed by, spread the fame of his beauty and his strength, and a vision having, informed Sam that he was his son, he set out for Elburz to claim him from the Seemurgh. It was with grief that Zal quitted the maternal nest. The Seemurgh, when parting with her foster-son, gave him one of her feathers, and bade him, whenever he should be in trouble or danger, to cast it into the fire, and he would have proof of her power; and she charged him at the same time strictly never to forget his nurse.

[k] see *Arabian Romance.*

[l] a pearl. Life, soul also, according to Wilkins.

[m] Ferdousee's great heroic poem. It is remarkable that the Peries are very rarely spoken of in this poem. They rarely appear in it with the birds and beasts among the subjects of the first Iranian monarchs.

[n] Chap. xx. translation of Jonathan Scott, 1799.

[o] see below, *Shetland.*

The Peri-Wife

The son of a merchant in a city of Hindostan, having been driven from his father's house on account of his undutiful conduct, assumed the garb of a Kalenderee or wandering Derweesh, and left his native town. On the first day of his travels, being overcome with fatigue before he reached any place of rest, he went off the high road and sat down at the foot of a tree by a piece of water: while he sat there, he saw at sunset four doves alight from a tree on the edge of the pond, and resuming their natural form (for they were Peries) take off their clothes and amuse themselves by bathing in the water. He immediately advanced softly, took up their garments, without being seen, and concealed them in the hollow of a tree, behind which he placed himself. The Peries when they came out of the water and missed their clothes were distressed beyond measure. They ran about on all sides looking for them, but in vain. At length, finding the young man and judging that he had possessed himself of them, they implored him to restore them. He would only consent on one condition, which was that one of them should become his wife. The Peries asserted that such a union was impossible between them whose bodies were formed of fire and a mortal who was composed of clay and water; but he persisted, and selected the one which was the youngest and handsomest. They were at last. obliged to consent, and having endeavoured to console their sister, who shed copious floods of tears at the idea of parting with them and spending her days with one of the sons of Adam; and having received their garments, they took leave of her and flew away.

The young merchant then led home his fair bride and clad her magnificently; but he took care to bury her Peri-raiment in a secret place, that she might not be able to leave him. He made every effort to gain her affections, and at length succeeded in his object: "she placed her foot in the path of regard, and her head on the carpet of affection." She bore him children, and gradually began to take pleasure in the society of his female relatives and neighbours. All doubts of her affection now vanished from his mind, and he became assured of her love and attachment.

At the end of ten years the merchant became embarrassed in his circumstances, and he found it necessary to undertake a long voyage. He committed the Peri to the care of an aged matron in whom he had the greatest confidence, and to whom he revealed the secret of her real nature, and showed the spot where he had concealed her raiment. He then "placed the foot of departure in the stirrup of travel," and set out on his journey. The Peri was now overwhelmed with sorrow for his absence, or for some more secret cause, and continually uttered expressions of regret. The old woman sought to console her, assuring her that "the dark night of absence would soon come to an end, and the bright dawn of interview gleam from the horizon of divine bounty." One day when the Peri had bathed, and was drying her amber-scented tresses with a corner of her veil, the old woman burst out into expressions of admiration at her dazzling beauty. "Ah, nurse," replied she, "though you think my present charms great, yet had you seen me in my native raiment, you would have witnessed what beauty and grace the Divine Creator has bestowed upon Peries; for know that we are among the most finished portraits on the tablets of existence. If then thou desirest to behold the skill of the divine artist, and admire the wonders of creation, bring the robes which my husband has kept concealed, that I may wear them for an instant, and show thee my native beauty, the like of which no human eye, but my lord's, hath gazed upon."

The simple woman assented, and fetched the robes and presented them to the Peri. She put them on, and then, like a bird escaped from the cage, spread her wings, and, crying Farewell, soared to the sky and was seen no more. When the merchant returned from his voyage "and found no signs of the rose of enjoyment on the tree of hope, but the lamp of bliss extinguished in the chamber of felicity, he became as one Peri-stricken, [possessed, insane] a recluse in the cell of madness. Banished from the path of understanding, he remained lost to all the bounties of fortune and the useful purposes of life."

The Peri has been styled "the fairest creation of poetical imagination." No description can equal the beauty of the female Peri,[a] and the highest compliment a Persian poet can pay a lady is to liken her to one of these lovely aerial beings. [b] Thus Sadee, in the lines prefixed to this section, declares that only the beauty of a Peri can be compared with that of the fair one he addresses; and more lately, Aboo Taleeb Khan says to Lady Elgin, as he is translated by M. von Hammer, [c]

> The sun, the moon, the Peries, and mankind,
> Compared with you, do far remain behind;
> For sun and moon have never form so mild,
> The Peries have, but roam in deserts wild.

Sir W. Ouseley is at a loss what to compare them to. They do not, he thinks, resemble the Angels, the Cherubim and Seraphim of the Hebrews, the Daemons of the Platonists, or the Genii of the Romans; neither do they accord with the Houri of the Arabs. Still less do they agree with the Fairies of Shakspeare; for though fond of fragrance, and living on that sweet essential food, we never find them employed in

> Killing cankers in the musk-rose buds,
> or obliged
> To serve the fairy queen
> To dew her orbs upon the green.

Neither is their stature ever represented so diminutive as to make key-holes pervious to their flight, or the bells of flowers their habitations. But Milton's sublime idea of a 'faery vision,' he thinks, corresponds more nearly with what the Persian poets have conceved of the Peries.

> Their port was more than human, as they stood;
> I took it for a faery vision
> Of some gay creatures of the element
> That in the colours of the rainbow live
> And play i' the plighted clouds. I was awestruck,
> And as I pass'd I worshipp'd.—*Comus.*

"I can venture to affirm," concludes Sir William gallantly, "that he will entertain a pretty just idea of a Persian Peri, who shall fix his eyes on the charms of a beloved and beautiful mistress."

If poetic imagination exhausted itself in pourtraying the beauty of the Peries, it was no less strenuous in heaping attributes of deformity on the Deevs. They may well vie in ugliness with the devils of our forefathers. "At Lahore, in the Mogul's palace," says William Finch, "are pictures of Dews, or Dives, intermixed in most ugly shapes, with long horns, staring eyes, shaggy hair, great fangs, ugly paws, long tails, with such horrible difformity and deformity, that I wonder the poor women are not frightened therewith." [d]

Such then is the Peri-system of the Mohammedan Persians, in which the influence of Islam is clearly perceptible, the very names of their fabled country and its kings being Arabic. Had we it as it was before the Arabs forced their law on Persia, we should doubtless find it more consistent in all its parts, more light, fanciful, and etherial.

NOTES

[a] It must be recollected that the Peries are of both sexes: we have just spoken of Peri *kings,* and of the *brothers* of Merjan.

[b] in the Shah Nameh it is said of Prince Siyawush, that when be was born he was *bright as a Peri.* We find the poets everywhere comparing female beauty to that of superior beings. The Greeks and Romans compared a lovely woman to Venus, Diana, or the nymphs; the Persians to a Peri: the ancient Scandinavians would say she was Frith sem Alfkone, "fair as an Alf-woman;" and an Anglo-Saxon poet says of Judith that she was *Elf-sheen,* or fair as an Elf. In the lay of Gugemer it is said,
Dedenz la Dame unt trovée
Ki de biauté resanbloit *Fée.*
The same expression occurs In Méon (3, 412); and in the Remant de la Rose we meet, *jure que plus belle est que fée* (10, 425). In the Pentamerone it is said of a king's son, *lo quale essenno bello comme a no fato.*

[c] Mines de l'Orient, vol. iii. p. 40. To make his version completely English, M. von Hammer uses the word Fairies; we have ventured to change it.

[d] In Purchas' Pilgrims, vol. 1., quoted by Sir W. Ouseley.

Arabian Romance

The Prophet is the centre round which every thing connected with Arabia revolves. The period preceding his birth is regarded and designated as the times of ignorance, and our knowledge of the ancient Arabian mythology comprises little more than he has been pleased to transmit to us. The Arabs, however, appear at no period of their history to have been a people addicted to fanciful invention. Their minds are acute and logical, and their poetry is that of the heart rather than of the fancy. They dwell with fondness on the joys and pains of love, and with enthusiasm describe the courage and daring deeds of warriors, or in moving strains pour forth the plaintive elegy; but for the description of gorgeous palaces and fragrant gardens, or for the wonders of magic, they are indebted chiefly to their Persian neighbours. [a]

What classes of beings the popular creed may have recognised before the establishment of Islam we have no means of ascertaining. [b] The Suspended Poems, and Antar, give us little or no information; we only know that the tales of Persia were current among them, and were listened to with such avidity as to rouse the indignation of the Prophet. We must, therefore, quit the tents of the Bedoween, and the valleys of 'Araby the Blest,' and accompany the khaleefehs to their magnificent capital on the Tigris, whence emanated all that has thrown such a halo of splendour around the genius and language of Arabia. It is in this seat of empire that we must look to meet with the origin of the marvels of Arabian literature.

Transplanted to a rich and fertile soil, the sons of the desert speedily abandoned their former simple mode of life; and the court of Bagdad equalled or surpassed in magnificence any thing that the East has ever witnessed. Genius, whatever its direction, was encouraged and rewarded, and the musician and the story-teller shared with the astronomer and historian the favour of the munificent khaleefehs. The tales which had amused the leisure of the Shahpoors and Yezdejirds were not disdained by the Haroons and Almansoors. The expert narrators altered them so as to accord with the new faith. And it was thus, probably, that the delightful Thousand and One Nights [c] were gradually produced and modified.

As the Genii or Jinn [d] are prominent actors in these tales, where they take the place of the Persian Peries and Deevs, we will here give some account of them.

According to Arabian writers, there is a species of beings named Jinn or Jan (Jinnee *m.*, Jinniyeh *f. sing.*), which were created and occupied the earth several thousand years before Adam. A tradition from the Prophet says that they were formed of "smokeless fire," *i.e.* the fire of the wind Simoom. They were governed by a succession of forty, or, as others say, seventy-two monarchs, named Suleyman, the last of whom, called Jan-ibn-Jan, built the Pyramids of Egypt. Prophets were sent from time to time to instruct and admonish them; but on their continued disobedience, an army of angels appeared, who drove them from the earth to the regions of the islands, making many prisoners, and slaughtering many more. Among the prisoners, was a young Jinnee, named 'Azazeel, or El-Harith (afterwards called Iblees, from his *despair),* who grew up among the angels, and became at last their chief. When Adam was created, God commanded the angels to worship him; and they all obeyed except Iblees, who, for his disobedience, was tuned into a Sheytan or Devil, and he became the father of the Sheytans.[e]

The Jinn are not immortal; they are to survive mankind, but to die before the general resurrection. Even at present many of them are slain by other Jinn, or by men; but chiefly by shooting-stars hurled at them from Heaven. The fire of which they were created, circulates in their veins instead of blood, and when they receive a mortal wound, it bursts forth and consumes them to ashes. They eat and drink, and propagate their species. Sometimes they unite with human beings, and the offspring partakes of the nature of both parents. Some of the Jinn are obedient to the will of God, and believers in the Prophet, answering to the Peries of the Persians; others are like the Deevs, disobedient and malignant. Both kinds are divided into communities, and ruled over by princes. They have the power to make themselves visible and invisible at pleasure. They can assume the form of various animals, especially those of serpents, cats, and dogs. When they appear in the human form, that of the good Jinnee is usually of great beauty; that of the evil one, of hideous deformity, and sometimes of gigantic size.

When the Zôba'ah, a whirlwind that raises the sand in the form of a pillar of tremendous height, is seen sweeping over the desert, the Arabs, who believe it to be caused by the flight of an evil Jinnee, cry, Iron! Iron! *(Hadeed! Hadeed!)* or Iron! thou unlucky one! *(Hadeed! ya meshoom!)* of which metal the Jinn are believed to have a great dread. Or else they cry, God is most great!*(Allahu akbar!)* They do the same when they see a water-spout at sea; for they assign the same cause to its origin. [f]

The chief abode of the Jinn of both kinds is the Mountains of Kaf, already described. But they also are dispersed through the earth, and they occasionally take up their residence in baths, wells, latrinae, ovens, and. ruined houses. [g]

They also frequent the sea and rivers, cross-roads, and market-places. They ascend at times to the confines of the lowest heaven, and by listening there to the conversation of the angels, they obtain some knowledge of futurity, which they impart to those men who, by means of talismans or magic arts, have been able to reduce them to obedience. [h]

The following are anecdotes of the Jinn, given by historians of eminence. [I]

It is related, says El-Kasweenee, by a certain narrator of traditions, that he descended into a valley with his sheep, and a wolf carried off a ewe from among them; and he arose and raised his voice, and cried, "O inhabitant of the valley!" whereupon he heard a voice saying, "O wolf, restore him his sheep!" and the wolf came with the ewe and left her, and departed.

Ben Shohnah relates, that in the year 456 of the Hejra, in the reign of Kaiem, the twenty-sixth khaleefeh of the house of Abbas, a report was raised in Bagdad, which immediately spread throughout the whole province of Irak, that some Turks being out hunting saw in the desert a black tent, beneath which there was a number of people of both sexes, who were beating their cheeks, and uttering loud cries, as is the custom in the East when any one is dead. Amidst their cries they heard these words—*The great king of the Jinn is dead, woe to this country!* and then there came out a great troop of women, followed by a number of other rabble, who proceeded to a neighbouring cemetery, still beating themselves in token of grief and mourning.

The celebrated historian Ebn Athir relates, that when he was at Mosul on the Tigris, in the year 600 of the Hejra, there was in that country an epidemic disease of the throat; and it was said that a woman, of the race of the Jinn, having lost her son, all those who did not condole with her on account of his death were attacked with that disease; so that to be cured of it men and women assembled, and with all their strength cried out, *O mother of Ankood, excuse us! Ankood is dead, and we did not mind it!*

NOTES

[a] compare Antar and the Suspended Poems (translated by Sir W. Jones) with the later Arabic works. Antar, though written by Asmai the court-poet of Haroon-er-Rasheed, gives the manners and ideas of the Arabs of the Desert.

[b] the Jinn are mentioned in the Kurân and also in Antar.

[c] see Tales and Popular Fictions, p. 37, *seq.* Lane, Thousand and One Nights, *passim.*

[d] Genius and Jinn, like Fairy and Peri, is a curious coincidence. The Arabian Jinnee bears no resemblance whatever to the Roman Genius.

[e] "When we said unto the Angels, Worship ye Adam, and they worshiped except Iblees (who) was of the Jinn."—Kuran. chap. xviii. v. 48. Worship is here prostration. The reply of Iblees was, "Thou hast created *me* of fire, and hast created *him* of earth."—*Ib.* vii. 11; xxxviii. 77.

[f] it was the belief of the irish peasantry, that whirlwinds of dust on the roads were raised by the Fairies, who were then on a journey. On such occasions, unlike the Arabs, they used to raise their hats and say, "God speed you, gentlemen!" For the power of iron, see *Scandinavia.*

[g] the Arabs when they pour water on the ground, let down a bucket into a well, enter a bath, etc., say, "Permission!" *(Destoor!)* or, Permission, ye blessed! *(Destoor, ya mubdrakeen!)*

[h] for the preceding account of the Jinn, we are wholly indebted to Lane's valuable translation of the Thousand and One Nights, i. 30, *seq.*

[i] the first is given by Lane, the other two by D'Herbelot.

MIDDLE-AGE ROMANCE

Ecco quet che le carte empton di sogni,
Lancliotto, Tristano e gil altri erranti,
Onde conven che il voigo errante agogni.
—PETRARCA.

FEW WILL now endeavour to trace romantic and marvellous fiction to any individual source. An extensive survey of the regions of fancy and their productions will incline us rather to consider the mental powers of man as having an uniform operation under every sky, and under every form of political existence, and to acknowledge that identity of invention is not more to be wondered at than identity of action. It is strange how limited the powers of the imagination are. Without due consideration of the subject, it might be imagined that her stores of materials and powers of combination are boundless; yet reflection, however slight, will convince us that here also 'there is nothing new, and charges of plagiarism will in the majority of cases be justly suspected to be devoid of foundation. The finest poetical expressions and similes of occidental literature meet us when we turn our attention to the East, and a striking analogy pervades the tales and fictions of every region. The reason is, the materials presented to the inventive faculties are scanty. The power of combination is therefore limited to a narrow compass, and similar combinations must hence frequently occur.

Yet still there is a high degree of probability in the supposition of the luxuriant fictions of the East having through Spain and Syria operated on European fancy. The poetry and romance of the middle ages are notoriously richer in detail, and more gorgeous in invention, than the more correct and chaste strains of Greece and Latium; the island of Calypso, for example, is in beauty and variety left far behind by the retreats of the fairies of romance. Whence arises this difference? No doubt

> When ancient chivalry display'd
> The pomp of her heroic games,
> And crested knights and tissued dames
> Assembled at the clarion's call,
> In some proud castle's high-arch'd hall,

that a degree of pomp and splendour met the eye of the minstrel and romancer on which the bards of the simple republics of ancient times had never gazed, and this might account for the difference between the poetry of ancient and of middle-age Europe. Yet, notwithstanding, we discover such an Orientalism in the latter as would induce us to acquiesce in the hypothesis of the fictions and the manner of the East having been early transmitted to the West; and it is highly probable that along with more splendid habits of life entered a more lavish use of the gorgeous stores laid open to the plastic powers of fiction. The tales of Arabia were undoubtedly known in Europe from a very early period. The romance of Cleomades and Claremonde, which was written in the thirteenth century, [a] not merely resembles, but actually is the story of the Enchanted Horse in the Thousand and One Nights. Another tale in the same collection, The two Sisters who envied their younger Sister, may be found in Straparola, and is also a popular story in Germany; and in the Pentamerone and. other collections of tales published long before the appearance of M. Galland's translation of the Eastern ones, numerous traces of an oriental origin may be discerned. The principal routes they came by may also be easily shown. The necessities of commerce and the pilgrimage to Mecca occasioned a constant intercourse between the Moors of Spain and their fellow-sectaries of the East; and the Venetians, who were the owners of Candia, carried on an extensive trade with Syria and Egypt. It is worthy of notice, that the Notti Piacevoli of Straparola were first published in Venice, and that Basile, the author of the Pentamerone, spent his youth in Candia, and was afterwards a long time at Venice. Lastly, pilgrims were notorious narrators of marvels, and each, as he visited the Holy Land, was anxious to store his memory with those riches, the diffusal of which procured him attention and hospitality at home.

We think, therefore, that European romance may be indebted, though not for the name, yet for some of the attributes and exploits of its fairies to Asia. This is more especially the case with the romances composed or turned into prose in the fourteenth, fifteenth, and sixteenth centuries; for in the earlier ones the Fairy Mythology is much more sparingly introduced.

But beside the classic and oriental prototypes of its fairies, romance may have had an additional one in the original mythology of the Celtic tribes, of which a being very nearly allied to the fay of romance appears to have formed a part. Such were the damoiselles who bestowed their favours upon Lanval and Graelent. This subject shall, however, be more fully considered under the head of Brittany.

Romances of chivalry, it is well known, may be divided into three principal classes; those of Arthur and his Round Table, of Charlemagne and his Paladins, and those of Amadis and Palmerin, and their descendants and kindred. In the first, with the exception of Isaie le Triste, which appears to be a work of the fifteenth century, the fairies appear but seldom; the second exhibits them in all their brilliancy and power; in the third, which all belong to the literature of Spain, the name at least does not occur, but the enchantress Urganda la Desconecida seems equal in power to La Dame du Lac, in the romance of Lancelot du Lac. [b]

Among the incidents of the fine old romance just alluded to, [c] is narrated the death of King Ban, occasioned by grief at the sight of his castle taken and in flames through the treachery of his seneschal. His afflicted queen had left her new-born infant on the margin of a lake, while she went to soothe the last moments of the expiring monarch. On her return, she finds her babe in the arms of a beautiful lady. She entreats her pathetically to restore the orphan babe; but, without heeding her entreaties, or even uttering a single word, she moves to the edge of the lake, into which she plunges and disappears with the child. The lady was the celebrated Dame du Lac: the child was Lancelot, afterwards styled Du Lac. The name of the lady was Vivienne, and she had dwelt "en la marche de la petite Bretaigne." Merlin the demon-born, the renowned enchanter, became enamoured of her, and taught her a portion of his art; and the ill-return she made is well known in the annals of female treachery. [d] In consequence of the knowledge thus acquired she became a fairy; for the author informs us that "the damsel who carried Lancelot to the lake was a fay, and in those times all those women were called fays who had to do with enchantments and charms—and there were many of them then, principally in Great Britain—and knew the power and virtues of words, of stones, and, of herbs, by which they were kept in youth and in beauty, and in great riches, as they devised." [e]

The lake was *feerie,* an illusion raised by the art which the devil had taught Merlin, and Merlin the lady. The romance says: "The lady who reared him conversed only in the forest, and dwelt on the summit of a hill, which was much lower than that on which King Ban had died. In this place, where it seemed that the wood was large and deep, the lady had many fair houses, and very rich; and in the plain beneath there was a gentle little river well-stored with fish; and this place was so secret and so concealed, that right difficult was it for any one to find, for the semblance of the said lake covered it so that it could not be perceived." [f]

When her young *protégé* had gone through his course of knightly education, she took him to King Arthur's court, and presented him there; and his subsequent history is well known.

In the romance of Maugis d'Aygremont et de Vivian son Frère, when Tapinel and the female slave had stolen the two children of Duke Bevis of Aygremont, the former sold to the wife of Sorgalant the child which he had taken, whose name was Eselarmonde, and who was about fifteen years of age, and was "plus belle et plus blanche qu'une fée." The slave having laid herself to rest under a white-thorn *(aubespine),* was devoured by a lion and a leopard, who killed one another in their dispute for the infant. "And the babe lay under the thorn, and cried loudly, during which it came to pass that Oriande la Fée, who abode at Rosefleur with four other fays, came straight to this thorn; for every time she passed by there she used to repose under that white-thorn. She got down, and hearing the child cry, she came that way and looked at him, and said, 'By the god in whom we believe, this child here is lying badly *(mal gist),* and this shall be his name;' and from that time be was always called Maugis."

Oriande la Fée brought the child home with her and her damsels; and having examined him, and found, by a precious ring that was in his ear, that he was of noble lineage, "she prayed our Lord that he would be pleased of his grace to make known his origin *(nation)."* When she had finished her prayer, she sent for her nephew Espiet, "who was a dwarf, and was not more than three feet high, and had his hair yellow as fine gold, and looked like a child of seven years, but he was more than a hundred; and he was one of the falsest knaves in the world, and knew every kind of enchantment." Espiet informed her whose child he was; and Oriande, having prayed to our Lord to preserve the child, took him with her to her castle of Rosefleur, where she had him baptised and named Maugis. She and her damsels reared him with great tenderness; and when he was old enough she put him under the care of her brother Baudris, "who knew all the arts of magic and necromancy, and was of the age of a hundred years;" and he taught what he knew to Maugis.

When Maugis was grown a man, the Fay Oriande clad him in arms, and he became her *ami;* and she loved him "de si grand amour qu'elle doute fort qu'il ne se departe d'avecques elle."

Maugis shortly afterwards achieved the adventure of gaining the enchanted horse Bayard, in the isle of Boucaut. Of Bayard it is said, when Maugis spoke to him, "Bayard estoit *feyé,*si entendoit aussi bien Maugis comme s'il *(Bayard)* eust parlé." On his return from the island, Maugis conquers and slays the Saracen admiral Anthenor, who had come to win the lands and castle of Oriande, and gains the sword Flamberge (Floberge), which, together with Bayard, he afterwards gave to his cousin Renaud.

In Perceforest, Sebille la Dame du Lac, whose castle was surrounded by a river on which lay so dense a fog that no one could see across the water, though not called so, was evidently a fay. The fortnight that Alexander the Great and Floridas abode with her, to be cured of their wounds, seemed to them but as one night. During that night, "la dame demoura enceinte du roy dung filz, dont de ce lignage yssit le roi Artus." [8]

In the same romance [h] we are told that "en lysle de Zellande jadis fut demourante une *faee* qui estoit appellee Morgane." This Morgane was very intimate with "ung esperit (named Zephir) qui repairoit es lieux acquatiques, mais jamais nestoit veu que de nuyt." Zephir had been in the habit of repairing to Morgane is Face from her youth up, "car elle estoit malicieuse et subtille et tousjours avoit moult desire a aucunement sçavoir des enchantemens et des conjurations." He had committed to her charge the young Passelyon and his cousin Bennucq, to be brought up, and Passelyon was detected in an intrigue with the young Morgane, daughter of the fay. The various adventures of this amorous youth form one of the most interesting portions of the romance.

In Tristan de Leonois, [i] king Meliadus, the father of Tristan, is drawn to a chase *par mal engin et negromance* of a fairy who was in love with him, and carries him off and from whose thraldom he was only released by the power of the great enchanter Merlin.

In Parthenopex of Blois,[j] the beautiful fairy Melior, whose magic bark carries the knight to her secret island, is daughter to the emperor of Greece.

In no romance whatever is the fairy machinery more pleasingly displayed than in Sir Launfal, a metrical romance, composed [k] by Thomas Chestre, in the reign of Henry VI.

Before, however, we give the analysis of this poem, which will be followed by that of another, and by our own imitations of this kind of verse, we will take leave to offer some observations on a subject that seems to us to be in general but little understood, namely, the structure of our old English verse, and the proper mode of reading it.

Our forefathers, like their Gotho-German kindred, regulated their verse by the number of accents, not of syllables. The foot, therefore, as we term it, might consist of one, two, three, or even four syllables, provided it had only one strongly marked accent. Further, the accent of a word might be varied, chiefly by throwing it on the last syllable, as *natúre* for *náture, honoúr* for *hónour,* etc. (the Italians, by the way, throw it back when two accents come into collision, as, *Il Pástor Fido* [l]*);* they also sounded what the French call the feminine *e* of their words, as, *In oldè dayès of the King Artoúr;* and so well known seems this practice to have been, that the copyists did not always write this *e,* relying on the skill of the reader to supply it. [m] There was only one restriction, namely, that it was never to come before a vowel, unless where there was a pause. In this way the poetry of the middle ages was just as regular as that of the present day; and Chaucer, when properly read, is fully as harmonious as Pope. But the editors of our ancient poems, with the exception of

Tyrwhitt, seem to have been ignorant or regardless of this principle; and in the Canterbury Tales alone is the verse properly arranged.

We will now proceed to the analysis of the romance of Sir Launfal.

Sir Launfal was one of the knights of Arthur, who loved him well, and made him his steward. But when Arthur married the beautiful but frail Gwennere, daughter of Ryon, king of Ireland, Launfal and other virtuous knights manifested their dissatisfaction when she came to court. The queen was aware of this, and, at the first entertainment given by the king,

> The queen yaf *(gave)* giftès for the nones,
> Gold and silver, precious stones,
> Her courtesy to kythe *(show):*
> Everiche knight she yaf broche other *(or)* ring,
> But Sir Launfel she yaf no thing,
> That grieved him many a sythe *(time).*

Launfal, under the feigned pretext of the illness of his father, takes leave of the king, and retires to Karlyoun, where he lives in great poverty. Having obtained the loan of a horse, one holyday, he rode into a fair forest, where, overcome by the heat, he lay down under the shade of a tree, and meditated on his wretched state. In this situation he is attracted by the approach of two fair damsels splendidly arrayed.

> Their faces were white as snow on down,
> Their rode [n] was red, their eyne were brown;
> I saw never none swiche.
> That one bare of gold a basin,
> That other a towel white and fine,

Of silk that was good and riche;
Their kerchevès were welè skire *(clear)*
Araid *(striped)* with richè goldè wire—
Launfal began to siche—
They comè to him over the hoth *(heath),*
He was curtèis, and against them goeth,
And greet them mildeliche.

They greet him courteously in return, and invite him to visit their mistress, whose pavilion is at hand. Sir Launfal complies with the invitation, and they proceed to where the pavilion lies. Nothing could exceed this pavilion in magnificence. It was surmounted by an *erne* or eagle, adorned with precious stones so rich, that the poet declares, and we believe, that neither Alexander nor Arthur possessed "none swiche jewel."

He foundè in the paviloun
The kingès daughter of Oliroun,
Dame Tryamour that hight;
Her father was king of Faerie,
Of occientè [o] fer and nigh,
A man of mickle might.
The beauty of dame Tryamour was beyond conception.
For heat her cloathès down she dede
Almostè to her girdle stede *(place),*
Than lay she uncover't;
She was as white as lily in May,
Or snow that snoweth in winter's day:
He seigh *(saw)* never none so pert *(lively).*
The redè rose, when she is new,
Against her rode was naught of hew
I dare well say in cert;
Her hairè shone as goldè wire:
May no man rede her attire,
Ne naught well think in hert *(heart).*

This lovely dame bestows her heart on Sir Launfal, on condition of his fidelity. As marks of her affection, she gives him a never-failing purse and many other valuable presents, and dismisses him next morning with the assurance, that whenever he wished to see her, his wish would be gratified on withdrawing into a private room, where she would instantly be with him. This information is accompanied with a charge of profound secrecy on the subject of their loves.

The knight returns to court, and astonishes every one by his riches and his munificence. He continues happy in the love of the fair Tryamour, until an untoward adventure interrupts his bliss. One day the queen beholds him dancing, with other knights, before her tower, and, inspired with a sudden affection, makes amorous advances to the knight. These passages of love are received on his part with an indignant repulse, accompanied by a declaration more enthusiastic than politic or courteous, that his heart was given to a dame, the foulest of whose maidens surpassed the queen in beauty. The offence thus given naturally effected an entire conversion in the queen's sentiments; and, when Arthur returned from hunting, like Potiphar's wife, she charges Launfal with attempting her honour. The charge is credited, and the unhappy knight condemned to be burned alive, unless he shall, against a certain day, produce that peerless beauty. The fatal day arrives; the queen is urgent for the execution of the sentence, when ten fair damsels, splendidly arrayed, and mounted on white palfreys, are descried advancing toward the palace. They announce the approach of their mistress, who soon appears, and by her beauty justifies the assertion of her knight. Sir

Launfal is instantly set at liberty, and, vaulting on the courser his mistress had bestowed on him, and which was held at hand by his squire, he follows her out of the town.

> The lady rode down Cardevile,
> Fer into a jolif île,
> Oliroun that hight; [p]
> Every year upon a certain day,
> Men may heare Launfales steedè neighe,
> And him see with sight.
> He that will there axsy *(ask)* justes
> To keep his armès fro the rustes,
> In turnement other *(or)* fight,
> Dar *(need)* he never further gon;
> There he may find justès anon,
> With Sir Launfal the knight.
> Thus Launfal, withouten fable,
> That noble knight of the roundê table,
> Was taken into the faerie;
> Since saw him in this land no man,
> Ne no more of him tell I ne can,
> For soothè, without lie. [q]

No romance is of more importance to the present sub. ject than the charming Huon de Bordeaux. [r] Generally known, as the story should be, through Wieland's poem and Mr. Sotheby's translation, we trust that we shall be excused for giving some passages from the original French romance, as Le petit roy Oberon appears to form a kind of connecting link between the fairies of romance and the Elves or Dwarfs of the Teutonic nations. When we come to Germany it will be our endeavour to show how the older part of Huon de Bordeaux has been taken from the story of Otnit in the Heldenbuch, where the dwarf king Elberich performs nearly the same services to Otnit that Oberon does to Huon, and that, in fact, the name Oberon is only Elberich slightly altered. [s]

Huon, our readers must know, encounters in Syria an old follower of his family named Gerasmes; and when consulting with him on the way to Babylon he is informed by him that there are two roads to that city, the one long and safe, the other short and dangerous, leading through a wood, "which is sixteen leagues long, but is so full of Fairie and strange things that few people pass there without being lost or stopt, because therewithin dwelleth a king, Oberon the Fay. He is but three feet in height; he is all humpy; but he hath an angelic face; there is no mortal man who should see him who would not take pleasure in looking at him, he hath so fair a face. Now you will hardly have entered the wood, if you are minded to pass that way, when he will find how to speak to you, but of a surety if you speak to him, you are lost for evermore, without ever returning; nor will it lie in you, for if you pass through the wood, whether straightforwards or across it, you will always find him before you, and it will be impossible for you to escape at all without speaking to him, for his words are so pleasant to hear, that there is no living man who can escape him. And if so be that he should see that you are nowise inclined to speak to him, he will be passing wroth with you. For before you have left the wood he, will cause it so to rain on you, to blow, to hail, and to make such right marvellous storms, thunder and lightning, that you will think the world is going to end. Then you will think that you see a great flowing river before you, wondrously black and deep; but know, sire, that right easily will you. be able to go through it without wetting. the feet of your horse, for it is nothing but a phantom and enchantments that the dwarf will make for you, because he wishes to have you with him, and if it so be that you keep firm to your resolve, not to speak to him, you will be surely able to escape," etc. [t]

Huon for some time followed the sage advice of Gerasmes, and avoided Oberon le fayé. The storms of rain and thunder came on as predicted, the magic horn set them all dancing, and at last the knight determined to await and accost the dwarf.

"The Dwarf Fay came riding through the wood, and was clad in a robe so exceeding fine and rich, that it would be a marvel to relate it for the great and marvellous riches that were upon it; for so much was there of precious stones, that the great lustre that they cast was like unto the sun when he shineth full clear. And therewithal he bare a right fair bow in his fist, so rich that no one could value it, so fine it was; and the arrow that he bare was of such sort and manner, that there was no beast in the world that he wished to have, that it did not stop at that arrow. He had at his neck a rich horn, which was hung by two rich strings of fine gold." [u]

This horn was wrought by four Fairies, who had endowed it with its marvellous properties.

Oberon, on bringing Huon to speech, informed him that he was the son of Julius Caesar, and the lady of the Hidden Island, afterwards called Cephalonia. This lady's first love had been Florimont of Albania, a charming young prince, but being obliged to part from him, she married, and had a son named Neptanebus, afterwards King of Egypt, who begot Alexander the Great, who afterwards put him to death. Seven hundred years later, Caesar, on his way to Thessaly, was entertained in Cephalonia by the lady of the isle, and he loved her, for she told him he would defeat Pompey, and he became the father of Oberon. Many a noble prince and noble fairy were at the birth, but one Fairy was unhappily not invited, and the gift she gave was that he should not grow after his third year, but repenting, she gave him to be the most beautiful of nature's works. Other Fairies gave him the gift of penetrating the thoughts of men, and of transporting himself and others from place to place by a wish; and the faculty, by like easy means, of raising and removing castles, palaces, gardens, banquets, and such like. He further informed the knight, that he was king and lord of Mommur; and that when he should leave this world his seat was prepared in Paradise—for Oberon, like his prototype Elberich, was a veritable Christian.

When after a variety of adventures Oberon comes to Bordeaux to the aid of Huon, and effects a reconciliation between him and Charlemagne, he tells Huon that the time is at hand that he should leave this world and take the seat prepared for him in Paradise, "en faerie ne veux plus demeurer." He directs him to appear before him within four years in his city of Mommur, where he will crown him as his successor.

Here the story properly ends, but an addition of considerable magnitude has been made by a later hand, in which the story is carried on.

Many are the perils which Muon encounters before the period appointed by Oberon arrives. At length, however, he and the fair Esclairmonde (the Rezia of Wieland) come to Mommur. Here, in despite of Arthur (who, with his sister Morgue la faée and a large train, arrives at court, and sets himself in opposition to the will of the monarch, but is reduced to order by Oberon's threat of turning him into a *Luyton de Mer* [v]), Huon is crowned king of all Faerie "tant du pais des Luytons comme des autres choses secretes reservées dire aux hommes." Arthur gets the kingdom of Bouquant, and that which Sybilla held of Oberon, and all the Faeries that were in the plains of Tartary. The good king Oberon then gave Huon his last instructions, recommending his officers and servants to him, and charging him to build an abbey before the city, in the mead which the dwarf had loved, and there to bury him. Then, falling asleep in death, a glorious troop of angels, scattering odours as they flew, conveyed his soul to Paradise.

Isaie le Triste is probably one of the latest romances, certainly posterior to Huon de Bordeaux, for the witty but deformed dwarf Trone, who is so important a personage in it, is, we are told, Oberon, whom Destiny compelled to spend a certain period in that form. And we shall, as we have promised, prove Oberon to be the handsome dwarf-king Elberich. In Isaie the Faery ladies approach to the Fées of Perrault, and Madame D'Aulnoy. Here, as at the birth of Oberon and of Ogier le Danois, they interest themselves for the new-born child, and bestow their gifts upon it. The description in this romance of the manner in which the old hermit sees them occupied about the infant Isaie is very pleasing. It was most probably Fairies of this kind, and not the diminutive Elves, that Milton had in view when writing these lines:

Good luck betide thee, son, for, at thy birth,
The Faery ladies danced upon the hearth.
Thy drowsy nurse hath sworn she did them spy
Come tripping to the room where thou didst lie,
And, sweetly singing round about thy bed,
Strew all their blessings on thy sleeping head.

The description of the Vergier des Fées in Isaie le Triste, and of the beautiful valley in which it was situated, may rival in richness and luxuriancy similar descriptions in Spenser and the Italian poets. [x]

We have now, we trust, abundantly proved our position of the Fairies of romance being, at least at the commencement, only 'human mortals,' endowed with superhuman powers, though we may perceive that, as the knowledge of Oriental fiction increased, the Fairies began more and more to assume the character of a distinct species. Our position will acquire additional strength when in the course of our inquiry we arrive at France and Italy.

Closely connected with the Fairies is the place of their abode, the region to which they convey the mortals whom they love, 'the happy lond of Faery.'

NOTES

[a] On the subjects mentioned is this paragraph, see Tales and Popular Fictions, chap. ii. and iii.

[b] in the Amadigi of B. Taaso, she is La Fata Urganda.

[c] Lancelot is regarded as probably the earliest prose romance of chivalry. It was first printed in 1494. The metrical romance called La Charrette, of which Lancelot is the hero, was begun by Chrestien de Troyes, who died in 1191, and finished by Geoffrey de Ligny. We may here observe that almost all the French romances of chivalry were written originally in verse in the twelfth and thirteenth centuries, principally by Chrestien de Troyes and Huon de Vilieneuve. The prose romances in general were made from them in the fifteenth century.

[d] For while It was in hand, by loving of an elf,
  For all his wondrous skill was cozened of himself:
  For walking with his Fay, her to the rock he brought,
  In which he oft before his nigromancies wrought.
  And going in thereat, his magics to have shown,
  She stopt the cavern's mouth with an enchanted stone,
  Whose cunning strongly crossed, amazed while he did stand,
  She captive him conveyed unto the Fairy-land.
  Drayten, *Poly-Olb.* Song IV.

[e] La damoiseile qui Lancelot ports au lac estoit une *fée*, et en cellui temps estoient appellées *fees* toutes celles qui seutremeloient denchantements et de charmes, et moult en estoit pour loss principallement en la Grand Bretaigne, et savoient la force et la vertu dee parolles, des pierres, et des herbes, parquoi elles estoient en jeunesse, et en beaulte, et en grandes richesses, comment elles divisoient.

[f] La dame qui le nourissoit ne conversoit que en forest, et estoit au plain de ung tetre plus bas assez que celui ou le roy Ban estoit mort: en ce lieu en ce lieu que il sembloit que le bois fust grant et parfont *(profond)* avoit la dame moult de belles maisons et moult riches; et au plain dessoubs y avoit une gente petite riviere moult plantureuse de poissons; et estoit ce lieu et cele et secret que bien difficille estoit a homme de le trouver, car la semblance du dit lac le couvroit si que il ne pouvoit estre apperceu. And farther, La damoiselle nestoit mie seulle, mais y avoit grande compaignie de chevaliers et de dames et demoiselles.

[g] Vol. i. ch. 42.

[h] Vol. iii. cli. 31.

[i] Tristan was written in verse by Chrestien do Troyes. The prose romance was first printed in 1489.

[j] Parthenopex was written in French in the twelfth century, according to Le Grand; in the thirteenth, according to Roquefort.

[k] *Composed*—for to call it, with Ellis, Ritson, and others, a translation, would be absurd. How Ellis, who had at least read Le Grand's and Way's Fabliaux, could say of Chestre, that he "seems to have given a *faithful* as well as spirited version of this old Breton story," is surprising. It is in fact no translation, but a poem on the adventures of Sir Launfal, founded chiefly on the Lais de Lanval and de Graelent, in Marie de France, with considerable additions of Chestre's own invention, or derived from other sources. These Lais will be considered under Brittany.

[l] Thus we ourselves say *the Pri'ncess Royal, éxtreme need,* etc. This, by the way, is the cause why the Greeks put a grave and not an acute accent on words accented on the last syllable, to show that it is easily moveable.

[m] As this seems to be one of the lost arts, we will here and elsewhere mark the feminine *e* and the change of accent.

[n] Rode—complexion; from *red.*

[o] Occient—occident or *océan?* The Gaston peasantry call the Bay a Biscay *La Mer d' Occient.* The Spaniards say *Mar Oceano.*

[p] It Is strange to find the English poet changing the Avalon of the Lai de Lanval into the well-known island of Oléron. It is rather strange too, that Mr. Ritson, who has a note on "Oliroun," did not notice this.

[q] The Lai ends thus:

Od (avec) li seat vait en Avalun,
Ceo nus recuntent. le Bretun;
En une isle que mut eat beaus,
La fut ravi li dameiseaus,
Nul humme nen ot plus parler,
Na jeo nan sai avant cunter.

In Graelent It is said that the horse of the knight used to return annually to the river where he lost his master. The rest is Thomas Chestre's own, taken probably from the well-known story in Gervase of Tilbury.

[r] Huon, Hue, or Hullin (for he is called by these three names in the poetic romance) is, there can be little doubt, the same person with Yon king of Bordeaux in the Quatre Filz Aymon, another composition of Huon de Villeneuve, and with Lo Re Ivone, prince or duke of Guienne in Bojardo and Ariosto. See the Orl, Inn. l i. c. iv. st. 46. I Cinque Canti, c. v. st. 42

[s] Otait was supposed to hare been written by Wolfram von Esehembach, in the early part of the thirteenth century. It is possibly much older. Huon de Bordeaux was, it is said, written in French verse by Huon do Villeneuve, some time in the same century. It does not appear in the list of Huon do Villenenve's works given by Mons. de Roquefort. At the end of the prose romance we are told that it was written at the desire of Charles seigneur do Rochefort, and completed on the 29th of January, 1454.

[t] Qui a de long seizes lieues, mais tant est plain de faerie et chose estrange que peu de gens y passent qui n'y soient perdus ou arrestez, pour ce que la dedans demeure un roi, Oberon le fayé. Il n'a que trois pieds de hauteur; il est tout bossu; mais il a un visage angelique; il n'est homme mortel que le voye que plaisir no prengne a le regarder tant a beau visage. Ja si tost ne serez entrez au bois se par ls voulez passer qu'il ne trouve maniere de parler a vous, si ainsi que a luy parliez perdu estus a tousjours sans jamais plus revenir; ne il ne sera en vous, car se par le bois passez, soit de long ou de travers, vous le trouverez tousjours au devant de vous, et vous sera impossible que eschappiez nullement que ne parliez a luy, car ses parolles sont tant plaisantes a ouyr qu'il n'est homme mortel qui de luy se puisse eschapper. Et se chose est qu'il voye que nullement ne vueillez parler a luy, il sera moult troublé envers vous. Car avant que du bois soyez parti vous fera pleuvoir, ventrer, gresiller, et faire si tres-mervueilleux orages, tonnerres, et esclairs, que advis vous sera que le monde doive finir. Puis vous sera advis que par devant vous verrez une grande riviere courante, noire et parfonde a grand merveilles; mais sachez, sire, que bien y pourrez aller sans mouiller les pieds de vostre cheval, car ce n'est que fantosme et

enchantemens que le nain vous fera pour vous cuider avoir avec lui, et se chose est que bien tenez propos en vous de non parler a luy, bien pourrez eschapper, etc.

[u] La Nain Fee s'en vint chevauchant par le bois, et estoit vestu d'une robbe si tres-belle et riche, que merveilles sera ce racompter pour la grand et merveilleuse richesse que dessus estoit, car tant y avoit de pierres precieuses, que la grand clarté qu'elles jettoient estoit pareille au soleil quant il luit bien clair. Et avec ce portoit un moult bel arc en son poing, tant riche que on ne le sauroit estimer tant estoit beau. Et la fleche qu'ii portoit estoit do telle sorto et maniere, qu'il n'estoit beste au monde qu'il vousist souhaiter qu'a icelle fleche elle ne s'arrestast. Il avoit a son cou un riche cor, lequel estoit pendu a deux riches attaches de fin or.

[v] This sort of transformation appears to have been a usual mode of punishing in a Fairy land. It may have come from Circe, but the Thousand and One Nights is full of such transformations. For *luyton* or *lutin,* see below, *France.*

[x] We are only acquainted with this romance through Mr. Dunlop's analysis.

FAIRY-LAND

There, renewed the vital spring,
Again he reigns a mighty king
And many a fair and fragrant clime,
Blooming in immortal prime,
By gales of Eden ever fanned,
Owns the monarch's high command.
–T. Warton.

AMONG ALL nations the mixture of joy and pain, of exquisite delight and intense misery in the present state, has led the imagination to the conception of regions of unmixed bliss destined for the repose of the good after the toils of this life, and of climes where happiness prevails, the abode of beings superior to man. The imagination of the Hindoo paints his Swergas as 'profuse of bliss,' and all the joys of sense are collected into the Paradise of the Mussulman. The Persian lavished the riches of his fancy in raising the Cities of Jewels and of Amber that adorn the realms of Jinnestân; the romancer erected castles and palaces filled with knights and ladies in Avalon and in the land of Faerie; while the Hellenic bards, unused to pomp and glare, filled the Elysian Fields and the Island of the Blest with tepid gales and brilliant flowers. We shall quote without apology two beautiful passages from Homer and Pindar, that our readers may at one view satisfy themselves of the essential difference between classic and romantic imagination. In Homer, Proteus tells Menelaus that, because he had had the honour of being the son-in-law of Zeus, he should not die in "horse-feeding Argos."

But thee the ever-living gods will send
Unto the Elysian plain and distant bounds
Of Earth, where dwelleth fair-hair'd Rhadamanthus.
There life is easiest unto men; no snow,
Or wintry storm, or rain, at any time,
Is there; but evermore the Ocean sends
Soft-breathing airs of Zephyr to refresh
The habitants—*Od.* iv. 563.

This passage is finely imitated by Pindar, and connected with that noble tone of pensive morality, so akin to the Oriental spirit, and by which the 'Dircaean Swan' is distinguished from all his fellows.

They speed their *way*
To Kronos' palace, where around
The Island of the Blest, the airs
Of Ocean breathe, and golden flowers
Blaze; some on land
From shining trees, and other kinds
The water feeds. Of these
Garlands and bracelets round their arms they bind,
Beneath the righteous sway
Of Rhadamanthus.—*Ol.* ii. 126.

Lucretius has transferred these fortunate fields to the superior regions, to form the abode of his *fainéans,* gods; and Virgil has placed them, with additional poetic splendour, in the bosom of the earth.

Widely different from these calm and peaceful abodes of parted warriors are the Faeries of the minstrels and romancers. In their eyes, and in those of their auditors, nothing was beautiful or good divested of the pomp and pride of chivalry; and chivalry has, accordingly, entered deeply into the composition of their pictures of these ideal realms.

The Feeries of romance may be divided into three kinds Avalon, placed in the ocean, like the Island of the Blest; those that, like the palace of Pan Banou, are within the earth; and, lastly, those that, like Oberon's domains, are situate 'in wilderness among the holtis hairy.'

Of the castle and isle of Avalon, [a] the abode of Arthur and Oberon, and Morgue lit faye, the fullest description is to be seen in the romance of Ogier le Danois, from which, as we know no sure quarter but the work itself to refer to for the part connected with the present subject, we will make some extracts. [b]

At the birth of Ogier several Fairies attended, who bestowed on him various gifts. Among them was Morgue la Faye, who gave him that he should be her lover and friend. Accordingly, when Ogier had long distinguished himself in love and war, and had. attained his hundredth year, the affectionate Morgue thought it was time to withdraw him from the toils and dangers of mortal life, and transport him to the joys and the repose of the castle of Avalon. In pursuance of this design, Ogier and king Caraheu are attacked by a storm on their return from Jerusalem, and their vessels separated. The bark on which Ogier was "floated along the sea till it came near the castle of loadstone, which is called the castle of Avalon, which is not far on this side of the terrestrial paradise, whither were rapt in a flame of fire Enock and Helias; and where was Morgue la Faye, who at his birth had endowed him with great gifts, noble and virtuous." [c]

The vessel is wrecked against the rock; the provisions are divided among the crew, and it is agreed that every man, as his stock failed, should be thrown into the sea. Ogier's stock holds out longest, and he remains alone. He is nearly reduced to despair, when a voice from heaven cries to him:

"God commandeth thee that, as soon as it is night, thou go unto a castle that thou wilt see shining, and pass from bark to bark till thou be in an isle which thou wilt find. And when thou wilt be in that isle thou wilt find a little path, and of what thou mayest see within be not dismayed at anything. And then Ogier looked, but he saw nothing." [d]

When night came, Ogier recommended himself to God, and seeing the castle of loadstone all resplendent with light, he went from one to the other of the vessels that were wrecked there, and so got into the island where it was. On arriving at the gate he found it guarded by two fierce lions. He slew them and entered; and making his way into a hall found a horse sitting at a table richly supplied. The courteous animal treats him with the utmost respect, and the starving hero makes a hearty supper. The horse then prevails on him to get on his back, and carries him into a splendid chamber, where Ogier sleeps that night. The name of this horse is Papillon, "who was a Luiton, and had been a great prince, but king Arthur conquered him, so he was condemned to be three hundred years a horse without speaking one single word, but after the three hundred years he was to have the crown of joy which they wore in Faerie." [e]

Next morning he cannot find Papillon, but on opening a door he meets a huge serpent, whom he also slays, and follows a little path which leads him into an orchard "tant bel et tant plaisant, que cestoit ung petit paradis a veoir." He plucks an apple from one of the trees and eats it, but is immediately affected by such violent sickness as to be put in fear of speedy death. He prepares himself for his fate, regretting "le bon pays de France, le roi Charlemaigne... et principallement la bonne royne dangleterre, sa bonne espouse et vraie amie, ma dame Clarice, qui tant estoit belle et noble." While in this dolorous state, happening to turn to the east, he perceived "une moult belle dame, toute vestue de blanc, si bien et si richement aornee que cestoit ung grant triumphe que de la veoir."

Ogier, thinking it is the Virgin Mary, commences an Ave; but the lady tells him she is Morgue la Faye, who at his birth had kissed him, and retained him for her loyal amoureux, though forgotten by him. She places then on his finger a ring, which removes all infirmity, and Ogier, a hundred years old, returns to the vigour and beauty of thirty. She now leads him to the castle of Avalon, where were her brother king Arthur, and Auberon, and Mallonbron, "ung luiton de mer."

"And when Morgue drew near to the said castle of Avalon, the Fays came to meet Ogier, singing the most melodiously that ever could be heard, so he entered into the hail to solace himself completely. There he saw several Fay ladies adorned and all crowned with crowns most sumptuously made, and very rich, and evermore they sung, danced, and led a right joyous life, without thinking of any evil thing whatever, but of taking their mundane pleasures." [f] Morgue here introduces the knight to Arthur, and she places on his head a crown rich and splendid beyond estimation, but which has the Lethean quality, that whoso wears it,

> Forthwith his former state end being forgets,
> Forgets both joy and grief, pleasure and pain;

for Ogier instantly forgot country and friends. He had no thought whatever *"ni de la dame Clarice, qui tant estoit belle et noble,"* nor of Guyon his brother, nor of his nephew Gauthier, *"ne de creature vivante."* His days now rolled on in never-ceasing pleasure. "Such joyous pastime did the Fay ladies make for him, that there is no creature in this world who could imagine or think it, for to hear them sing so sweetly it seemed to him actually that he was in Paradise; so the time passed from day to day, from week to week, in such sort that a year did not last a month to him." [8]

But Avalon was still on earth, and therefore its bliss was not unmixed. One day Arthur took Ogier aside, and informed him that Capalus, king of the Luitons, incessantly attacked the castle of Faerie with design to eject king Arthur from its dominion, and was accustomed to penetrate to the basse court, calling on Arthur to come out and engage him. Ogier asked permission to encounter this formidable personage, which Arthur willingly granted. No sooner, however, did Capalus see Ogier than he surrendered to him; and the knight had the satisfaction of leading him into the castle, and reconciling him to its inhabitants.

Two hundred years passed away in these delights, and seemed to Ogier but twenty: Charlemagne and all his lineage had failed, and even the race of Ogier was extinct, when the Paynims invaded France and Italy in vast numbers; and Morgue no longer thought herself justified in withholding Ogier from the defence of the faith. Accordingly, she one day took the Lethean crown from off his head: immediately all his old ideas rushed on his mind, and inflamed him with an ardent desire to revisit his country. The Fairy gave him a brand which was to be preserved from burning, for so long as it was unconsumed, so long should his life extend. She adds to her gift the horse Papillon and his comrade Benoist. "And when they were both mounted, all the ladies of the castle came to take, leave of Ogier, by the command of king Arthur and of Morgue la Faye, and they sounded an aubade of instruments, the most melodious thing to hear that ever was listened to; then, when the aubade was finished, they sung with the voice so melodiously, that it was a thing so melodious that it seemed actually to Ogier that he was in Paradise. Again, when that was over, they sung with the instruments in such sweet concordance that it seemed rather to be a thing divine than mortal." [h] The knight then took leave of all, and a cloud, enveloping him and his companion, raised them, and set them down by a fair fountain near Montpellier. Ogier displays his ancient prowess, routs the infidels, and on the death of the king is on the point of espousing the queen, when Morgue appears and takes him back to Avalon. Since then Ogier has never reappeared in this world.

Nowhere is a Faerie of the second kind so fully and circumstantially described as in the beautiful romance of Orfeo and Heurodis. There are, indeed, copious extracts from this poem in Sir Walter Scott's Essay on the Fairies of Popular Superstition; and we have no excuse to offer for repeating what is to be found in a work so universally diffused as the Minstrelsy of the Scottish Border, but that it is of absolute necessity for our purpose, and that romantic poetry is rarely unwelcome.

Orfeo and Heurodis were king and queen of Winchester. The queen happening one day to sleep under an ymp [i] tree in the palace orchard, surrounded by her attendants, had a dream, which she thus relates to the king:

> As I lay this undertide *(afternoon)*
> To sleep under the orchard-side,
> There came to me two faire knightes
> Well arrayed allè rightes,
> And bade me come without letting
> To speaké with their lord the king;
> And I answér'd with wordès bolde
> That I ne durstè ne I nolde:
> Fast again they can *(did)* drive,
> Then came their kingè nil no blive *(quick)*
> With a thousand knights and mo,
> And with ladies fifty also,
> And riden all on snow-white steedes,
> And also whitè were their weedes.
> I sey *(saw)* never sith I was borne
> So fairè knightés me by forne.
> The kingè had a crown on his head,
> It was not silver ne gold red;
> All it was *of* precious stone,
> As bright as sun forsooth it shone.
> All so soon he to me came,
> Wold I, nold I he me name *(took)*,
> And made me with him ride
> On a white palfrey by his side,
> And brought me in to his palis,
> Right well ydight over all ywis.
> He showed me castels and toures,
> Meadows, rivers, fields and flowres,
> And his forests everiche ones
> And sith he brought me again home.

The fairy-king orders her, under a dreadful penalty, to await him next morning under the ymp tree. Her husband and ten hundred knights stand in arms round the tree to protect her,

And yet amiddés them full right
The queenè was away y-twight *(snatched)*;
With Faery forth y-nome *(taken)*;
Men wist never where she was become.

Oribo in despair abandons his throne, and retires to the wilderness, where he solaces himself with his harp, charming with his melody the wild beasts, the inhabitants of the spot. Often while here,

He mightè see him besides
Oft in hot undertides
The king of Faery with his rout
Come to hunt him all about,
With dim cry and blowing,
And houndes also with him barking.
Ac *(yet)* no beastè they no nome,
Ne never he nist whither they become;
And other while he might them see
As a great hostè by him. te. [i]
Well atourned ten hundred knightes
Each well y-armed to his rightes,
Of countenancè stout. and fierce,
With many displayéd bannérs,
And each his sword y-drawè hold;
Ac never he nistè whither they wold.
And otherwhile ho seigh *(saw)* other thing,
Knightès and levedis *(ladses)* come dauncing
In quaint attire guisely,
Quiet pace and softely.
Tabours and trumpès gede *(went)* him by,
And allè manere minstracy.
And on a day he neigh him beside
Sixty levedis on horse ride,
Gentil and jolif as brid on ris *(bird on branch)*,
Nought o *(one)* man amonges hem ther nis,
And each a faucoun on hond bare,
And riden on hauken by o rivér.

Of game they found well good haunt,
Mallardes, heron, and cormeraunt.
The fowlès of the water ariseth,
Each faucoun them well deviseth,
Each faucoun his preyè slough [k] *(slew).*

Among the ladies he recognises his lost queen, and he determines to follow them, and attempt her rescue.

In at a roche *(rock)* the levedis rideth,
And he after and nought abideth.
When he was in the roche y-go
Well three milès other *(or)* mo,
Re came into a fair countráy
As bright soonne summers day,
Smooth and plain and allè grene,
Hill ne dale nas none y-seen.
Amiddle the lond a castel he seigh,
Rich and real and wonder high.
Allè the utmostè wall
Was clear and shinè of cristal.
An hundred towers there wore about,
Deguiselich and batailed stout.
The buttras come out of the ditch,
Of reds gold y-arched rich.
The bousour was anowed all
Of each manere diverse animal.
Within there were widè wones
All of precious stones.
The worstè pillar to behold
Was all of burnished gold.
All that lond was ever light,
For when it should be therk *(dark)* and night,
The richè stones lightè gonne *(yield* [l]*)*
Bright as doth at nonne the sonne,
No man may tell ne think in thought
The richè work that there was wrought.

Orfeo makes his way into this palace, and so charms the king with his minstrelsy, that he gives him back his wife. They return to Winchester, and there reign, in peace and happiness.

Another instance of this kind of Feerie may be seen in Thomas the Rymer, but, restricted by our limits, we must omit it, and pass to the last kind.

Sir Thopas was written to ridicule the romancers; its incidents must therefore accord with theirs, and the Feerie in it in fact resembles those in Huon de Bordeaux. It has the farther merit of having suggested incidents to Spencer; and perhaps of having given the idea of a queen regnante of Fairy Land. Sir Thopas is chaste as Graelent.

> Full many a maidè bright in bour
> They mourned for him *par amour;*
> When hem were bete to slepe;
> But he was chaste and no lechour,
> And sweet as is the bramble flour
> That bereth the red hepe.

He was therefore a suitable object for the love of a gentle elf-queen. So Sir Thopas one day "pricketh through a faire forest" till he is weary, and he then lies down to sleep on the grass, where he dreams of an elf-queen, and awakes, declaring

> An elf-queen wol I love, ywis.
> All other women I forsake,
> And to an elf-queen I me take
> By dale and eke by down.
> He determines to set out in quest of her.
> Into his sadel he clombe anon,
> And pricked over style and stone,
> An elf-quene for to espie;
> Till be so long had ridden and gone,

That he found in a privee wone
The countree of Faerie, [m]
Wherein he soughtè north and south,
And oft he spied with his mouth
In many a forest wilde;
For in that countree n'as there none
That to him dorst ride or gon,
Neither wif ne childe.
The "gret giaunt" Sire Oliphaunt, however, informs him that
Here is the quene of Faerie,
With harpe and pipe and simphonie,
Dwelling in this place.

Owing to the fastidiousness of "mine hoste," we are unable to learn how Sir Thopas fared with the elf-queen, and we have probably lost a copious description of Fairy Land.

From the glimmering of the morning star of English poetry, the transition is natural to its meridian splendour, the reign of Ellzabeth, and we will now make a few remarks on the poem of Spenser.

NOTES

[a] Avalon was perhaps the Island of the Blest, of Celtic mythology, and then the abode
of the Fees, through the Breton Korrigan. Writers, however, seem to be unanimous in
regarding it and Glastonbury as the same place, called an isle, it is stated, as being made
nearly such by the "river's embracement." It was named Avalon, we are told, from the
British word *Aval*, an apple, as it abounded with orchards and *Ynys gwydrin;* Saxon Glaytn-
ey, glassy isle; Latin, Glastonia, from the green hue of the water surrounding it.

[b] see Tales and Popular Fictions, ch. ix., for a further account of Ogier.

[c] Tant nagea en mer qu'il arriva pres du chastel daymant quon nomme le chastean
davallon, qui nest gueres deca paradis terrestre la ou furent ravis en une raye de feu Enoc
et Helye, et la ou estoit Morgue la faye, qui a sa naisance lui avoit donne de grands dons,
nobles et vertueux.

[d] Dieu te mande que si tost que sera nuit que tu allies en ung chasteau que tu verras luire,
et passe de bateau en bateau tant que tu soies en une isle que tu trouveras. Et quand tu
seras en lisle tu trouveras une petite sente, et de chose que tu voies leans ne tesbahis de
rien. Et adonc Ogier regarda mais il ne vit rien.

[e] Lequel estoit luiton, et avoit este ung grant prince; mais le roi Artus le conquist, si fust
condampne a estre trois cens ans cheval sans parler ung tout seul mot; mais apres lea
trois cens ans, il devoit avoir la couronne de joye do laquelle ils usuient en faerie.

[f] Et quand Morgue approcha du dit chasteau, les Faes vindrent an devant dogier, chantant
le plus melodieusement quon scauroit jamais ouir, si entra dedans in salle pour me
deduire totallement. Adonc vist plusieurs dames Faees sournees et toutes courrunnees
de couronnes tressomptueusement faictes, et moult riches, et tout jour chantoient,
dansoient, et menoient vie treajoyeuse, sans penser a nulle quelconque meschante
chose, fors prandre leurs moudains plaisirs.

[g] Tant de joyeulx passetemps lui faisoient les dames Faees, quil nest creature en ce monde
quil le sceust imaginer ne penser, car les ouir si doulcement chanter il lui sembloit
propprement quil fut en Paradis, si passoit temps de jour en jour, de sepmaine en
sepmaine, tellement que ung an ne lui duroit pas ung mois.

[h] Et quand ils furent tous deux montes, toutes les dames du chasteau vindrent a la
departie dogier, par le commandement du roi Artus et de Morgue la fae, et sonnerent
une aubade dinstrumeus, la plus melodieuse chose a ouir que on entendit jamais; puis,
l'aubade achevee, chanterent de gorge si melodieusement que cestoit une chose si
melodieuse que il sembloit propremont a Ogier quil estoit en Paradis. De rechief, cela
fini, ils chanterent avecques les instrumens par si doulce concordance quil sembloit
mieulx chose divine que humaine.

[i] Imp tree is a grafted tree. Sir W. Scott queries if it be not a tree consecrated to the imps or
fiends. Had imp that sense so early? A grafted tree had perhaps the same relation to the
Fairies that the linden in Gennany end the North had to the dwarfs.

[j] *Te* or *tao* (Dayton, Poly-Olb. xxv.) is to draw, to march ...

[k] Beattie probably knew nothing of Orfeo and Heurodis, and the Fairy Vision in the
Minstrel (a dream that would never have occurred to any minstrel) was derived from
the Flower and the Leaf, Dryden's, not Chaucer's, for the personages in the latter are not
called Fairies. In neither are they Elves.

[l] *Günnen*, Germ.

[m] The "countrie of Faerie," situated in a "privee wone," plainly accords rather with the Feeries of'
Huon de Bordeaux than with Avalon, or the region into which Dame Heurodis was taken.

SPENSER'S FÆRIE QUEENE

A braver lady never tript on land,
Except the ever-living Faerie Queene,
Whose virtues by her swain so written been
That time shall call her high enhanced story,
In his rare song, the Muse's chiefest glory.
—BROWN.

DURING THE sixteenth century the study of classical literature, which opened a new field to imagination, and gave it a new impulse, was eagerly and vigorously pursued. A classic ardour was widely and extensively diffused. The compositions of that age incessantly imitate and allude to the beauties and incidents of the writings of ancient Greece and Rome.

Yet amid this diffusion of classic taste and knowledge, romance had by no means lost its influence. The black-letter pages of Lancelot du Lac, Perceforest, Mort d'Arthur, and the other romances of chivalry, were still listened to with solemn attention, when on winter-evenings the family of the good old knight or baron 'crowded round the ample fire,' to hear them made vocal, and probably no small degree of credence was given to the wonders they recorded. The passion for allegory, too, remained unabated. Fine moral webs were woven from the fragile threads of the Innamorato and the Furioso; and even Tasso was obliged, in compliance with the reigning taste, to extract an allegory from his divine poem; which Fairfax, when translating the Jerusalem, was careful to preserve. Spenser, therefore, when desirous of consecrating his genius to the celebration of the glories of the maiden reign, and the valiant warriors and grave statesmen who adorned it, had his materials ready prepared. Fairy-land, as described by the romancers, gave him a scene; the knights and dames with whom it was peopled, actors; and its court, its manners, and usages, a facility of transferring thither whatever real events might suit his design.

It is not easy to say positively to what romance the poet was chiefly indebted for his Faery-land. We might, perhaps, venture to conjecture that his principal authority was Huon de Bordeaux, which had been translated some time before by Lord Berners, and from which it is most likely that Shakespeare took his Oberon, who was thus removed from the realms of romance, and brought back among his real kindred, the dwarfs or elves. Spenser, it is evident, was acquainted with this romance, for he says of Sir Guyon,

> He was an elfin born of noble state
> And mickle worship in his native land;
> Well could he tourney and in lists debate,
> And knighthood took of good *Sir Huon's* hand,
> When with King Oberon he came to Fairy-land.
> B. ii. c. 1. st. vi.

And here, if such a thing were to be heeded, the poet commits an anachronism in making Sir Huon, who slew the son of Charlemagne, a contemporary of Arthur.

Where "this delightful, land of Faery" lies, it were as idle to seek as for Oberon's realm of Mommur, the island of Calypso, or the kingdom of Lilliput. Though it shadow forth England, it is distinct from it; for Cleopolis excels Troynovant in greatness and splendour, and Elfin, the first Fairy king, ruled over India and America. To the curious the poet says,

> Of Faerylond yet if he more inquire,
> By certain signes here sett in sondrie place,
> He may it fynd ne let him then admyre,
> But yield his sence to be too blunt and bace,
> That no'te without an hound fine footing trace.

The idea of making a queen sole regnante of Fairy-land was the necessary result of the plan of making "the fayrest princesse under sky" view her "owne realmes in lond of faery." Yet there may have been sage authority for this settlement of the fairy throne. Some old romancers may have spoken only of a queen; and the gallant Sir Thopas does not seem to apprehend that he is in pursuit of the wedded wife of another. This doughty champion's dream was evidently the original of Arthur's.

> Forwearied with my sportes, I did alight
> From loftie steede, and downe to sleepe me layd;
> The verdant grass my couch did goodly dight,
> And pillow was my helmett fayre displayd;
> Whiles every sence the humour sweet embayd,
> Me seemed by my side a royall mayd
> Her dainty limbes full softly down did lay,
> So faire a creature yet saw never sunny day.
> Most goodly glee and lovely blandishment
> She to me made, and badd me love her deare,
> For dearly, sure, her love was to me bent,
> As, when iust time expired, should appeare:
> But whether dreames delude, or true it were,
> Was never hart so raviaht with delight,
> Ne living man such wordes did never heare
> As she to me delivered all that night,
> And at her parting said, she queen of Faires hight.

* * * * *

From that day forth I cast in carefull mynd
To seek her out with labor and long tyne,
And never vow to rest till her I fynd—
Nyne months I seek in vain, yet n'ill that vow unbynd.
B. i. c. 9. st. xiii, xiv., xv.

The names given by Spenser to these beings are Fays (*Feés*), Farys or Fairies, Elfes and Elfins, of which last words the former had been already employed by Chaucer, and in one passage it is difficult to say what class of beings is intended. Spenser's account of the origin of his Fairies is evidently mere invention, as nothing in the least resembling it is to be found in any preceding writer. It bears, indeed, some slight and distant analogy to that of the origin of the inhabitants of Jinnestan, as narrated by the Orientals. According to the usual practice of Spenser, it is mixed up with the fables of antiquity.

Prometheus did create
A man of many parts from beasts deryved;
That man so made he called Elfe, to weet,
Quick, [a] the first author of all Elfin kynd,
Who, wandring through the world with wearie feet,
Did in the gardins of Adonis fynd
A goodly creature, whom he deemed in mynd
To be no earthly wight, but either spright
Or angell, the anthour of all woman-kynd;
Therefore a Fay he her according hight,
Of whom all Faryes spring, and fetch their lignage right.
Of these a mighty people shortly grew,
And puissant kings, which all the world warrayd,
And to themselves all nations did subdue.
B. ii. c. 9. st. lxx., lxxi., lxxii.

Sir Walter Scott remarks with justice (though his memory played him somewhat false on the occasion), that "the stealing of the Red Cross Knight while a child, is the only incident in the poem which approaches to the popular character of the Fairy." It is not exactly the *only* incident; but the only other, that of Arthegal, is a precisely parallel one:-

> He wonneth in the land of Fayëree,
> Yet is no Fary born, ne sib at all
> To Elfes, but sprung of seed terrestriall,
> And whyleome by false Faries stolne away,
> Whyles yet in infant cradle he did crall:
> We other to himself is knowne this day,
> But that he by an Elfe was gotten of a Fay.
> B. iii. c.3. st xxvi.

Sir Walter has been duly animadverted on for this dangerous error by the erudite Mr. Todd. It would be as little becoming as politic in us, treading, as we do, on ground where error ever hovers around us, to make any remark. Freedom from misconception and mistake, unfortunately, forms no privilege of our nature.

We must here observe, that Spenser was extremely injudicious in his selection of the circumstances by which he endeavoured to confound the two classes of Fairies. It was quite incongruous to style the progeny of the subjects of Gloriane a "base elfin brood," or themselves "false Fairies," especially when we recollect that such a being as Belphoebe, whose

> whole creation did her shew
> Pure and unspotted from all loathly crime,
> That is ingenerate in fleshly slime,
> was born of a Fairie.

Our poet seems to have forgotten himself also in the Legend of Sir Calidore; for though the knight is a Faerie himself; and though such we are to suppose were all the native inhabitants of Faerie-land, yet to the "gentle flood" that tumbled down from Mount Acidale,

> ne mote the ruder clown
> Thereto approach ne filth mote therein drown;
> But Nymphs and Faeries on the banks did sit
> In the woods shade which did the waters crown.
> B. vi. c. 10. st vii.

And a little farther, when Calidore gazes on the "hundred naked maidens lily white," that danced around the Graces, he wist not

> Whether it were the train of beauty's queen,
> Or Nymphs or Faeries, or enchanted show,
> With which his eyes mote have deluded been.
> - St xvii.

The popular Elves, who dance their circlets on the green, were evidently here in Spenser's mind. [b]

It is now, we think, if not certain, at least highly probable, that the Fairy-land and the Fairies of Spenser are those of romance, to which the term Fairy properly belongs, and that it is without just reason that the title of his poem has been styled a *misnomer*. [c] After the appearance of his Faerie Queene, all distinction between the different species was rapidly lost, and Fairies became the established name of the popular Elves.

Here, then, we will take our leave of the potent ladies of romance, and join the Elves of the popular creed, tracing their descent from the Duergar of northern mythology, till we meet them enlivening the cottage fireside with the tales of their pranks and gambols.

NOTES

[a] That is, *elfe* is *alive*.

[b] These Fairies thus coupled with Nymphs remind us of the Fairies of the old translators. Spenser, in the Shepherd's Calendar, however, had united them before, as
Nor elvish ghosts nor ghastly owls do flee,
But friendly Faeries met with many Graces,
And light-foot Nymphs.—AEg. 6.

[c] "Spenser's Fairy Queen, which is one of the grossest misnomers in romance or history, bears no features of the Fairy nation."—Gifford, note on B. Jonson, vol. ii. p. 202.

EDDAS AND SAGAS

En sång om strålende Valhalla,
Om Gudar och Gudinnar alla.
    –TREGNER.

A song of Vallhall's bright abodes,
Of all the goddesses and gods.

THE ANCIENT religion of Scandinavia, and probably of the whole Gotho-German race, consisted, like all other systems devised by man, in personifications of the various powers of nature and faculties of mind. Of this system in its fulness and perfection we possess no record. It is only from the poems of the elder or poetic Edda, [a] from the narratives of the later or prose Edda and the various Sagas or histories written in the Icelandic language, [b] that we can obtain any knowledge of it.

The poetic or Saemund's Edda was, as is generally believed, collected about the end of the eleventh or beginning of the twelfth century by an Icelander named Saemund, and styled Hinns Fròda, or The Wise. It consists of a number of mythological and historical songs, the production of the ancient Scalds or poets, all, or the greater part, composed before the introduction of Christianity into the north. The measure of these venerable songs is alliterative rime, and they present not unfrequently poetic beauties of a high and striking character. [c]

The prose Edda is supposed to have been compiled in the thirteenth century by Snorro Sturleson, the celebrated historian of Norway. It is a history of the gods and their actions formed from the songs of the poetic Edda, and from other ancient poems, several stanzas of which are incorporated in it. Beside the preface and conclusion, it consists of two principal parts, the first consisting of the Gylfaginning *(Gylfa's Deception),* or Hárs Lygi *(Har's* i.e. *Odin's Fiction),* and the Braga-raedur *(Braga's Narrative),* each of which is divided into several Daemi-sagas or Illustrative Stories; and the second named the Kenningar or list of poetic names and periphrases. [d]

The Gylfa-ginning narrates that Gylfa king of Sweden, struck with the wisdom and power of the Aeser, [e] as Odin and his followers were called, journeyed in the likeness of an old man, and under the assumed name of Ganglar, to Asgard their chief residence, to inquire into and fathom their wisdom. Aware of his design, the Aeser by their magic art caused to arise before him a lofty and splendid palace, roofed with golden shields. At the gate he found a man who was throwing up and catching swords, seven of which were in the air at one time. This man inquires the name of the strange; whom he leads into the palace, where Ganglar sees a number of persons drinking and playing, and three thrones, each set higher than the other. On the thrones sat Har *(High),* Jafnhar *(Equal-high),* and Thridi *(Third).* Ganglar asks if there is any one there wise and learned. Har replies that he will not depart in safety if he knows more than they [f]. Ganglar then commences his interrogations, which embrace a variety of recondite subjects, and extend from the creation to the end of all things. To each he receives a satisfactory reply. At the last reply Ganglar hears a loud rush and noise: the magic illusion suddenly vanishes, and he finds himself alone on an extensive plain.

The Braga-raedur is the discourse of Braga to Aegir, the god of the sea, at the banquet of the Immortals. This part contains many tales of gods and heroes old, whose adventures had been sung by Skalds, of high renown and lofty genius.

Though both the Eddas were compiled by Christians, there appears to be very little reason for suspecting the compilers of having falsified or interpolated the mythology of their forefathers. Saemund's Edda may be regarded as an Anthology of ancient Scandinavian poetry; and the author of the prose Edda (who it is plain did not always understand the true meaning of the tales he related) wrote it as a northern Pantheon and Gradus ad Parnassum, to supply poets with incidents, ornaments, and epithets. Fortunately they did so, or impenetrable darkness had involved the ancient religion of the Gothic stock!

Beside the Eddas, much information is to be derived from the various Sagas or northern histories. These Sagas, at times transmitting true historical events, at other times containing the wildest fictions of romance, preserve much valuable mythic lore, and the Ynglinga, Volsunga, Hervarar, and other Sagas, will furnish many important traits of northern mythology.

It is not intended here to attempt sounding the depths of Eddaic mythology, a subject so obscure, and concerning which so many and various opinions occur in the works of those who have occupied themselves with it. Suffice it to observe that it goes back to the most remote ages, and that two essential parts of it are the Alfar (*Alfs* or *Elves*) and the Duergar (*Dwarfs*), two classes of beings whose names continue to the present day in all the languages of the nations descended from the Gotho-German race.

"Our heathen forefathers," says Thorlacius, [8] "believed, like the Pythagoreans, and the farther back in antiquity the more firmly, that the whole world was filled with spirits of various kinds, to whom they ascribed in general the same nature and properties as the Greeks did to their Daemons. These were divided into the Celestial and the Terrestrial, from their places of abode. The former were, according to the ideas of those times, of a good and elevated nature, and of a friendly disposition toward men, whence they also received the name of White or Light Alfs or Spirits. The latter, on the contrary, who were classified after their abodes in air, sea, and earth, were not regarded in so favourable a light. It was believed that they, particularly the *land ones,* the δαίμονες ἐπιχθόνιοι of the Greeks, constantly and on all occasions sought to torment or injure mankind, and that they had their dwelling partly on the earth in great thick woods, whence came the name Skovtrolde [h] *(Wood Trolls),* or in other desert and lonely places, partly in and under the ground, or in rocks and hills; these last were called Bjerg-Trolde*(Hill Trolls):* to the first, on account of their different nature, was given the name of Dverge *(Dwarf's),* and Alve, whence the word Ellefolk, which is still in the Danish language. These Daemons, particularly the underground ones, were called Svartálfar, that is Black Spirits, and inasmuch as they did mischief, Trolls."

This very nearly coincides with what is to be found in the Edda, except that there would appear to be some foundation for a distinction between the Dwarfs and the Dark Alfs. [i]

NOTES

[a] *Edda* signifies grandmother. Some regard it as the feminine of *othr,* or *odr,* wisdom.

[b] This language is so called because still spoken in Iceland. Its proper name is the Norraena Tunga *(northern tongue).* It was the common language of the whole North.

[c] see Tales and Popular Fictions, chap. ix.

[d] It was first published by Resenius in 1665.

[e] By the Aeser are understood the Asiatics, who with Odin brought their arts and religion into Scandinavia. This derivation of the word, however, is rather dubious. Though possibly the population and religion of Scandinavia came originally from Asia there seems to be no reason whatever for putting any faith in the legend of Odin. It is not unlikely that the name of their gods, Aeser, gave birth to the whole theory. It is remarkable that the ancient Etrurians also should have called the gods Aesar.

[f] So the Iötunn or Giant Vafthrudnir to Odin in the Vafthrudninual—Strophe vii.

[g] Thorlacius, Noget om Thor og hans Hammer, in the Skandinavisk Museum for 1803.

[h] Thorlacius, *ut supra,* says the thundering Thor was regarded as particularly inimical to the Skovtrolda, against whom be continually employed his mighty weapon. He thinks that the *Bidental*of the Romans, and the rites connected with it, seem to suppose a similar superstition, and that in the well-known passage of Horace,

Tu parum castis inimica mittes

Fulmina lucis,

the words *parum castis lucis* may mean groves or parts of woods, the haunt of unclean spirits or Skovtrolds, *satyri lascivi et salaces.* The word *Trold* will be explained below.

[i] The Dark Alfs were probably different from the Duergar, yet the language of the prose Edda is in some places such as to lead to a confusion of them. The following passage, however, seems to be decisive;

Náir, Dvergar

Ok Döck-A'lfar.

Hrafna-Galdr Othins, xxiv. 7.

Ghosts, Dwarfs

And Dark Alfs.

Yet the Scandinavian llterati appear unanimous in regarding them as the same. Grimm, however, agrees with us in viewing the Döck-Alfar as distinct from the Duergar. As the abode of these last is named Svartálfaheimr, lie thinks that the Svartálfar and the Duergar were the same.—Deutsche Mythologie, p. 413, *seq.* See below, *Isle of Rügen.*

The Alfar

Ther ro meth Alfum.
Brynhildar Quida.

(Those are with the Alfs.)

In the prose Edda, Ganglar inquires what other cities beside that in which the Nornir dwelt were by the Urdar fount, under the Ash Yggdrasil. [a] Hár replies,

"There are many fair cities there. There is the city which is called Alf-heim, where dwelleth the people that is called Liosálfar (*Light Alfs*). But the Döckálfar (*Dark Alfs*) dwell below under ground, and are unlike them in appearance, and still more unlike in actions. The Liosálfar are whiter than the sun in appearance, but the Döckálfar are blacker than pitch." [b]

The Nornir, the Parcae, or Destinies of Scandinavian mythology, are closely connected with the Alfar.

"Many fair cities are there in Heaven," says Hár, "and the divine protection is over all. There standeth a city under the ash near the spring, and out of its halls came three maids, who are thus named, Udr, Verthandi, Skulld (*Past, Present, Future*). These maids shape the life of man. We call them Nornir. But there are many Nornir; those who come to each child that is born, to shape its life, are of the race of the gods; but others are of the race of the Alfs; and the third of the race of dwarfs. As is here expressed,

Sundry children deen l
The Nornir to be—the same
Race they have not
Some are of Aeser-kin,
Some are of Alf-kin,
Some are the daughters of Dualin" (*i.e.* of the Dwarfs.)

"Then," said Ganglar, "if the Nornir direct the future destiny of men, they shape it very unequally. Some have a good life and rich, but some have little wealth and praise, some long life, some short." "The good Nornir, and well descended," sags Hár, "shape a good life; but as to those who meet with misfortune, it is caused by the malignant Nornir."

These Nornir bear a remarkable resemblance to the classical Parcae and to the fairies of romance. They are all alike represented as assisting at the birth of eminent personages, as bestowing gifts either good or evil, and as foretelling the future fortune of the being that has just entered on existence. [c] This attribute of the fairies may have been derived from either the north or the south, but certainly these did not borrow from each other.

Of the origin of the word Alf nothing satisfactory is to be found. Some think it is akin to the Latin *albus*, white; others, to *alpes*, Alps, mountains. There is also supposed to be some mysterious connexion between it and the word Elf or Elv, signifying water in the northern languages; an analogy which has been thought to correspond with that between the Latin Nympha and Lympha. Both relations, however, are perhaps rather fanciful than just. Of the derivation of Alf; as just observed, we know nothing certain, [d] and the original meaning of Nympha would appear to be a new-married woman, [e] and thence a marriageable young woman; and it. was applied to the supposed inhabitants of the mountains, seas, and streams, on the same principle that the northern nations gave them the appellation of men and women, that is, from their imagined resemblance to the human form.

Whatever its origin, the word Alf has continued till the present day in all the Teutonic languages. The Danes have *Elv,* pl. *Elve;* the Swedes, *Elf* pl. *Elfvar* m. *Elfvor* f.; and the words*Elf-dans* and *Elf-blaest,* together with *Olof* and other proper names, are derived from them. The Germans call the nightmare *Alp*; and in their old poems we meet with *Elbe* and*Elbinne,* and *Elbisch* occurs in them in the bad sense of *elvish* of Chaucer and our old romancers; and a number of proper names, such as Alprecht, Alphart, Alpinc, Alpwin [f] were formed from it, undoubtedly before it got its present ill sense. [g] In the Anglo-Saxon, Aelp or Aelpen, with its feminine and plural, frequently occurs. The Oreas, Naias, and Hamodryas of the Greeks and Romans are rendered in an Anglo-Saxon glossary by Munt-al-pen, *rae*-aelpen, and *pelb*-aelpen [h] Aelp is a component part of the proper names Aelfred and Aelfric; and the author of the poem of Judith says that his heroine was Aelp-rcine *(Elf-sheen),* bright or fair as an elf. But of the character and acts of the elfs no traditions have been preserved in Anglo-Saxon literature. In the English language, Elf; Elves, and their derivatives are to be found in every period, from its first formation down to this present time.

NOTES

[a] the ash-tree, Yggdrasil, is the symbol of the universe, the Urdar-fount Is the fount of light and heat, which invigorates and sustains it. A good representation of this myth is given in Mr. Bohn's edition of Mallet's " Northern Antiquities," which the reader is recommended to consult.

[b] this Grimm *(ut sup.)* regards as an error of the writer, who confounded the *Döck* and the *Svartálfar*

[c] see Tales and Popular Fictions, p. 274

[d] the analogy of Deev, and other words of like import, might lead to the supposition of Spirit being the primary meaning of Alf.

[e] see Mythology of Greece and Italy, p. 248, second edition.

[f] after the introduction of Christianity, *Engel,* angel, was employed for *Alp* in most proper names, as Engelrich, Engelhart, etc.

[g] see MM. Grimm's learned Introduction to their translation of the Irish Fairy Legends, and the Deutsche Mythologie of J. Grimm.

[h] MM. Grimm suppose with a good deal of probability, that these are compounds formed to render the Greek ones, and are not expressive of a belief in analogous classes of spirits.

The Duergar

By ek fur jőrth nethan,
A ek, undir stein, stath.
Alvis—Mal.

(I dwell the earth beneath,
I possess, under the stone, my seat.)

These diminutive beings, dwelling in rocks and hills, and distinguished for their skill in metallurgy, seem to be peculiar to the Gotho-German mythology [a] Perhaps the most probable account of them is, that they are personifications of the subterraneous powers of nature; for it may be again observed, that all the parts of every ancient mythology are but personified powers, attributes, and moral qualities. The Edda thus describes their origin:-

"Then the gods sat on their seats, and held a council, and called to mind how the Duergar had become animated in the clay below in the earth, like maggots in flesh. The Duergar had been first created, and had taken life in Ymir's [b] flesh, and were maggots in it, and by the will of the gods 'they became partakers of human knowledge, and had the likeness of men, and yet they abode in the ground and in stones. Modsogner was the first of them, and then Dyrin."

The Duergar are described as being of low stature, with short legs and long arms, reaching almost down to the ground when they stand erect. [c] They are skilful and expert workmen in gold, silver, iron, and the other metals. They form many wonderful and extraordinary things for the Aeser, and for mortal heroes, and the arms and armour that come from their forges are not to be paralleled. Yet the gift must be spontaneously bestowed, for misfortune attends those extorted from them by violence [d]

In illustration of their character we bring forward the following narratives from the Edda and Sagas. The homely garb in which they are habited, will not, it is hoped, be displeasing to readers of taste. We give as exact & copy as we are able of the originals in all their rudeness. The tales are old, their date unknown, and they therefore demand respect. Yet it is difficult to suppress a smile at finding such familiar, nay almost vulgar terms [e] applied to the great supernal powers of nature, as occur in the following tale from the Edda.

NOTES

[a] some think, but with little reason, they were originally a part of the Finnish mythology, and were adopted into the Gothic system

[b] the giant Ynsir is a personification of Chaos, the undigested primal matter. The sons of Börr (other personifications) slew him. Out of him they formed the world; his blood made the sea, his flesh the land; his bones the mountains; rocks and cliffs were his teeth, jaws, and broken pieces of bones; his skull formed the heavens.

[c] Gudmund Andreas in notis ad Völsupá.

[d] that they are not insensible to kindness one of the succeeding tales will show.

[e] the habitual reader of the northern and German writers, or even our old English ones, will observe with surprise his gradually diminished contempt for many expressions now become vulgar. He will find himself imperceptibly falling into the habit of regarding thorns in the light of their pristine-dignity.

Loki and the Dwarf

Loki the son of Laufeiar, had out of mischief cut off all the hair of Sif. When Thor found this out he seized Loki, and would have broken every bone in his body, only that he swore to get the Suartalfar to make for Sif hair of gold, which would grow like any other hair.

Loki then went to the Dwarfs that are called the sons of Ivallda. They first made the hair, which as soon as it was put on the head grew like natural hair; then the ship Skidbladni, [a] which always had the wind with it, wherever it would sail; and, thirdly, the spear Gugner, which always hit in battle.

Then Loki laid his head against the dwarf Brock, that his brother Eitri could not forge three such valuable things as these were. They went to the forge; Eitri set the swine. skin (bellows) to the fire, and bid his brother Brock to blow, and not to quit the fire till he should have taken out the things he had put into it.

And when he was gone out of the forge, and that Brock was blowing, there came a fly and settled upon his hand, and bit him; but he blew without stopping till the smith took the work out of the fire; and it was a boar, and its bristles were of gold.

He then put gold into the fire, and bid him not to stop blowing till be came back. He went away, and then the fly came and settled on his neck, and bit him more severely than before; but he blew on till the smith came back and took out of the fire the gold-ring which is called Drupner. [b]

Then he put iron into the fire, and bid him blow, and said that if he stopped blowing all the work would be lost. The fly now settled between his eyes, and bit so hard that the blood ran into his eyes, so that he could not see; so when the bellows were down be caught at the fly in all haste, and tore off its wings; but then came the smith, and said that all that was in the fire had nearly been spoiled. He then took out of the fire the hammer Miölner, [c] gave all the things to his brother Brock, and bade him go with them to Asgard and settle the wager.

Loki also produced his jewels, and they took Odin, Thor, and Frey, for judges. Then Loki gave to Odin the spear Gugner, and to Thor the hair that Sif was to have, and to Frey Skidbladni, and told their virtues as they have been already related. Brock took out his jewels, and gave to Odin the ring, and said that every ninth night there would drop from it eight other rings as valuable as itself. To Frey he gave the boar, and said that he would run through air and water, by night and by day, better than any horse, and that never was there night so dark that the way by which he went would not be light from his hide. He gave the hammer to Thor, and said that it would never fail to hit a Troll, and that at whatever he threw it it would never miss it; and that he could never fling it so far that it would not of itself return to his band; and when he chose, it would become so small that he might put it into his pocket. But the fault of the hammer was that its handle was too short.

Their judgment was, that the hammer was the best, and that the Dwarf had won the wager. Then Loki prayed hard not to lose his head, but the Dwarf said that could not be. "Catch me then," said Loki; and when he went to catch him he was far away, for Loki had shoes with which he could run through air and water. Then the Dwarf prayed Thor to catch him, and Thor did so. The Dwarf now went to cut off his head, but Loki said he was to have the head only, and not the neck. Then the Dwarf took a knife and a thong, and went to sew up his mouth; but the knife was bad, so the Dwarf wished that his brother's awl were there; and as soon as he wished itit was there, and he sewed his lips together. [d]

*

Northern mythologists thus explain this very ancient fable. Sif is the earth, and the wife of Thor, the heaven or atmosphere; her hair is the trees, bushes, and plants, that adorn the surface of the earth. Loki is the Fire-God, that delights in mischief, *bene servit, male imperat.* When by immoderate heat he has burned off the hair of Sif, her husband compels him so by temperate heat to warm the moisture of the earth, that its former products may spring up more beautiful than ever. The boar is given to Freyr, to whom and his sister Freya, as the gods of animal and vegetable fecundity, the northern people offered that animal, as the Italian people did, to the earth. Loki's bringing the gifts from the under-ground people seems to indicate a belief that metals were prepared by subterranean fire, and perhaps the forging of Thor's hammer, the mythic emblem of thunder, by a terrestrial demon, on a subterranean anvil, may suggest that the natural cause of thunder is to be sought in the earth.

[a] Skidbladni, like Pari Banou's tent, could expand and contract as required. It would carry all the Aeser and their arms, and when not in use it could be taken asunder and put in a purse. "A good ship," says Ganglar, " is Skidbladni, but great art must have been employed in making it." Mythologists say it is the clouds.

[b] *i. e.* The *Dripper.*

[c] *i. E.* The *Bruiser* or *Crusher,* from *Myla,* to bruise or crush. Little the Fancy know of the high connexions of their phrase *Mill.*

[d] Edda Resenii, Daemisaga 59.

Thorston and the Dwarf

When spring came, Thorston made ready his ship, and put twenty-four men on board of her. When they came to Vinland, they ran her into a harbour, and every day he went on shore to amuse himself.

He came one day to an open part of the wood, where he saw a great rock, and out a little way from it a Dwarf, who was horridly ugly, and was looking up over his head with his mouth wide open; and it appeared to Thorston that it ran from ear to ear, and that the lower jaw came down to his knees. Thorston asked him, why he was acting so foolishly. "Do not be surprised, my good lad," replied the Dwarf; "do you not see that great dragon that is flying up there? He has taken off my son, and I believe that it is Odin himself that has sent the monster to do it. But I shall burst and die if I lose my son." Then Thorston shot at the dragon, and bit him under one of the wings, so that he fell dead to the earth; but Thorston caught the Dwarf's child in the air, and brought him to his father.

The Dwarf was exceeding glad, and was more rejoiced than any one could tell; and he said, "A great benefit have I to reward you for, who are the deliverer of my son; and now choose your recompense in gold and silver." "Cure your son;" said Thorston, "but I am not used to take rewards for my services." "It were not becoming," said the Dwarf, "if I did not reward you; and let not my shirt of sheeps' -wool, which I will give you, appear a contemptible gift, for you will never be tired when swimming, or get a wound, if you wear it next your skin."

Thorston took the shirt and put it on, and it fitted him well, though it had appeared too short for the Dwarf. The Dwarf now took a gold ring out of his purse and gave it to Thorston, and bid him to take good care of it, telling him that he never should want for money while be kept that ring. He next took a black stone and gave it to Thorston, and said, "If you hide this stone in the palm of your hand no one will see you. I have not many more things to offer you, or that would be of any value to you; I will, however, give you a fire-stone for your amusement."

He then took the stone out of his purse, and with a steel point. The stone was triangular, white on one side and red on the other, and a yellow border ran round it. The Dwarf then said, "If you prick the stone with the point in the white side, there will come on such a hail-storm that no one will be able to look at it; but if you want to stop this shower, you have only to prick on the yellow part, and there will come so much sunshine that the whole will melt away. But if you should like to prick the red side, then there will come out of it such fire, with sparks and crackling, that no one will be able to look at it, You may also get whatever you will by means of this point and stone, and they will come of themselves back to your band when you call them. I can now give you no more such gifts."

Thorston then thanked the Dwarf for his presents, and re-turned to his men, and it was better for him to have made this voyage than to have stayed at home.

[Thorston's Saga, c. 3, in the Kampa Däter.]

The Dwarf-Sword Tirfing

Suaforlami, the second in descent from Odin, was kin over Gardarike (Russia). One day he rode a-hunting, an sought long after a hart, but could not find, one the whole day. When the sun was setting he found himself immersed so deep in the forest that he knew not where he was. There lay a hill on his right hand, and before it he saw two Dwarfs; he drew his sword against them, and cut off their retreat by getting between them and the rock. They proffered him ransom for their lives, and he asked them then their names, and one of them was called Dyren, and the other Dualin. He knew then that they were the most ingenious and expert of all the Dwarfs, and he therefore imposed on them that they should forge him a sword, the best that they could form; its hilt should be of gold, and its belt of the same metal. He moreover enjoined, that the sword should never miss a blow, and should never rust; and. should cut through iron and stone, as through a garment; and should be always victorious in war and in single combat for him who bare it. These were the conditions on which he gave them their lives.

On the appointed day he returned, and the Dwarfs came forth and delivered him the sword; and when Dualin stood in the door he said, "This sword shall be the bane of a man every time it is drawn; and with it shall be done three of the greatest atrocities. It shall also be thy bane." Then Suaforlami struck at the Dwarf so, that the blade of the sword penetrated into the solid rock. Thus Suaforlami became possessed of this sword, and he called it Tirfing, and he bare it in war and in single combat, and he slew with it the Giant Thiasse, and took his daughter Fridur.

Suaforlami was shortly after slain by the Berserker [a] And-grim, who then became master of the sword. When the twelve sons of Andgrim were to fight with Hialmar and Oddur for Ingaborg, the beautiful daughter of King Inges, Angantyr bore the dangerous Tirf-ing; but all the brethren were slain in the combat, and were buried with their arms.

Angantyr left an only daughter, Hervor, who, when she grew up, dressed herself in man's attire, and took the name of Hervardar, and joined a party of Vikinger, or Pirates. Knowing that Tirfing lay buried with her father, she determined to awaken the dead, and obtain the charmed blade; and perhaps nothing in northern poetry equals in interest and sublimity the description of her landing alone in the evening on the island of Sams, where her father and uncles lay in their sepulchral mounds, and at night ascending to the tombs, that were enveloped in flame, [b] and by force of entreaty obtaining from the reluctant Angantyr the formidable Tirfing.

Hervor proceeded to the court of King Gudmund, and there one day, as she was playing at tables with the king, one of the ser-vants chanced to take up and draw Tirfing, which shone like a sun-beam. But Tirfing was never to see the light but for the bane of man, and Hervor, by a sudden impulse, sprang from her seat, snatched the sword and struck off the head of the unfortunate man. Hervor, after this, returned to the house of her grandfather, Jarl Biartmar, where she resumed her female attire, and was married to Haufud, the son of King Gudmund. She bare him two sons, Angantyr and Heidreker; the former of a mild and gentle disposition, the latter violent and fierce. Haufud would not permit Heidreker to remain at his court; and as he was departing, his mother, with other gifts, presented him Tirfing. His brother accompanied him out of the castle. Before they parted, Heidreker drew out his sword to look at and admire it; but scarcely did the rays of light fall on the magic blade, when the Berserker rage came on its owner, and he slew his gentle brother.

After this be joined a body of Vikinger, and became so distinguished, that King Harold, for the aid he lent him, gave him his daughter Helga in marriage. But it was the destiny of Tirfing to commit crime, and Harold fell by the hand of his son-in-law. Heidreker was afterwards in Russia, and the son of the king was his foster-son. One day, as they were out hunting, Heidreker and his foster-son happened to be separated from the rest of the party, when a wild boar appeared before them; Heidreker ran at him with his spear, but the beast caught it in his mouth and broke it across. He then alighted and drew Tirfing, and killed the boar; but on looking around, he could see no one but his foster-son, and Tirfing could only be appeased with warm human blood, and he slew the unfortunate youth. Finally, King Heidreker was murdered in his bed by his Scottish slaves, who carried off Tirfing; but his son Angantyr, who succeeded him, discovered and put them to death, and recovered the magic blade. In battle against the Huns he afterwards made great slaughter; but among the slain was found his own brother Laudur. And so ends the history of the Dwarf-sword Tirfing. [c]

Like Alf, the word Duergr has retained its place in .the Teutonic languages. Dverg [d] is the term still used in the north; the Germans have Zwerg, and we Dwarf [e] which, however, is never synonymous with Fairy, as Elf is. Ihre rejects all the etymons proposed for it, such, for example, as that of Gudmund Andreae, θέοη ἐργον; and with abundant reason.

Some have thought that by the Dwarfs were to be understood the Finns, the original inhabitants of the country, who were driven to the mountains by the Scandinavians, and who probably excelled the new-comers in the art of working their mines and manufacturing their produce. Thorlacius, on the contrary, thinks that it was Odin and his followers, who came from the country of the Chalybes, that brought the metallurgic arts into Scandinavia.

Perhaps the simplest account of the origin of the Dwarfs is, that when, in the spirit of all ancient religions, the subterranean powers of nature were to be personified, the authors of the system, from observing that people of small stature usually excel in craft and ingenuity, took occasion to represent the beings who formed crystals and purified metals within the bowels of the earth as of diminutive size, which also corresponded better with the power assigned them of slipping through the fissures and interstices of rocks and stones. Similar observations led to the representation of the wild and awful powers of brute nature under the form of huge giants.

NOTES

[a] The Berserkers were warriors who used to be inflamed with such rage and fury at the thoughts of combats as to bite their shields, run through fire, swallow burning coals, and perform such like mad feats. "Whether the avidity for fighting or the ferocity of their nature;" says Saxo, "brought this madness on then is uncertain."

[b] The northern nations believed that the tombs of their heroes emitted a kind of lambent flame, which was always visible in the night, and served to guard the ashes of the dead; they called it *Hauga Elldr,* or The Sepulchral Fire. It was supposed more particularly to surround such tombs as contained hidden treasures.—*Bartholin, Contempt. a Dan. Morte,* p. 275.

[c] Hervarar Saga *passim.* The Tirfing Saga would be Its more proper appellation. In poetic and romantic interest it exceeds all the northern Sagas.

[d] In Swedish Dverg also signifies a spider.

[e] In the old Swedish metrical history of Alexander, the word *Duerf* occurs. The progress in the English word is as follows: Anglo-Saxon—thence *dwerke;*
A maid that is a messingere
And a *dwerke* me brought here,
Her to do socoúr.
Lybeaus Disconus
lastly, *dwarf,* as in old Swedish.

118

SCANDINAVIA

Du vare syv og hundrede Trolde,
De vera bade grumme og lede,
De vilde gjöre Bonden et Gjaesterle,
Med hannem baade drikke og aede.
−ELINE AF VILLENSKOV.

There were seven and a hundred Trolls,
They were both ugly and grim,
A visit they would the farmer make,
Both eat and drink with him.

UNDER THE name of Scandinavia are included the kingdoms of Sweden, Denmark, and Norway, which once had a common religion and a common language. Their religion is still one, and their languages differ but little; we therefore feel that we may safely treat of their Fairy Mythology together.

Our principal authorities are the collection of Danish popular trañitions, published by Mr. Thiele, [a] the select Danish ballads of Nyerup and Rahbek, [b] and the Swedish ballads of Geijer and Afzelius. [c] As most of the principal Danish ballads treating of Elves, etc., have been already translated by Dr. Jamieson, we will not insert; them here; but translate, instead, the corresponding Swedish ones, which are in general of greater simplicity, and often contain additional traits of popular belief. As we prefer fidelity to polish, the reader must not be offended at antique modes of expression and imperfect rimes. Our rimes we can, however, safely say shall be at least as perfect as those of our originals.

These ballads, none of which are later than the fifteenth century, are written in a strain of the most artless simplicity not the slightest attempt at ornament is to be discerned in them; the same ideas and expressions continually recur; and the rimes are the most careless imaginable, often a mere *assonance* in vowels or consonants; sometimes not possessing even that slight similarity of sound. Every Visa or ballad has its single or double Omquaed [d] or burden, which, like a running accompaniment in music, frequently falls in with the most happy effect; sometimes recalling former joys or sorrows; sometimes, by the continual mention of some attribute of one of the seasons, especially the summer, keeping up in the mind of the reader or hearers the forms of external nature.

It is singular to observe the strong resemblance between the Scandinavian ballads and those of England and Scotland, not merely in manner but in subject. The Scottish ballad first mentioned below is an instance; it is to be met with in England, in the Feroes, in Denmark, and in Sweden, with very slight differences. Geijer observes, that the two last stanzas of 'William and Margaret,' in Percy's Reliques, are nearly word for word the same as the two last in the Swedish ballad of 'Rosa Lilla,' [e] and in the corresponding Danish one. This might perhaps lead to the supposition of many of these ballads having come down from the time when the connexion was so intimate between this country and Scandinavia.

We will divide the Scandinavian objects of popular belief into four classes:- 1. The Elves; 2. The Dwarfs, or Trolls, as they are usually called; 3. The Nisses; and 4. The Necks, Mermen, and Mermaids. [f]

NOTES

[a] Danske Folkesagn, 4 vols. l2mo. Copenh. 1818—22.

[b] Udvalgde Danske Viser fra Middelaldaren, 5 vols. l2mo. Copenh. 1812.

[c] Svenska Folk-Visor fran Forntiden, 3 vols. 8vo, Stockholm, 1814—16. We have not seen the late collection of Arvideson named Svenska Fornsangur, in 3 vols. 8vo.

[d] The reader will find a beautiful instance of a double Omquaed in the Scottish ballad of the Cruel Sister.

There were two sisters sat in a bower,
Binnörie o Binnörie
There came a knight to be their wooer
By the bonny mill-dams of Binnörie.

And in the Cruel Brother,

There were three ladies played at the ba',
With a heigh ho and a lily gay;
There came a knight and played o'er them a',
As the primrose spreads so sweetly.

The second and fourth lines are repeated in every stanza.

[e] These are the Swedish verses:

Det växte upp *Liljor* på begge deres graf,
Med äran och med dygd—
De växte tilsamman med alla sina blad.
J vinnen väl, J vinnen väl både rosor och liljor.
Det växte upp *Roser* ur bäda deras mun,
De växte tilsammans i fagreste lund.
J vinnen väl, J vinnen väl både rosor och liljor.

[f] Some readers may wish to know the proper mode of pronouncing such Danish and Swedish words as occur in the following legends. For their satisfaction we give the following information. J is pronounced as our y; when it comes between a consonant and a vowel, it is very short, like the y that is expressed, but not written, in many English words after c and g: thus *kjaer* is pronounced very nearly as *care:* ö sounds like the German ö, or French *eu: d* after another consonant is rarely sounded, Trold is pronounced Troll: *aa*, which the Swedes write å, as o in *more, tore.* Aarhuus is pronounced *Ore-hoos.*

ELVES

Säg, kännar du Elfvornas glada slägt?
De bygga ved fiodernas rand;
De spinna af månsken sin högtidsdrägt,
Med liljehvit spelande hand.
−STAGNELIUS.

Say, knowest thou the Elves' gay and joyous race?
The banks of streams are their home;
They spin of the moonshine their holiday-dress,
With their lily-white hands frolicsome.

The Alfar still live in the memory and traditions of the peasantry of Scandinavia. They also, to a certain extent, retain their distinction into White and Black. The former, or the Good Elves, dwell in the air, dance on the grass, or sit in the leaves of trees; the latter, or Evil Elves, are regarded as an underground people, who frequently inflict sickness or injury on mankind; for which there is a particular kind of doctors called *Kloka män,* [a] to be met with in all parts of the country.

The Elves are believed to have their kings, and to celebrate their weddings and banquets, just the same as the dwellers above ground. There is an interesting intermediate class of them in popular tradition called the Hill-people *(Högfolk),* who are believed to dwell in caves and small hills: when they show themselves they have a handsome human form. The common people seem to connect with them a deep feeling of melancholy, as if bewailing a half-quenched hope of redemption. [b]

There are only a few old persons now who can tell any thing more about them than of the sweet singing that may occasionally on summer nights be beard out of their hills, when one stands still and listens, or, as it is expressed in the ballads, "lays his ear to the Elve-hill" *(lägger sit öra till Elfvehögg)*: but no one must be so cruel as, by the slightest word, to destroy their hopes of salvation, for then the spritely music will be turned into weeping and laanentation. [c]

The Norwegians call the Elves Huldrafolk, and their music Huldraslaat: it is in the minor key, and of a dull and mournful sound. The mountaineers sometimes play it, and pretend they have learned it by listening to the underground people among the hills and rocks. There is also a tune called the Elf-king's tune, which several of the good fiddlers know right well, but never venture to play, for as soon as it begins both old and young, and even inanimate objects, are impelled to dance, and the player cannot stop unless be can play the air backwards, or that some one comes behind him and cuts the strings of his fiddle. [d]

The little underground Elves, who are believed to dwell under the houses of mankind, are described as sportive and mischievous, and as imitating all the actions of men. They are said to love cleanliness about the house and place, and to reward such servants as are neat and. cleanly.

There was one time, it is said, a servant girl, who was for her cleanly, tidy habits, greatly beloved by the Elves, particularly as she was careful to carry away all dirt and foul water to a distance from the house, and they once invited her to a wedding. Every thing was conducted in the greatest order, and they made her a present of some chips, which she took good-homouredly and put into her pocket. But when the bride-pair was coming there was a straw unluckily lying in the way, the bridegroom got cleverly over it, but the poor bride fell on her face. At the sight of this the girl could not restrain herself, but burst out a-laughing, and that instant the whole vanished from her sight. Next day, to her utter amazement, she found that what she had taken to be nothing but chips, were so many pieces of pure gold. [e]

A dairy-maid at a place called Skibshuset *(the Ship-house)*, in Odense, was not so fortunate. A colony of Elves had taken up their abode under the floor of the cowhouse, or it is more likely, were there before it was made a cowhouse. However, the dirt and filth that the cattle made annoyed them beyond measure, and they gave the dairy-maid to understand that if she did not remove the cows, she would have reason to repent it. She gave little heed to their representations; and it was not very long till they set her up on top of the hay-rick, and killed all the cows. It is said that they were seen on the same night removing in a great hurry from the cowhouse down to the meadow, and that they went in little coaches; and their king was in the first coach, which was far more stately and magnificent than the rest. They have ever since lived in the meadow. [f]

The Elves are extremely fond of dancing in the meadows, where they form those circles of a livelier green which from them are called Elf-dance *(Elfdans)*. When the country people see in the morning stripes along the dewy grass in the woods and meadows, they say the Elves have been dancing there. If any one should at midnight get within their circle, they become visible to him, and they may then illude him. It is not every one that can see the Elves; and one person may see them dancing while another perceives nothing. Sunday children, as they are called, *i. e.* those born on Sunday, are remarkable for possessing this property of seeing Elves and similar beings. The Elves, however, have the power to bestow this gift on whomsoever they please. People also used to speak of Elf-books which they gave to those whom they loved, and which enabled them to foretell future events.

The Elves often sit in little stones that are of a circular form, and are called Elf-mills *(Elf-quärnor);* the sound of their voice is said to be sweet and soft like the air. [8]

The Danish peasantry give the following account of their Elle-folk or Elve-people.

The Elle-people live in the Elle-moors. The appearance of the man is that of an old man with a low-crowned hat on his head; the Elle-woman is young and of a fair and attractive countenance, but behind she is hollow like a dough-trough. Young men should be especially on their guard against her, for it is very difficult to resist her; and she has, moreover, a stringed instrument, which, when she plays on it, quite ravishes their hearts. The man may be often seen near the Elle-moors, bathing himself in the sunbeams, but if any one comes too near him, he opens his mouth wide and breathes upon them, and his breath produces sickness and pestilence. But the women are most frequently to be seen by moonshine; then they dance their rounds in the high grass so lightly and so gracefully, that they seldom meet a denial when they offer their hand to a rash young man. It is also necessary to watch cattle, that they may not graze in any place where the Elle-people have been; for if any animal come to a place where the Elle-people have spit, or done what is worse, it is attacked by some grievous disease which can only be cured by giving it to eat a handful of St. John's wort, which had been pulled at twelve o'clock on St. John's night. It might also happen that they might sustain some injury by mixing with the Elle-people's cattle, which are very large, and of a blue colour, and which may sometimes be seen in the fields licking up the dew, on which they live. But the farmer has an easy remedy against this evil; for he has only to go to the Elle-hill when he is turning out his cattle and to say, "Thou little Troll! may I graze my cows on thy hill?" And if he is not prohibited, he may set his mind at rest. [h]

The following ballads and tales will fully justify what baa been said respecting the tone of melancholy connected with the subject of the Elves. [i]

NOTES

[a] That is, Wise People or Conjurors. They answer to the Fairy-women of Ireland.

[b] Afzelius is of opinion that this notion respecting the Hill-people is derived from the time of the introduction of Christianity into the north, and expresses the sympathy of the first converts with their forefathers, who had died without a knowledge of the Redeemer, and lay buried in heathen earth, and whose unhappy spirits were doomed to wander about these lower regions, or sigh within their mounds till the great day of redemption.

[c] "About fifteen years ago," says Odman (Bahuslän, p. 80), "people used to hear, out of the hill under Gärun, in the parish of Tanum, the playing, as it were, of the very best musicians. Any one there who had a fiddle, and wished to play, was taught in an instant, provided they promised them salvation; but whoever did not do so, might hear them within, in the hill, breaking their violins to pieces, sad weeping bitterly." See Grimm. Deut. Myth. 461.

[d] Arndt, Reise nach Schweden, iv. 241.

[e] Svenska Folk-Visor, vol. iii. p. 159. There is a similar legend in Germany. A servant, one time, seeing one of the little ones very hard-set to carry a single grain of wheat, burst out laughing at him. In a rage, he threw it on the ground, and it proved to be the purest gold. But he and his comrades quitted the house, and it speedily went to decay.—Strack. Beschr. v. Eilsen, p. 124, ap.Grimm, Introd., etc., p. 90.

[f] Thiele, vol. iv. p. 22. They are called Trolls in the original. As they had a king, we think they must have been Elves. The Dwarfs have long since abolished monarchy.

[g] The greater part of what precedes has been taken from Afzelius in the Svenska Visor, vol. iii.

[h] Thiele, iv. 26.

[i] In the distinction which we have made between the Elves and Dwarfs we find that we are justified by the popular creed of the Norwegians—Faye, p. 49, ap. Grimm, Deutsche Mythologie, p. 412.

Sir Olof in the Elve-Dance

Sir Olof he rode out at early day,
And so came he unto an Elve-dance gay.
The dance it goes well,
So well in the grove.
The Elve-father reached out his white hand free,
"Come, come, Sir Olof, tread the dance with me."
The dance it goes well,
So well in the grove.
"O nought I will, and nought I may,
To-morrow will be my wedding-day.'
The dance it goes well,
So well in the grove.
And the Elve-mother reached out her white hand free,
"Come, come, Sir Olof, tread the dance with me."
The dance it goes well,
So well in the grove.
"O nought I will, and nought I may,
To-morrow will be my wedding-day."
The dance.it goes well,
So well in the grove.
And the Elve-sister reached out her white hand free,
"Come, come, Sir Olof, tread the dance with me."
The dance it goes well,
So well in the grove.
"O nought I will, and nought I may,
To-morrow will be my wedding-day."
The dance it goes well,
So well in the grove.
And the bride she spake with her bride-maids so,
"What may it mean that the bells thus go?"
The dance it goes well,
So well in the grove.
"Tis the custom of this our isle," they replied;
"Each young swain ringeth home his bride."
The dance it goes well,
So well in the grove.

"And the truth from you to conceal I fear,
Sir Olof is dead, and lies on his bier."
The dance it goes well,
So well in the grove.
And on the morrow, ere light was the day,
In Sir Olof's house three corpses lay.
The dance it goes well,
So well in the grove.
It was Sir Olof, his bonny bride,
And eke his mother, of sorrow she died.
The dance it goes well,
So well in the grove. [a]

NOTE

[a] Svenska Visor, iii. 158, as sung iii Upland and East Gothland.

The Elf Woman and Sir Olof

Sir Olof rideth out ere dawn,
Breaketh day, falleth rime;
Bright day him came on.
Sir Olof cometh home,
When the wood it is leaf-green.
Sir Olof rides by Borgya,
Breaketh day, falleth rime;
Meets a dance of Elves so gay.
Sir Olof cometh home,
When the wood it is leaf-green.
There danceth Elf and Elve-maid,
Breaketh day, falleth rime;
Elve-king's daughter, with her flying hair.
Sir Olof cometh home,
When the wood it is leaf-green.
Elve-king's daughter readieth her hand free,
Breaketh day, falleth rime;
"Come here, Sir Olof, tread the dance with me."
Sir Olof cometh home,
When the wood it is leaf-green.
"Nought I tread the dance with thee,"
Breaketh day, falleth rime;
"My bride hath that forbidden me."
Sir Olof cometh home,
When the wood it is leaf-green.
"Nought I will and nought I may,"
Breaketh day, falleth rime;
"To-morrow is my wedding-day."
Sir Olof cometh home,
When the wood it is leaf-green.
"Wilt thou not tread the dance with me?"
Breaketh day, falleth rime;
"An evil shall I fix on thee."
Sir Olof cometh home,
When the wood it is leaf-green.
Sir Olof turned his horse therefrom,

Breaketh day, falleth rime;
Sickness and plague follow him home.
Sir Olof cometh home,
When the wood it is leaf-green.
Sir Olof to his mother's rode,
Breaketh day, falleth rime;
Out before him his mother stood.
Sir Olof cometh home,
When the wood it is leaf-green.
"Welcome, welcome, my dear son,"
Breaketh day, falleth rime;
"Why is thy rosy cheek so wan?"
Sir Olof cometh home,
When the wood it is leaf-green.
"My colt was swift and I tardy,"
Breaketh day, faileth rime;
"I knocked against a green oak-tree."
Sir Olof cometh home,
When the wood it is leaf-green.
"My dear sister, prepare my bed,"
Breaketh day, faileth rime;
"My dear brother, take my horse to the mead."
Sir Olof cometh home,
When the wood it is leaf-green.
"My dear mother, brush my hair,"
Breaketh day, falleth rime;
"My dear father, make me a bier."
Sir Olof cometh home,
When the wood it is leaf-green.
"My dear son, that do not say,"
Breaketh day, falleth rime;
To-morrow is thy wedding-day."
Sir Olof cometh home,
When the wood it is leaf-green.
"Be it when it will betide,"
Breaketh day, falleth rime;
"I ne'er shall come unto my bride."
Sir Olof cometh home,
When the wood it is leaf-green. [a]

[a] Svenska Visor, iii. 165, from a MS. in the Royal Library. This and the preceding one are variations of the Danish Ballad of Elveskud, which has been translated by Dr. Jamieson (Popular Ballads, 1. 219), and by Lewis in the Tales of Wonder. The Swedish editors give a third variation from East Gothland. A comparison of the two ballads with each other, and with the Danish one, will enable the reader to judge of the modifications a subject undergoes in different parts of a country.

The Young Swain and the Elves

I was a handsome young swain,
And to the court should ride.
I rode out in the evening-hour;
In the rosy grove I to sleep me laid.
Since I her first saw.
I laid me under a lind so green,
My eyes they sunk in sleep;
There came two maidens going along,
They fain would with me speak.
Since I her first saw.
The one she tapped me on my cheek,
The other whispered in my ear:
"Stand up, handsome young swain,
If thou list of love to hear."
Since I her first saw.
They led then forth a maiden,
Whose hair like gold did shine:
"Stand up, handsome young swain,
If thou to joy incline."
Since I her first saw.
The third began a song to sing,
With good will she did so;
Thereat stood the rapid stream,
Which before was wont to flow.
Since I her first saw.
Thereat stood the rapid stream,
Which before was wont to flow;
And the hind all with her hair so brown,
Forgot whither she should go.
Since I her first saw.
I got me up from off the ground,
And leaned my sword upon;
The Elve-women danced in and out,
All had they the Elve fashión.
Since I her first saw.
Had not fortune been to me so good,

That the cock his wings clapped then,
I had slept within the hill that night,
All with the Elve-womén.
Since I her first saw. [a]

NOTE

[a] Svenska Visor, iii. p. 170. This is the Elvesböj of the Danish ballads, translated by
Jamieson (i. 225), and by Lewis. In the different Swedish variations, they are Hafsfruen,
i. e. Mermaids, who attempt to seduce young men to their love by the offer of costly
presents.

A Danish legend (Thiele, i. 22) relates that a poor man, who was working near Gillesbjerg,
a haunted hilt, my down on it to rest himself in the middle of the day. Suddenly there
appeared before him a beautiful maiden, with a gold cup in her hand. She made signs
to him to come near, but when the man in his fright made the sign of the cross, she was
obliged to turn round and then he saw her back that it was hollow.

Svend Faelling and the Elle-Maid

Svend Faelling was, while a little boy, at service in Sjeller-wood-house in Framley; and it one time happened that he had to ride of a message to Ristrup. It was evening before he got near home, and as he came by the hill of Borum Es, he saw the Elle-maids, who were dancing without ceasing round and round his horse. Then one of the Elle-maids stept up to him, and readied him a drinking cup, bidding him at the same time to drink. Svend took the cup, but as he was dubious of the nature of the contents, he flung it out over his shoulder, where it fell on the horse's back, and singed off all the hair. While he had the horn fast in his band, be gave his horse the spurs and rode off full speed. The Elle-maid pursued him till he came to Trigebrand's mill, and rode through the running water, over which she could not follow him. She then earnestly conjured Svend to give her back the horn, promising him in exchange twelve men's strength. On this condition he gave back the horn, and got what she had promised him; but it very frequently put him to great inconvenience, for he found that along with it be had gotten an appetite for twelve. [a]

NOTE

[a] Thiele, ii. 67. Framley is in Jutland. Svend (i.e. *Swain)* Faelling is a celebrated character in Danish tradition; he is regarded as a second Holger Danake, and he is the hero of two of the Kjempe Viser. In Sweden he is named Sven Färling or Fotling. Grimm has shown that he and Sigurd are the same person. Deutsche Mythologie, p. 345. In the Nibelungen Lied (st. 345) Sifret (Sigurd) gets the strength of twelve men by wearing the *tarnkappe* of the dwarf Albrich. Another tradition, presently to be mentioned, says it was from a Dwarf he got his strength, for aiding him in battle against another Dwarf. It is added, that when Svend came home in the evening, after his adventure with the Elle-maids, the people were drinking their Yule-beer, and they sent him down for a fresh supply. Svend went without saying anything, and returned with a barrel in each hand and one under each arm.

The Elle-Maids

There lived a man in Aasum, near Odense, who, as be was coming home one night from Seden, passed by a hill that was standing on red pillars, and underneath there was dancing and great festivity. He hurried on past the hill as fast as he could, never venturing to cast his eyes that way. But as he went along, two fair maidens came to meet him, with beautiful hair floating over their shoulders, and one of them held a cup in her hand, which she reached out to him that he might drink of it. The other then asked him if he would come again, at which he laughed, and answered, Yes. But when he got home he became strangely affected in his mind, was never at ease in himself, and was continually saying that he had promised to go back. And when they watched him closely to prevent his doing so, he at last lost his senses, and died shortly after. [a]

NOTE

[a] Thiele, iii. 43. Odense is in Funen.

Maid Va

There was once a wedding and a great entertainment at Oesterhae-singe. The party did not break up till morning, and the guests took their departure with a great deal of noise and bustle. While they were putting their horses to their carriages, previous to setting out home, they stood talking about their respective bridal-presents. And while they were talking loudly, and with the utmost earnestness, there came from a neighbouring moor a maiden clad in green, with plaited rushes on her head; she went up to the man who was loud-est, and bragging most of his present, and said to him: "What wilt thou give to maid Vae?" The man, who was elevated with all the ale and brandy he had been drinking, snatched up a whip, and replied: "Ten cuts of my whip;" and that very moment he dropt down dead on the ground. [a]

NOTE

[a] Thiele, 1. 109. *(communicated)*. Such legends, as Mr. Thiele learned directly from the mouths of the peasantry, he terms *oral;* those he procured from his friends, *communicated.* Oesterhaesinge, the scene of this legend, is in the island of Funen.

The Elle-Maid near Ebeltoft

A farmer's boy was keeping cows not far from Ebeltoft. There came to him a very fair and pretty girl, and she asked him if he was hungry or thirsty. But when he perceived that she guarded with the greatest solicitude against his getting a sight of her back, he immediately suspected that she must be an Elle-maid, for the Elle-people are hollow behind. He accordingly would give no heed to her, and endeavoured to get away from her; but when she perceived this, she offered him her breast that be should suck her. And so great was the enchantment that accompanied this action, that he was unable to resist it. But when he had done as she desired him, he had no longer any command of himself; so that she had now no difficulty in enticing him with her.

He was three days away, during which time his father and mother went home, and were in great affliction, for they were well assured that he must have been enticed away. But on the fourth day his father saw him a long way off coming home, and he desired his wife to set a pan of meat on the fire as quick as possible. The son then came in at the door, and sat down at the table without saying a word. The father, too, remained quite silent, as if every thing was as it ought to be. His mother then set the meat before him, and his father bid him eat, but he let the food lie untouched, and said that he knew now where he could get much better food. The father then became highly enraged, took a good large switch, and once more ordered him to take his food. The boy was then obliged to eat, and as soon as he had tasted the flesh he ate it up greedily, and instantly fell into a deep sleep. He slept for as many days as the enchantment had lasted, but he never after recovered the use of his reason. [a]

NOTE
[a] Thiele. i. 118. *(communicated)*. Ebeltoft is a village in North Jutland.

Hans Puntleder

There are three hills on the lands of Bubbelgaard in Funen, which are to this day called the Dance-bills, from the following occurrence. A lad named Hans was at service in Bubbelgaard, and as he was coming one evening past the hills, he saw one of them raised on red pillars, and great dancing and much merriment underneath. He was so enchanted with the beauty and magnificence of what he saw, that he could not restrain his curiosity, but was in a strange and wonderful manner attracted nearer and nearer, till *at* last the fairest of all the fair maidens that were there came up to him and gave him a kiss. From that moment be lost all command of himself, and became so violent, that he used to tear to pieces all the clothes that were put on him, so that at last they were obliged to make him a dress of sole-leather, which he could, not pull off him; and ever after he went by the name of Hans Puntleder, i. e. Sole-leather. [a]

According to Danish tradition, the Elle-kings, under the denomination of Promontory-kings, *(Klintekonger),* keep watch and ward over the country. Whenever war, or any-other misfortune, threatens to come on the land, there may be seen, on the promontory, complete armies, drawn up in array to defend the country.

One of these kings resides at Möen, on the spot which still bears the name of King's-hill *(Kongsbjerg).* His queen is the most beautiful of beings; and she dwells at the Queen's Chair *(Dronningstolen).* This king is a great friend of the king of Stevns, and they are both at enmity with Grap, the promontory-king of Rűgen, who must keep at a distance, and look out over the sea to watch their approach.

Another tradition, however, says, that there is but one king, who rules over the headlands of Möen, Stevns, and Rügen. He has a magnificent chariot, which is drawn by four black horses. In this he drives over the sea, from one promontory to another. At such times the sea grows black, and is in great commotion, and the loud snorting and neighing of his horses may be distinctly heard. [b]

It was once believed that no mortal monarch dare come to Stevns; for the Elle-king would not permit him to cross the stream that bounds it. But Christian IV passed it without opposition, and since his time several Danish monarchs have been there.

At Skjelskör, in Zealand, reigns another of these jealous promontorial sovereigns, named king Tolv *(Twelve)*. He will not suffer a mortal prince to pass the bridge of Kjelskör. Wo, too, betide the watchman who should venture to cry twelve o'clock in the village, he might chance to find himself transported to the village of Borre or to the Windmills.

Old people that have eyes for such things, declare they frequently see Kong Tolv rolling himself on the grass in the sunshine. On New-year's night he takes from one smith's forge or another nine new shoes for his horses; they must be always left ready for him, and. with them the necessary complement of nails.

The Elle-king of Bornholm [c] lets himself be occasionally heard with fife and drum, especially when war is at hand; he may then be seen in the fields with his soldiers. This king will not suffer an earthly monarch to pass more than three nights on his isle.

In the popular creed there is some strange connexion between the Elves and the trees. They not only frequent them, but they make an interchange of form with them. In the church-yard of Store Hed-dinge, [d] in Zealand, there are the remains of an oak wood. These, say the common people, are the Elle-king's soldiers; by day they are trees, by night valiant warriors. In the wood of Rugaard, in the same island, is a tree which by night becomes a whole Elle-people, and goes about all alive. It has no leaves upon it, yet it would be very unsafe to go to break or fell it, for the underground-people frequently hold their meetings under its branches. There is, in another place, an elder-tree growing in a farm-yard, which frequently takes a walk in the twilight about the yard, and peeps in through the window at the children when they are alone.

It was, perhaps, these elder-trees that gave origin to the no-tion. In Danish *Hyld* or *Hyl*—a word not far removed from Elle—is Elder, and the peasantry believe that in or under the elder-tree dwells a being called Hyldemoer *(Elder-mother)*, or Hyldequinde *(Elder-woman)*, with her ministrant spirits. [e] A Danish peasant, if he wanted to take any part of an elder-tree, used previously to say, three times—"O, Hyldemoer, Hyldemoer! let me take some of thy elder, and I will let thee take something of mine in return." If this was omitted he would be severely punished. They tell of a man who cut down an elder-tree, but he soon after died suddenly. It is, moreover, not prudent to have any furniture made of elder-wood. A child was once put to lie in a cradle made of this wood, but Hyldemoer came and pulled it by the legs, and gave it no rest till it was put to sleep elsewhere. Old David Monrad relates, that a shepherd, one night, heard his three children crying, and when he inquired the cause, they said some one had been sucking them. Their breasts were found to be swelled, and they were removed to another room, where they were quiet. The reason is said to have been that that room was floored with elder.

The linden or lime tree is the favourite haunt of the Eves and cognate beings; and it is not safe to be near it after sunset. [f]

NOTES

[a] Thiele, iv. 32. From the circumstances, it would appear that these were Elves and not Dwarfs; but one cannot be positive in these matters.

[b] Möen and Stevns are in Zealand. As Rügen does not belong to the Danish monarchy, the former tradition is probably the more correct one. Yet the latter may be the original one.

[c] Bornbolm is a *holm*, or small island, adjacent to Zealand.

[d] The Elle-king of Stevns has his bedchamber in the wall of this church.

[e] This is evidently the Frau Holle of the Germans.

[f] The preceding particulars are all derived from M. Thiele's work.

DWARFS OR TROLLS

Ther bygde folk i the bärg,
Quinnor och män, för mycken duerf.
–HIST. ALEX. MAG. *Suedice.*

Within the hills folk did won,
Women and men, dwarfs many a one.

The more usual appellation of the Dwarfs is Troll or Trold, [a] word originally significant of any evil spirit, [b] giant monster, magician [c] or evil person; but now in a good measure divested of its ill senses, for the Trolls are not in general regarded as noxious or malignant beings.

The Trolls are represented as dwelling inside of hills, mounds, and hillocks—whence they are also called Hill-people (*Bjergfolk*)— sometimes in single families, sometimes in societies. In the ballads they are described as having kings over them, but never so in the popular legend. Their character seems gradually to have sunk down to the level of the peasantry, in proportion as the belief in them was consigned to the same class. They are regarded as extremely rich for when, on great occasions of festivity, they have their hills raised up on red pillars, people that have chanced to be passing by have seen them shoving large chests full of money to and fro, and opening and clapping down the lids of them. Their hill-dwellings are very magnificent inside. "They live," said one of Mr. Arndt's guides, "in fine houses of gold and crystal. My father saw them once in the night, when the hill was open on St. John's night. They were dancing and drinking, and it seemed to him as if they were making signs to him to go to them, but his horse snorted, and carried him away, whether he would or no. There is a great number of them in the Guldberg *(Goldhill)*, and they have brought into it all the gold and silver that people buried in the great Russian war." [d]

They are obliging and neighbourly; freely lending and borrowing, and elsewise keeping up a friendly intercourse with mankind. But they have a sad propensity to thieving, not only stealing provisions, but even women and children.

They marry, have children, bake and brew, just as the peasant himself does. A farmer one day met a bill-man and his wife, and a whole squad of stumpy little children, in his fields; [e] and people used often to see the children of the man who lived in the hill of Kund, in Jutland, climbing up the hill, and rolling down after one another, with shouts of laughter.

The Trolls have a great dislike to noise, probably from a recollection of the time when Thor used to be flinging his hammer after them; so that the hanging of bells in the churches has driven them almost all out of the country. The people of Ebeltoft were once sadly plagued by them, as they plundered their pantries in a most unconscionable manner; so they consulted a very wise and pious man; and his advice was, that they should hang a bell in the steeple of the church. They did so, and they were soon eased of the Trolls. [f]

These beings have some very extraordinary and useful properties; they can, for instance, go about invisibly, [g] or turn themselves into any shape; they can foresee future events; they can confer prosperity, or the contrary, on a family; they can bestow bodily strength on any one; and, in short, perform numerous feats beyond the power of man.

Of personal beauty they have not much to boast: the Ebeltoft Dwarfs, mentioned. above, were often seen, and they had immoderate humps on their backs, and long crooked noses. They were dressed in gray jackets, [h] and they wore pointed red caps. Old people in Zealand say, that when the Trolls were in the country, they used to go from their hill to the village of Gudmandstrup through the Stone-meadow, and that people, when passing that way, used to meet great tall men in long black clothes. Some have foolishly spoken to them, and wished them good evening, but they never got any other answer than that the Trolls hurried past them, saying, Mi! mi! mi! mi!

Thanks to the industry of Mr. Thiele, who has been indefatigable in collecting the traditions of his native country, we are furnished with ample accounts of the Trolls; and the following legends will fully illustrate what we have written concerning them. [i]

We commence with the Swedish ballads of the Hill-kings, as in dignity and antiquity they take precedence of the legends.

NOTES

[a] There is no etymon of this word. It is to be found in both the Icelandic and the Finnish languages; whether the latter borrowed or communicated it is uncertain. Ihre derives the name of the celebrated waterfall of Trollhaeta, near Gotenburg, from Troll, and Haute *Lapponice*, an abyss. It therefore answers to the Irish *Poul-a-Phooka*. See *Ireland*.

[b] In the following lines quoted in the Heimskringla, it would seem to signify the Dii Manes.
Tha gaf hann Trescegg Tröllum,
Torf-Einarr drap Scurfo.
Then gave he Trescegg to the Trolls,
Turf-Einarr slew Scurfo.

[c] The ancient Gothic nation was called Troll by their Vandal neighbours (Junii Batavia, c. 27); according to Sir J. Malcolm, the Tartars call the Chinese Deevs. It was formerly believed, says Ihre, that the noble family of Troll, in Sweden, derived their name from having killed a Troll, that is, probably, a Dwarf.

[d] Arndt, Reise nach Schweden, vol. III. p. 8.

[e] Like our Fairies the Trolls are sometimes of marvellously small dimensions: in the Danish ballad of Eline af Villenskov we read—
Det da meldte den mindste Trold,
Han var ikke större end en myre,
Her er kommet en Christen mand,
Den maa jag visseligen styre.
Out then spake the tinyest Troll,
No bigger than an emmet was he,
Hither is come a Christian man,
And manage him will I surelie.

[f] Thiele, i. 36.

[g] For this they seem to be indebted to their hat or cap. Eske Brok being one day in the fields, knocked off, without knowing it, the hat of a Dwarf who instantly became visible, and had, in order to recover it, to grant him every thing he asked. Thiele iii. 49. This hat answers to the Tarnkappe or Hel-kaplein of the German Dwarfs; who also become visible when their caps are struck off.

[h] In the Danish ballad of Eline af Villenskov the hero is called *Trolden graae,* the Gray Trold, probably from the colour of his habiliments.

[i] We deem it needless in future to refer to volume and page of Mr. Thiele's work. Those acquainted with the original will easily find the legends.

Sir Thynnè

And it was the knight Sir Thynnè,
He was a knight so grave;
Whether he were on foot or on horse,
He was a knight so brave. [a]
And it was the knight Sir Thynnè
Went the hart and the hind to shoot,
So he saw Ulva, the little Dwarf's daughter,
At the green linden's foot.
And it was Ulva, the little Dwarf's daughter,
Unto her handmaid she cried,
"Go fetch my gold harp hither to me,
Sir Thynnè I'll draw to my side."
The first stroke on her gold harp she struck,
So sweetly she made it ring,
The wild beasts in the wood and field
They forgot whither they would spring.
The next stroke on her gold harp she struck,
So sweetly she made it ring,
The little gray hawk that sat on the bough,
He spread out both his wings.
The third stroke on her gold harp she struck,
So sweetly she made it ring,
The little fish that went in the stream,
He forgot whither he would swim.
Then flowered the mead, then leafed all,
'Twas caused by the runic lay; [b]
Sir Thynnè he struck his spurs in his horse,
He no longer could hold him away.
And it was the knight Sir Thynnè,
From his horse he springs hastily,
So goeth he to Ulva, the little Dwarf's daughter,
All under the green linden tree.
"Here you sit, my maiden fair,
A rose all lilies above;
See you can never a mortal man
Who will not seek your love."

"Be silent, be silent, now Sir Thynnè,
With your proffers of love, I pray;
For I am betrothed unto a hill-king,
A king all the Dwarfs obey.
"My true love he sitteth the hill within,
And at gold tables plays merrily;
My father he setteth his champions in ring,
And in iron arrayeth them he.
"My mother she sitteth the hill within,
And gold in the chest doth lay;
And I stole out for a little while,
Upon my gold harp to play."
And it was the knight Sir Thynnè,
He patted her cheek rosie:
"Why wilt thou not give a kinder reply:
Thou dearest of maidens, to me?"
"I can give you no kinder reply;
I may not myself that allow;
I am betrothed to a hill-king,
And to him I must keep my vow."
And it was Thora, the little Dwarf's wife,
She at the hill-door looked out,
And there she saw how the knight Sir Thynnè,
Lay at the green linden's foot.
And it was Thora, the little Dwarf's wife,
She was vext and angry, God wot:
"What hast thou here in the grove to do?
Little business, I trow, thou hast got.
"'Twere better for thee in the hill to be,
And gold in the chest to lay,
Than here to sit in the rosy grove, [c]
And on thy gold harp to play.
"And 'twere better for thee in the hill to be,
And thy bride-dress finish sewing,
Than sit under the lind, and with runic lay
A Christian man's heart to thee win."
And it was Ulva, the little Dwarf's daughter,
She goeth in at the hill-door:

And after her goeth the knight Sir Thynnè,
Clothed in scarlet and fur.
And it was Thora, the little Dwarf's wife,
Forth a red-gold chair she drew:
Then she cast Sir Thynnè into a sleep
Until that the cock he crew.
And it was Thora, the little Dwarf's wife,
The five rune-books she took out;
So she loosed him fully out of the runes,
Her daughter had bound him about.
"And hear thou me, Sir Thynnè,
From the runes thou now art free;
This to thee I will soothly say,
My daughter shall never win thee.
"And I was born of Christian kind,
And to the hill stolen in;
My sister dwelleth in Iseland, [d]
And wears a gold crown so fine.
"And there she wears her crown of gold,
And beareth of queen the name;
Her daughter was stolen away from her,
Thereof there goeth great fame.
"Her daughter was stolen away from her,
And to Berner-land brought in;
And there now dwelleth the maiden free,
She is called Lady Hermolin.
"And never can she into the dance go,
But seven women follow her;
And never can she on the gold-harp play,
If the queen herself is not there.
"The king he hath a sister's son,
He hopeth the crown to possess,
For him they intend the maiden free,
For her little happiness.
"And this for my honour will I do
And out of good-will moreover,
To thee will I give the maiden free,
And part her from that lover."
Then she gave unto him a dress so new,

With gold and pearls bedight;
Every seam on the dress it was
With precious stones all bright.
Then she gave unto him a horse so good,
And therewith a new sell;
"And never shalt thou the way inquire,
Thy horse will find it well."
And it was Diva, the little Dwarf's daughter,
She would show her good-wifi to the knight;
So she gave unto him a spear so new,
And therewith a good sword so bright.
"And never shalt thou fight a fight,
Where thou shalt not the victory gain;
And never shalt thou sail on a sea
Where thou shalt not the land attain."
And it was Thor; the little Dwarf's wife,
She wine in a glass for him poured:
"Ride away, ride away, now Sir Thynnè,
Before the return of my lord."
And it was the knight Sir Thynnè,
He rideth under the green hill side,
There then met him the hill-kings two,
As slow to the hill they ride.
"Well met! Good day, now Sir Thynnè!
Thy horse can well with thee pace;
Whither directed is thy course?
Since thou 'it bound to a distant place."
"Travel shall I and woo;
Plight me shall I a flower;
Try shall I my sword so good,
To my weal or my woe in the stour."
"Ride in peace, ride in peace, away, Sir Thynnè,
From us thou hast nought to fear;
They are coming, the champions from Iseland,
Who with thee long to break a spear."
And it was the knight Sir Thynnè,
He rideth under the green hill side;
There met him seven Bernisk champions,
They bid him to halt and abide.

"And whether shall we fight to-day,
For the red gold and the silver;
Or shall we fight together to-day,
For both our true loves fair?"
And it was the king's sister's son,
He was of mood so hasty;
"Of silver and gold I have enow,
If thou wilt credit me."
"But hast thou not a fair true love,
Who is called Lady Hermolin?
For her it is we shall fight to-day,
If she shall be mine or thine."
The first charge they together rode,
They were two champions so tall;
He cut at the king's sister's son,
That his head to the ground did fall.
Back then rode the champions six,
And dressed themselves in fur;
Then went into the lofty hall,
The aged king before.
And it was then the aged king,
He tore his gray hairs in woe.
"Ye must avenge my sister's son's death;
I will sables and martins bestow.' [e]
Back then rode the champions six,
They thought the reward to gain,
But they remained halt and limbless:
By loss one doth wit obtain.
And he slew wolves and bears,
All before the high chamber;
Then taketh he out the maiden free
Who so long had languished there.
And now hath Lady Hermolin
Escaped from all harm;
Now sleeps she sweet full many a sleep,
On brave Sir Thynnè's arm.
And now has brave Sir Thynnè
Escaped all sorrow and tine;
Now sleeps he sweet full many a sleep,

Beside Lady Hermolin.
Most thanketh he Ulva, the little Dwarf's daughter,
Who him with the runes had bound,
For were he not come inside of the bill,
The lady he never had found. [f]

NOTES

[a] We have ventured to omit the Omqued. *I styren väll de Runor!* (Manage well the runes!)
The final *e* in Thynnè ia marked merely to indicate that it is to be sounded.

[b] *Runeslag,* literally Rune-stroke. Runes originally signified letters, and then songs. They
were of two kinds, Maalrunor *(Speech-runes),* and Trollrunor *(Magic-runes);* These last
were again divided into Skaderunur *(Mischief-runes)* and Hjelprunor *(Help-runes),* of each
of which there were five kinds. See Verelius' notes to the Hervarar Saga, cap. 7.
The power of music over all nature is a subject of frequent recurrence in northern poetry.
Here all the wild animals are entranced by the magic tones of the harp; the meads flower,
the trees put forth leaves; the knight, though grave and silent, is attracted, and even if
included to stay away, he cannot restrain his horse.

[c] *Rosendelund.* The word *Lund* signifies any kind of grove, thicket, &c.

[d] Not the island of Iceland, but a district in Norway of that name. By Berner-land, Geijer
thinks is meant the land of Bern (Verona), the country of Dietrich, so celebrated in
German romance.

[e] *Sabel och Mård.* These furs are always mentioned In the northern ballads, as the royal
rewards of distinguished actions.

[f] This fine ancient Visa was taken down from recitation in West Gothland. The
corresponding Danish one of Her Tönne is much later.

Proud Margeret

Proud Margaret's [a] father of wealth had store,
Time with me goes slow.—
And he was a king seven kingdoms o'er,
But that grief is heavy I know. [b]
To her came wooing good earls two,
Time with me goes slow.—
But neither of them would she hearken unto,
But that grief is heavy I know.
To her came wooing princes five,
Time with me goes slow.—
Yet not one of them would the maiden have,
But that grief is heavy I know.
To her came wooing kings then seven,
Time with me goes slow.—
But unto none her hand has she given,
But that grief is heavy I know.
And the hill-king asked his mother to read,
Time with me goes slow.—
How to win proud Margaret he might speed,
But that grief is heavy I know.
"And say how much thou wilt give unto me,"
Time with me goes slow.—
"That herself may into the hill come to thee?"
But that grief is heavy I know.
"Thee will I give the ruddiest gold,"
Time with me goes slow.—
"And thy chests full of money as they can hold,"
But that grief is heavy I know.
One Sunday morning it fell out so,
Time with me goes slow.—
Proud Margaret unto the church should go,
But that grief is heavy I know.
And all as she goes, and all as she stays,
Time with me goes slow.—
All the nearer she comes where the high hill lay,
But that grief is heavy I know.

So she goeth around the hill compassing,
Time with me goes slow.—
So there openeth a door, and thereat goes she in,
But that grief is heavy I know.
Proud Margaret stept in at the door of the hill,
Time with the goes slow.—
And the hill-king salutes her with eyes joyful,
But that grief is heavy I know.
So he took the maiden upon his knee,
Time with me goes slow.—
And took the gold rings and therewith her wed be,
But that grief is heavy I know.
So he took the maiden his arms between,
Time with me goes slow.—
He gave her a gold crown and the name of queen,
But that grief is heavy I know.
So she was in the hill for eight round years,
Time with me goes slow.—
There bare she two sons and a daughter so fair,
But that grief is heavy I know.
When she had been full eight years there,
Time with me goes slow.—
She wished to go home to her mother so dear,
But that grief is heavy I know.
And the hill-king spake to his footpages twain,
Time with me goes slow.—
"Put ye the gray pacers now unto the wain," [c]
But that grief is heavy I know.
And Margaret out at the hill-door stept,
Time with me goes slow.—
And her little children they thereat wept,
But that grief is heavy I know.
And the hill-king her in his arms has ta'en,
Time with me goes slow.—
So he lifteth her into the gilded wain,
But that grief is heavy I know.
"And hear now thou footpage what I unto thee say,"
Time with me goes slow.—
"Thou now shalt drive her to her mother's straightway,"

But that grief is heavy I know.
Proud Margaret stept in o'er the door-sill,
Time with me goes slow.—
And her mother saluteth her with eyes joyful,
But that grief is heavy I know.
"And where heat thou so long stayed?"
Time with me goes slow.—
"I have been in the flowery meads,"
But that grief is heavy I know.
"What veil is that thou wearest on thy hair?"
Time with me goes slow.—
"Such as women and mothers use to wear,"
But that grief is heavy I know.
"Well may I wear a veil on my head,"
Time with me goes slow.—
"Me hath the hill-king both wooed and wed,"
But that grief is heavy I know.
"In the hill have I been these eight round years,"
Time with me goes slow.—
"There have I two sons and a daughter so fair,"
But that grief is heavy I know.
"There have I two sons and a daughter so fair,"
Time with me goes slow.—
"The loveliest maiden the world doth bear,"
But that grief is heavy I know.
"And hear thou, proud Margaret, what I say unto thee,"
Time with me goes slow.—
"Can I go with thee home thy children to see?"
But that grief is heavy I know.
And the hill-king stept now in at the door,
Time with me goes slow.—
And Margaret thereat fell down on the floor,
But that grief is heavy I know.
"And stayest thou now here complaining of me,"
Time with me goes slow.—
"Camest thou not of thyself into the hill to me?"
But that grief is heavy I know.
"And stayest thou now here and thy fate dost deplore?"
Time with me goes slow.—

"Camest thou not of thyself in at my door?"
But that grief is heavy I know.
The hill-king struck her on the cheek rosie,
Time with me goes slow.—
"And pack to the hill to thy children wee,"
But that grief is heavy I know.
The hill-king struck her with a twisted root,
Time with me goes slow.—
"And pack to the hill without any dispute,"
But that grief is heavy I know.
And the hill-king her in his arms has ta'en,
Time with me goes slow.—
And lifted her into the gilded wain,
But that grief is heavy I know.
"And hear thou my footpage what I unto thee say,"
Time with me goes slow.—
"Thou now shalt drive her to my dwelling straightway,"
But that grief is heavy I know.
Proud Margaret stept in at the bill door,
Time with me goes slow.—
And her little children rejoiced therefore,
But that grief is heavy I know.
"It is not worth while rejoicing for me,"
Time with me goes slow.—
"Christ grant that I never a mother had been,"
But that grief is heavy I know.
The one brought out a gilded chair,
Time with me goes slow.—
"O rest you, my sorrow-bound mother, there,"
But that grief is heavy I know.
The one brought out a filled up horn,
Time with me goes slow.—
The other put therein a gilded corn,
But that grief is heavy I know.
The first drink she drank out of the horn,
Time with me goes slow.—
She forgot straightway both heaven and earth,
But that grief is heavy I know.
The second drink she drank out of the horn,

Time with me goes slow.—
She forgot straightway both God and his word,
But that grief is heavy I know.
The third drink she drank out of the horn,
Time with me goes slow.—
She forgot straightway both sister and brother,
But that grief is heavy I knew.
She forgot straightway both sister and brother,
Time with me goes slow.—
But she never forgot her sorrow-bound mother,
But that grief is heavy I know. [d]

NOTES

[a] Niebuhr, speaking of the Celsi Ramnes, says, "With us the salutation of blood relations
was *Willkommen stolze Vetter* (Welcome, proud cousins) and in the Danish ballads, proud
(stolt) is a noble appellation of a maiden."—Römische Geschichte, 2d edit. vol. i. p. 316.
It may be added, that in English, *proud* and the synonymous terni *stout (stolz, stolt)* had
also the sense of noble, high-born.
Do now your devoir, yonge knightes *proud.*
Knight's Tale.
Up stood the queen and ladies stout.
Launfal.

[b] *Men jag vet a sorge är tung.*

[c] Wain, our readers hardly need be informed, originally signified any kind of carriage: see
Faerie Queene, *passim.* It is the Ang. Sax. *páen,* and not a contraction of *waggon.*

[d] From Vermland and Upland

The Troll Wife

The grandfather of Reor, who dwelt at Fuglekärr (i.e. *Bird-marsh),* in the parish of Svartsborg *(Black-castle),* lived close to a hill, and one time, in the broad daylight, be saw sitting there on a stone a comely maiden. He wished to intercept her, and for this purpose *he threw steel* between her and the hill; whereupon her father laughed within the hill, and opening the hill-door asked him if he would have his daughter. He replied in the affirmative and as she was *stark naked* he took some of his own clothes and covered her with them, and he afterwards had her christened. As he was going away, her father said. to him, "When you are going to have your wedding *(bröllup)* you must provide twelve barrels of beer and bake a heap of bread and the flesh of four oxen, and drive to the barrow or hill where l keep, and when the bridal gifts are to be bestowed, depend on it l will give mine." This also came to pass; for when others were giving he raised the cover of the cart and cast into it so large a bag of money that the body of it nearly broke, saying at the same time:—"This is *my* gift!" He said, moreover, "When you want to have your wife's portion*(hemmagifta),*[a] you must drive to the hill with four horses, and get your share. When he came there afterwards at his desire he got copper-pots, the one larger than the other till the largest pot of all was filled with the smaller ones. He also gave him other things, [b] which were helmets, of that colour and fashion which are large and thick, and which are still remaining in the country, being preserved at the parsonage of Tanum. This man Reor's father surnamed l Foglekärsten, had a number of children by this wife of his, whom he fetched out of the hill, among whom was the aforesaid Reor. Olaf Stenson also in Stora Rijk, who died last year, was Reor's sister's son. [c]

NOTES

[a] This we suppose to be the meaning of *hemmagifta,* as it Is that of *hemgift,* the only word approaching to it that we have met in our dictionary.

[b] *Brandcreatur,* a word of which we cannot ascertain the exact meaning. We doubt greatly if the following *hielmeta* be helmets.

[c] Grimm (Deut. Mythol. p. 435) has extracted this legend from the Bahuslän of Odman, who, as he observes, and as we may see, relates it quite seriously, and with the real names of persons. It is we believe the only legend of the union of a *man* with one of the hill-folk.

The Altar-Cup in Aagerup

Between the villages of Marup and Aagerup in Zealand, there is said to have lain a great castle, the ruins of which are still to be seen near the strand. Tradition relates that a great treasure is concealed among them, and that a dragon there watches over three kings' ransoms. [a] Here, too, people frequently happen to get a sight of the underground folk, especially about festival-times, for then they have dancing and great jollity going on down on the strand.

One Christmas-eve, a farmer's servant in the village of Aagerup went to his master and asked him if he might take a horse and ride down to look at the Troll-meeting. The farmer not only gave him leave but desired him to take the best horse in the stable; so he mounted and rode away down to the strand. When he was come to the place he stopped his horse, and stood for some time looking at the company who were assembled in great numbers. And while he was wondering to see how well and how gaily the little dwarfs danced, up came a Troll to him, and invited him to dismount, and take a share in their dancing and merriment. Another Troll came jumping up, took his horse by the bridle, and held him while the man got off, and went down and danced away merrily with them the whole night long.

When it was drawing near day he returned them his very best thanks for his entertainment, and mounted his horse to return home to Aagerup. They now gave him an invitation to come again on New-year's night, as they were then to have great festivity; and a maiden who held a gold cup in her hand invited him to drink the stirrup-cup.

He took the cup; but, as he had some suspicion of them, he, while he made as if he was raising the cup to his mouth, threw the drink out over his shoulder, so that it fell on the horse's back, and it immediately singed off all the hair. He then clapped spurs to his horse's sides, and rode away with the cup in his hand over a ploughed field.

The Trolls instantly gave chase all in a body; but being hard set to get over the deep furrows, they shouted out, without ceasing,

"Ride on the lay,

And not on the clay." [b]

He, however, never minded them, but kept to the ploughed field. However, when he drew near the village he was forced to ride out on the level road, and the Trolls now gained on him every minute. In his distress he prayed unto God, and lie made a vow that if he should be delivered he would bestow the cup on the church.

He was now riding along just by the wall of the churchyard, and he hastily flung the cup over it, that it at least might be secure. He then pushed on at full speed, and at last got into the village; and just as they were on the point of catching hold of the horse, he sprung in through the farmer's gate, and the man clapt to the wicket after him. He was now safe; but the Trolls were so enraged, that, taking up a huge great stone, they flung it with such force against the gate, that it knocked four planks out of it.

There are no traces now remaining of that house, but the stone is still lying in the middle of the village of Aagerup. The cup was presented to the church, and the man got in return the best farm-house on the lands of Eriksholm. [c]

NOTES

[a] "Three kings' ransoms" is a common maximum with a Danish peasant when speaking of treasure.

[b] 'Rid paa det Bolde,
   Og ikke paa dot Knolde."

[c] *Oral.* This is an adventure common to many countries. The church of Vigersted in Zealand has a cup obtained in the same way. The man, in this case, took refuge in the church, and was there besieged by the Trolls till morning. The bridge of Hagbro in Jutland got its name from a similar event. When the man rode off with the silver jug from the beautiful maiden who presented it to him, an old crone set off in pursuit of him with such velocity, that she would surely have caught him, but that providentially he came to a running water. The pursuer, however, like Nannie with Tam o' Shanter, caught the horse's hind leg, but was only able to keep one of the cocks of his shoe: hence the bridge was called Hagbro, *i. e.* Cock Bridge.

Origin of this Lake

A Troll had once taken up his abode near the village of Kund, in the high bank on which the church now stands; but when the people about there had become pious, and went constantly to church, the Troll was dreadfully annoyed by their almost incessant ringing of bells in the steeple of the church. He was at last obliged, in consequence of it, to take his departure; for nothing has more contributed to the emigration of the Troll-folk out of the country than the increasing piety of the people, and their taking to bell-ringing. The Troll of Kund accordingly quitted the country, and went over to Funen, where he lived for some time in peace and quiet.

Now it chanced that a man who had lately settled in the town of Kund, coming to Funen on business, met on the road with this same Troll: "Where do you live?" said the Troll to him. Now there was nothing whatever about the Troll unlike a man, so he answered him, as was the truth, "I am from the town of Kund." "So?" said the Troll. "I don't know you, then! And yet I think I know every man in Kund. Will you, however," continued he, "just be so kind to take a letter from me back with you to Kund?" The man said, of course, he had no objection. The Troll then thrust the letter into his pocket, and charged him strictly not to take it out till he came to Kund church, and then to throw it over the churchyard wall, and the person for whom it was intended would get it.

The Troll then went away in great haste, and with him the letter went entirely out of the man's mind. But when he was come back to Zealand he sat down by the meadow where Tiis Lake now is, and suddenly recollected the Troll's letter. He felt a great desire to look at it at least. So be took it out of his pocket, and sat awhile with it in his hands, when suddenly there began to dribble a little water out of the seal. The letter now unfolded itself, and the water came out faster and faster, and it was with the utmost difficulty that the poor man was enabled to save his life; for the malicious Troll had enclosed an entire lake in the letter. The Troll, it is plain, had thought to avenge himself on Kund church by destroying it in this manner; but God ordered it so that the lake chanced to run out in the great meadow where it now flows. [a]

_____
NOTE

[a] *Oral.* Tiis Lake is in Zealand. It is the general belief of the peasantry that there are now very few Trolls in the country, for the ringing of bells has driven them all away, they, like the Stille-folk of the Germans, delighting in quiet and silence. It is said that a farmer having found a Troll sitting very disconsolate on a stone near Tiis Lake, and taking him at first for a decent Christian man, accosted him with—"Well! where are you going, friend?" "Ah!" said he, in a melancholy tone, "I am going off out of the country. I cannot live here any longer, they keep such eternal ringing and dinging!"
"There is a high hill," says Kalm (Resa, &c. p. 136), "near Botna in Sweden, in which formerly dwelt a Troll. When they got up bells in Botna church, and he heard the ringing of them, he is related to have said:
„Det är så godt i det Botnaberg at bo,
Vore ikke den leda Bjälleko."
"Pleasant it were in Botnahill to dwell,
Were it not for the sound of that plaguey bell,"

A Farmer Tricks a Troll

A farmer, on whose ground there was a little hill, resolved not to let it lie idle, so he began at one end to plough it up. The hill-man, who lived in it, came to him and asked him bow he dared to plough on the roof of his house. The farmer assured him that he did not know that it was the roof of his house, but at the same time represented to him that it was at present equally unprofitable to them both to let such a piece of land lie idle. He therefore took the opportunity of proposing to him that he should plough, sow, and, reap it every year on these terms: that they should take it year and year about, and the hill-man to have one year what grew over the ground, and the farmer what grew in the ground; and the next year the farmer to have what was over, and the hill-man what was under.

The agreement was made accordingly; but the crafty farmer took care to sow carrots and corn year and year about, and he gave the hill-man the tops of the carrots and the roots of the corn for his share, with which he was well content. They thus lived for a long time on extremely good terms with each other. [a]

NOTE

[a] This story is told by Rabelais with his characteristic humour and extravagance. As there are no Trolls in France, it is the devil who is deceived in the French version. A legend similar to this is told of the district of Lujhman in Afghanistan (Masson, Narrative, etc., iii. 297); but there it was the Shaitan (*Satan*) that cheated the farmers. The legends are surely independent fictions.

Skotte in the Fire

Near Gudmanstrup, in the district of Odd, is a hill called Hjulehöi *(Hollow-hill)*. The hill-folk that dwell in this mount are well known in all the villages round, and no one ever omits making a cross on his beer-barrels, for the Trolls are in the habit of slipping down from Hjulehöi to steal beer.

One evening late a farmer was passing by the hill, and he saw that it was raised up on red pillars, and that underneath there was music and dancing and a splendid Troll banquet. The man stood a long time gazing on their festivity; but while he was standing there, deeply absorbed in admiration of what he saw, all of a sudden the dancing stopped, and the music ceased, and he heard a Troll cry out, in a tone of the utmost anguish, "Skotte is fallen into the fire! Come and help him up!" The hill then sank, and all the merriment was at an end.

Meanwhile the farmer's wife was at home all alone, and while she was sitting and spinning her tow, she never noticed a Troll who had crept through the window into the next room, and was at the beer-barrel drawing off the liquor into his copper kettle. The room-door was standing open, and the Troll kept a steady eye on the woman. The husband now came into the house full of wonder at what he had seen and heard. "Hark ye, dame," he began, "listen now till I tell you what has happened to me!" The Troll redoubled his attention. "As I came just now by Hjulehöi," continued he, "I saw a great Troll-banquet there, but while they were in the very middle of their glee they shouted out within in the hill, 'Skotte is fallen into the fire;

come and help him up!"

At hearing this, the Troll, who was standing beside the beer-barrel, was so frightened, that he let the tap run and the kettle of beer fall on the ground, and tumbled himself out of the window as quickly as might be. The people of the house hearing all this noise instantly guessed what had been going on inside; and when they went in they saw the beer all running about, and found the copper kettle lying on the floor. This they seized, and kept in lieu of the beer that bad been spilled; and the same kettle is said to have been a long time to be seen in the villages round about there. [a]

NOTE

[a] *Oral.* Gudmanstrup is in Zealand. In Ouröe, a little Island close to Zealand, there is a hill whence the Trolls used to come down and supply themselves with provisions out of the farmers' pantries. Niel Jensen, who lived close to the hill, finding that they were making, as he thought, over free with his provisions, took the liberty of putting a lock on the door through which they had access. But he had better have left it alone, for his daughter grew stone blind, and never recovered her sight till the lock was removed.—*Resenii Atlas,* i. 10. There is a similar story in Grimm's Deutsche Sagen, i. p. 55.

The legend of Bodeys

There is a hill called Bodedys close to the road in the neighbourhood of Lynge, that is near Soröe. Not far from it lived an old farmer, whose only son was used to take long journeys on business. His father had for a long time heard no tidings of him, and the old man became convinced that his son was dead. This caused him much affliction, as was natural for an old man like him, and thus some time passed over.

One evening as he was coining with a loaded cart by Bodedys, the hill opened, and the Troll came out and desired him to drive his cart into it. The poor man was; to be sure, greatly amazed at this, but well knowing how little it would avail him to refuse to comply with the Troll's request, he turned about his horses, and drove his cart straight into the hill. The Troll now began to deal with him for his goods, and finally bought and paid him honestly for his entire cargo. When he had finished the unloading of his vehicle, and was about to drive again out of the hill, the Troll said to him, "If you will now only keep a silent tongue in your head about all that has happened to you, I shall from this time out have an eye to your interest; and if you come here again to-morrow morning, it may be you shall get your son." The farmer did not well know at first what to say to all this; but as he was, however, of opinion that the Troll was able to perform what he had promised, he was greatly rejoiced, and failed not to come at the appointed time to Bodedys.

He sat there waiting a long time, and at last he fell asleep, and when he awoke from his slumber, behold! there was his son lying by his side. Both father and son found it difficult to explain how this had come to pass. The son related how he had been thrown into, prison, and had there suffered great hardship and distress; but that one night, while he was lying asleep in his cell, there came a man to him, who said, "Do you still love your father?" And when he had answered that he surely did, his chains fell off and the wall burst open. While he was telling this he chanced to put his hand up to his neck, and he found that he had brought a piece of the iron chain away with him. They both were for some time mute through excess of wonder; and they then arose and went straightway to Lynge, where they hung up the piece of the chain in the church, as a memorial of the wonderful event that had occurred. [a]

NOTE
[a] This legend is oral.

Kallundborg Church

When Esbern Snare was about building a church in Kallundborg, he saw clearly that his means were not fully adequate to the task. But a Troll came to him and offered his services; and Esbern Snare made an agreement with him on these conditions, that he should be able to tell the Troll's name when the church was finished; or in case he could not, that he should give him his heart and his eyes.

The work now went on rapidly, and the Troll set the church on stone pillars; but when all was nearly done, and there was only half a pillar wanting in the church, Esbern began to get frightened, for the name of the Troll was yet unknown to him.

One day be was going about the fields all alone, and in great anxiety on account of the perilous state he was in; when, tired, and depressed, by reason of his exceeding grief and affliction, he laid him down on Ulshöi bank to rest himself a while. While he was lying there, he heard a Troll-woman within the hill saying these words:—

"Lie still, baby mine!
To-morrow cometh Fin,
Father thine,
And giveth thee Esbern Snare's eyes and heart to play with." [a]

When Esbern heard this, he recovered his spirits, and went back to the church. The Troll was just then coming with the half-pillar that was wanting for the church; but when Esbern saw him, he hailed him by his name, and called him "Fin." The Troll was so enraged at this, that he went off with the half-pillar through the air, and this is the reason that the church has but three pillars and a half. [b]

* * *

The same is told of a far greater than Esbern Snare. As St. Olaf; the royal apostle of the North, was one day going over hill and dale, thinking how he could contrive to build a splendid church without distressing his people by taxation, he was met by a man of a strange appearance, who asking him what he was thinking about, Olaf told him, and the Troll, or rather Giant(*Jätte*), for such he was, undertook to do it within a certain time, stipulating, for his reward, the sun and. moon, or else St. Olaf himself Olaf agreed, but gave such a plan for the church as it seemed to be impossible ever could be executed. It was to be so large that seven priests could preach in it at the same time without disturbing each other; the columns and other orna- ments both within and without should be of hard flintstone, and so forth. It soon, however, was finished, all but the roof and pinnacle. Olaf; now grown uneasy, rambled once more over hill and dale, when he chanced to bear a child crying within a hill, and a giantess, its mother, saying to it, "Rush, hush! Thy father, Wind-and-Weather, will come home in the morning, and bring with him the sun and moon, or else St. Olaf himself." Olaf was overjoyed, for the power of evil beings ceases when their name is known. He returned home, where he saw every thing completed—pinnacle and all. He immediately cried out, "Wind-and-Weather, you've set the pinnacle crooked! " [c] Instantly the Giant fell witn a great crash from the ridge of the roof, and broke into a thousand pieces, which were all flintstone. [d]

NOTES

[a] *Tie stille, barn min!*
Imorgen kommer Fin,
Fa'er din,
Og gi'er Esbern Snares öine og hjerte at lege med.

[b] *Oral.* Kallundborg is in Zealand. Mr. Thiele says he saw four pillars at the church. The same story is told of the cathedral of Lund in Funen, which was built by the Troll Finn at the desire of St. Laurentius.

Of Esbern Snare, Holberg says, " The common people tell wonderful stories of him, and how the devil carried him off; which, with other things, will servo to prove that he was an able man."

The German story of Rumpelstilzchen (Kinder and Haus-Märchen, No. 55) is similar to this legend. MM. Grimm, in their note on this story, notice the unexpected manner in which, in the Thousand and One Days, or Persian Tales, the princess Turandot learns the name of Calaf.

[c] *Wind och Veder!*
Du har satt spiran spedar!
Others say it was.
Bläster! sätt spiran väster!
Blester! set the pinnacle westwards!
Or,
Slät! sätt spiran rätt!
Slatt! set the pinnacle straight!

[d] Afzelius Sago-häfder, iii. 83. Grimm, Deut. Mythol. P. 515

The Hill-Man invited to the Christening

The hill-people are excessively frightened during thunder. When, therefore, they see bad weather coming on, they lose no time in getting to the shelter of their hills. This terror is also the cause of their not being able to endure the beating of a drum, as they take it to be the rolling of thunder. It is therefore a good receipt for banishing them to beat a drum every day in the neighbourhood of their hills; for they immediately pack up and depart to some more quiet residence.

A farmer lived once in great friendship and unanimity with a hill-man, whose hill was on his lands. One time when his wife was lying-in, it gave him some degree of perplexity to think that he could not well avoid inviting the hill-man to the christening, which might not improbably bring him into bad repute with the priest and the other people of the village. He was going about pondering deeply, but in vain, how he might get out of this dilemma, when it came into his head to ask the advice of the boy that kept his pigs, who was a great head-piece, and had often helped him before. The pig-boy instantly undertook to arrange the matter with the hill-man in such a manner that he should not only stay away without being offended, but moreover give a good christening-present.

Accordingly, when it was night be took a sack on his shoulder, went to the hill-man's hill, knocked, and was admitted. He delivered his message, giving his master's compliments, and requesting the honour of his company at the christening. The hill-man thanked him, and said, "I think it is but right that I should give you a christening-gift." With these words he opened his money-chests, bidding the boy to hold up his sack while he poured money into it. "Is there enough now?" said he, when he had put 'a good quantity into it. "Many give more, few give less," replied the boy.

The hill-man then fell again to filling the sack, and again asked, "Is there enough now?" The boy lifted up the sack a little off the ground to try if he was able to carry any more, and then answered, "It is about what most people give." Upon this the hill-man emptied the whole chest into the bag, and once more asked, "Is there enough now?" The guardian of the pigs saw that there was as much in it now as ever he was able to carry, so he made answer, "No one gives more, most people give less."

"Come, now," said the hill-man, "let us hear who else is to be at the christening?" "Ah," said the boy, "we are to have a great parcel of strangers and great people. First and foremost, we are to have three priests and a bishop!" "Hem!" muttered the hill-man; "however, these gentlemen usually look only after the eating and drinking: they will never take any notice of me. Well, who else?" "Then we have asked St. Peter and St. Paul." "Hem! hem! however, there will be a by-place for me behind the stove. Well, and then?" "Then our Lady herself is coming!" "Hem! hem! hem! however, guests of such high rank come late and go away early. But tell me, my lad, what sort of music is it you are to have?"' "Music!" said the boy, "why, we are to have drums." "Drums! "repeated he, quite terrified; "no, no, thank you, I shall stay at 'home in that case. Give my best respects to your master, and I thank him for the invitation, but I cannot come. I did but once go out to take a little walk, and some people beginning to beat a drum, I hurried home, and was just got to my door when they flung the drum-stick after me and broke one of my shins. 'I have been lame of that leg ever since, and I shall take good care in future to avoid that sort of music." So saying, he helped the boy to put the sack on his back, once more charging him to give his best respects to the farmer. [a]

NOTE

[a] This event happened in Jutland. The Troll's dread of thunder seems to be founded in the mythologic narratives of Thor's enmity to the Trolls.

The Troll turned Cat

About a quarter of a mile from Soröe lies Pedersborg, and a little farther on is the town of Lyng. Just between these towns is a hill called Bröndhöi *(Spring-hill)*, said to be inhabited by the Troll-people.

There goes a story that there was once among these Troll. people of Bröndhöi an old crossgrained curmudgeon of a Troll, whom the rest nick-named Knurremurre *(Rumble-grumble)*, because he was evermore the cause of noise and uproar within the hill. This Knurremurre having discovered what he thought to be too great a degree of intimacy between his young wife and a young Troll of the society, took this in such ill part, that he vowed vengeance, swearing he would have the life of the young one. The latter, accordingly, thought it would be his best course to be off out of the hill till better times; so, turning himself into a noble tortoise. shell tom-cat, he one fine morning quitted his old residence, and journeyed down to the neighbouring town of Lyng, where he established himself in the house of an honest poor man named Plat.

Here he lived for a long time comfortable and easy, with nothing to annoy him, and was as happy as any tom-cat or Troll crossed in love well could be. He got every day plenty of milk and good groute [a] to eat, and lay the whole day long at his ease in a warm arm-chair behind the stove.

Plat happened one evening to come home rather late, and as he entered the room the cat was sitting in his usual place, scraping meal-groute out of a pot, and licking the pot itself carefully. "Harkye, dame," said Plat, as he came in at the door, "till l tell you what happened to me on the road. Just as I was coming past Bröndhöi, there came out a Troll, and he called out to me, and said,

"Harkye Plat,
Tell your cat,
That Knurremurre is dead." [b]

The moment the cat heard these words, he tumbled the pot down on the floor, sprang out of the chair, and stood up on his hind-legs. Then, as he hurried out of the door, he cried out with exultation, "What! is Knurremurre dead? Then I may go home as fast as I please." And so saying he scampered off to the hill, to the amazement of honest Plat; and it is likely lost no time in making his advances to the young widow. [c]

NOTES

[a] Groute, Danish *Gröd,* is a species of food like furmety, made of shelled oats or barley. It is boiled and eaten with milk or butter.
[b] Hör du Plat,
Siig til din Kat,
At Knurremurre er död.
[c] The scene of this story is in Zealand. The same is related of a hill called Onrehöi in the same island. The writer has heard it in Ireland, but they were cats who addressed the man as he passed by the churchyard where they were assembled.

Kirsten's-hill

There is a hill on the lands of Skjelverod, near Ringsted, called Kirst-en's-hill *(Kirstens Bjerg)*. In it there lived a Hill-troll whose name was Skynd, who had from time to time stolen no less than three wives from a man in the village of Englerup.

It was late one evening when this man was riding hone from Ringsted, and his way lay by the hill. When he came there he saw a great crowd of Hill-folk who were dancing round it, and had great merriment among them. But on looking a little closer, what should he recognise but all his three wives among them! Now as Kirsten, the second of them, had been his favourite, and dearer to him than either of the others, he called out to her, and named her name. Troll Skynd then came up to the man, and asked him why he presumed to call Kirsten. The man told him briefly how she had been his favourite and best beloved wife, and entreated of him, with many tears and much lamentation, to let him have her home with him again. The Troll consented at last to grant the husband's request, with, however, the condition, that he should never hurry *(skynde)* her.

For a long time the husband strictly kept the condition; but one day, when the woman was above in the loft, getting something, and it happened that she delayed a long time, he called out, Make haste, Kirsten, make haste, *(Skynde dig Kirsten);* and scarcely had he spoken the words, when the woman was gone, compelled to return to the hill, which has ever since been called Kirsten's Bjerg. [a]

NOTE
[a] This legend was orally related to Mr. Thiele.

The Troll-Labourer

"In the year 1660, when I and my wife had gone to my farm *(fabod-erne),* which is three quarters of a mile from Ragunda parsonage, and we were sitting there and talking a while, late in the evening, there came a little man in at thà door, who begged of my wife to go and aid his wife, who was just then in the pains of labour. The fellow was of small size, of a dark complexion, and dressed in old grey clothes. My wife and I sat a while, and wondered at the man; for we were aware that he was a Troll, and we had heard tell that such like, called by the peasantry Vettar *(spirits),* always used to keep in the farmhouses, when people left them in harvest-time. But when he had urged his request four or five times, and we thought on what evil the country folk say that they have at times suffered from the Vettar, when they have chanced to swear at them, or with uncivil words bid them go to hell, I took the resolution to read some prayers over my wile, and to bless her, and bid her in God's name go with him. She took in haste some old linen with her, and went along with him, and I remained sitting there. When she returned, she told me, that when she went with the man out at the gate, it seemed to her as if she was carried for a time along in the wind, and so she came to a room, on one side of which was a little dark chamber, in which his wife lay in bed in great agony. My wife went up to her, and, after a little while, aided her till she brought forth the child after the same manner as other human beings. The man then offered her food, and when she refused it, he thanked her, and accompanied her out, and then she was carried along, in the same way in the wind, and after a while came again to the gate, just at ten o'clock. Meanwhile, a quantity of old pieces and clippings of silver were laid on a shelf, in the sitting-room, and my wife found them next day, when she was putting the room in order. It is to be supposed that they were laid there by the *Vettr*. That it in truth so happened, I witness, by inscribing my name. [a]

Ragunda, the 12th of April, 1671.
"PET. RAHM."

NOTE

[a] Hülpher, Samlingen om Jämtland. Westeras, 1775. p. 210 *ap*. Grimm, Deut. Mythol., p. 425.

The Hill Smith

Biörn Martinsson went out shooting, one day, with a gamekeeper, on the wooded hill of Ormkulla. They there found a hill-smith *(bergsmed)* lying fast asleep. Biörn directed the gamekeeper to secure him, but he refused, saying "Pray to God to protect you! The hill-smith will fling you down to the bottom of the hill." He was, however, bold and, determined, and he went up and seized the sleeping hill-smith, who gave a cry, and implored him to let him go, as he had a wife and seven little children. He said he would also do any iron work that should be required; it would only be necessary to leave iron and steel on the side of the hill, and the work would be found lying finished in the same place. Biörn asked him for whom he worked; he replied, "For my companions." When Biörn would not let him go, he said, "If I had my mist-cap *(uddehat)* you should not carry me away. But if you do not let me go, not one of your posterity will attain to the importance which you possess, but continually decline;" which certainly came to pass. Biörn would not, however, let him go, but brought him captive to Bahus. On the third day, however, he effected his escape out of the place in which he was confined. [a]

* * *

The following legend is related in Denmark:—

On the lands of Nyegaard lie three large hills, one of which is the abode of a Troll, who is by trade a blacksmith. If any one is passing that hill by night, he will see the fire issuing from the top, and going in again at the side. Should you wish to have any piece of iron-work executed in a masterly manner, you have only to go to the hill, and saying aloud what you want to have made, leave there the iron and a silver shilling. On revisiting the hill next morning, you will find the shilling gone, and the required piece of work lying there finished, and ready for use. [b]

NOTES

[a] Odmane Bahuslän, *ap*. Grimm. Deut. Mythol. p. 426. Odman also tells of a man who, as he was going along one day with his dog, came on a hill-smith at his work, using a stone as an anvil. He had on him a light grey coat and a black woollen hat. The dog began to bark at him, but he put on so menacing an attitude that they both deemed it advisable to go away.

[b] Thiele, iv. 120. In both these legends we find the tradition of the artistic skill of the Duergar and of Völundr still retained by the peasantry see Tales and Popular Fictions, p. 270.

The Girl at the Troll-Dance

A girl, belonging to a village in the isle of' Funen, went out, one evening, into the fields, and as she was passing by a small hill, she saw that it was raised upon red pillars, and a Troll-banquet going on beneath it. She was invited in, and such was the gaiety and festivity that prevailed, that she never perceived the flight of time. At length, however, she took her departure, after having spent, as she thought, a few hours among the joyous hill-people. But when she came to the village she no longer found it the place she had left. All was changed; and when she entered the house in which she had lived with her family, she learned that her father and mother had long been dead, and the house had come into the hands of strangers. She now perceived. that for every hour that she had been among the Trolls, a year had elapsed in the external world. The effect on her mind. was such that she lost her reason, which she never after recovered. [a]

NOTE

[a] Thiele, iv. 21. In Otmar's Volksagen, there is a German legend of Peter Klaus, who slept a steep of twenty years in the bowling-green of the Kyffhäuser, from which Washington Irving made his Ripp van Winkle. We shall also find it in the Highlands of Scotland. It is the Irish legend of Clough na Cuddy, so extremely well told by Mr. C. Croker (to which, by the way, we contributed a Latin song), in the notes to which further information will be found. The Seven Sleepers seems to be the original.

The Changeling

There lived once, near Tiis lake, two lonely people, who were sadly plagued with a changeling, given them by the underground-people instead of their own child, which had not been baptised in time. This changeling behaved in a very strange and uncommon manner, for when there was no one in the place, he was in great spirits, ran up the walls like a cat, sat under the roof, and shouted and bawled away lustily; but sat dozing at the end of the table when any one was in the room with him. He was able to eat as much as any four, and never cared what it was that was set before him; but though he regarded not the quality of his food, in quantity be was never satisfied, and gave excessive annoyance to every one in the house.

When they had tried for a long time in vain how they could best get rid of him, since there was no living in the house with him, a smart girl pledged herself that she would banish him from the house. She accordingly, while he was out in the fields, took a pig and killed it, and put it, hide, hair, and all, into a black pudding, and set it before him when he came home. He began, as was his custom, to gobble it up, but when he had eaten for some time, he began to relax a little in his efforts, and at last he sat quite still, with his knife in his hand, looking at the pudding.

At length, after sitting for some time in this manner, he began—"A pudding with hide!—and a pudding with hair! a pudding with eyes!—and a pudding with legs in it! Well, three times have I seen a young wood by Tiis lake, but never yet did I see such a pudding! The devil himself may stay here now for me!" So saying,he ran off with himself; and never more came back again.[a]

* * *

Another changeling was got rid of in the following manner. The mother, suspecting it to be such from its refusing food, and being so ill-thriven, heated the oven as hot as possible. The maid, as instructed, asked her why she did it. "To burn my child in it to death," was the reply. When the question had been put and answered three times, she placed the child on the peel, and was shoving it into the oven, when the Troll-woman came in a great fright with the real child, and took away her own, saying, "There's your child for you. I have treated it better than you treated mine," and in truth it was fat and hearty.

NOTE

[a] *Oral.* See the Young Piper and the Brewery of Egg-shells in the Irish Fairy Legends, with the notes. The same story is also to be found in Germany where the object is to make the changeling laugh. The mother breaks an egg in two and sets water down to boil in each half shell. The imp then cries out: "Well! I'm as old as the Westerwald, but never before saw I any one cooking in egg-shells," and bunt out laughing at it. Instantly the true child was returned.—Kinder and Haus—Märchen, iii. 39. Grose also tells the story in his Provincial Glossary. The mother there breaks a dozen of eggs and sets the shells before the child, who says, "I was seven years old when I came to nurse, and I have lived four since, and yet I never saw so many milkpans." See also Minstrelsy of the Scottish Border, and below, *Wales, Brittany, France.*

The Tile-Stove jumping over the Brook

Near Hellested in Zealand, lived a man, who from time to time re-marked that he was continually plundered. All his suspicions fell on the Troll-folk, who lived in the neighbouring hill of Ildshöi*(Fire-hill)*, and once hid himself to try and get a sight of the thief. He had waited there but a very short time when he saw, as he thought, his tile-stove jumping across the brook. The good farmer was all astonishment at this strange sight, and he shouted out "Hurra! there 'a a jump for a tile-stove!" At this exclamation the Troll, who was wading through the water with the stove on his head, was so frightened that he threw it down, and ran off as hard as he could to Ildshöi. But in the place where the stove fell, the ground got the shape of it, and the place is called Krogbek *(Hook-brook),* and it was this that gave rise to the common saying, "That was a jump for a tile-stove!"

"Det var et Spring af em Leerovn!" [a]

NOTE

[a] This legend is taken from Resenii Atlas, i. 36.

Departure of the Trolls from Vendsyssel

One evening, after sunset, there came a strange man to the ferry of Sund. He engaged all the ferry-boats there to go backwards and forwards the whole night long between that place and Vendsyssel, without the people's knowing what lading they had. He told them that they should take their freight on board half a mile to the east of Sund, near the alehouse at the bridge of Lange. At the appointed time the man was at that place, and the ferrymen, though unable to see anything, perceived very clearly that the boats sunk deeper and deeper, so that they easily concluded that they had gotten a very heavy freight on board. The ferry-boats passed in this manner to and fro the whole night long; and though they got every trip a fresh cargo, the strange man never left them, but staid to have everything regulated by his directions.

When morning was breaking they received the payment they had agreed for, and they then ventured to inquire what it was they had been bringing over, but on that head their employer would give them no satisfaction.

But there happened to be among the ferrymen a smart fellow who knew more about these matters than the others. He jumped on shore, took the clay from under his right foot, and put it into his cap, and when he had set it on his head he perceived that all the sand-hills east of Aalborg were completely covered with little Troll-people, who had all pointed red caps on their heads. Ever since that time there have been no Dwarfs seen in Vendsyssel. [a]

NOTE

[a] Vendsyssel and Aalborg are both in North Jutland—The story Is told by the ferrymen to travellers: see Mythology of Greece and Italy, p. 68.

Svend Faelling

Svend Faelling was a valiant champion. He was born in Faelling, and was a long time at service in Aakjaer house, Aarhuus, and as the roads were at that time greatly infested by Trolls and underground-people, who bore great enmity to all Christians, Svend undertook the office of letter-carrier.

As he was one time going along the road, he saw approaching him the Troll of Jels-hill, on the lands of Holm. The Troll came up to him, begging him to stand his friend in a combat with the Troll of Borum-es-hill. When Svend Faelling had promised to do so, saying that he thought himself strong and active enough for the encounter, the Troll reached him a heavy iron bar, and bade him show his strength on that. But not all Svend's efforts availed to lift it: whereupon the Troll handed him a horn, telling him to drink out of it. No sooner had he drunk a little out of it than his strength increased. He was now able to lift the bar, which, when he had drunk again, became still lighter; but when again renewing his draught he emptied the horn, he was able to swing the bar with ease, and he then learned from the Troll that he had now gotten the strength of twelve men. He then promised to prepare himself for combat with the Troll of Bergmond. As a token he was told that he should meet on the road a black ox and a red ox, and that he should fall with all his might on the black ox, and drive him from the red one.

This all came to pass just as he was told, and he found, after his work was done, that the black ox was the Troll from Borum-es-hill, and the red ox was the Troll himself of Jelshill, who, as a reward for the assistance he had given him, allowed him to retain for his own use the twelve men's strength with which he had endowed him. This grant was, however, on this condition—that if ever he should reveal the secret of his strength, he should be punished by getting the appetite of twelve.

The fame of the prodigious strength of Svend soon spread through the country, as he distinguished himself by various exploits, such, for instance, as throwing a dairy-maid, who had offended him, up on the gable of the house, and similar feats. So when this report came to the ears of his master, he had Svend called before him, and inquired of him whence his great strength came. Svend recollected the words of his friend the Troll, so he told him if he would promise him as much food as would satisfy twelve men, he would tell him. The master promised, and Svend told his story; but the word of the Troll was accomplished, for from that day forth Svend ate and drank as much as any twelve. [a]

NOTE

[a] According to what Mr. Thiele was told in Zealand, Svend Faelling must have been of prodigious size, for there is a hill near Steenstrup on which he used to sit while he washed his feet tnd hands in the sea, about half a quarter of a mile distant. The people of Holmstrup dressed a dinner for him, and brought it to him in large brewing vessels, much as the good people of Lilliput did with Gulliver, This reminds us of Holger Danske, who once wanted a new suit of clothes. Twelve tailors were employed: they set ladders to his back and shoulders, as was done to Gulliver, and they measured away; but the man that was highest on the right side ladder chanced, as he was cutting a mark in the measure, to clip Holger's ear. Holger, forgetting what it was, hastily put up his hand to his head, caught the poor tailor, and crushed him to death between his fingers.

The Dwarfs' Banquet
A Norwegian Tale [a]

There lived in Norway, not far from the city of Drontheim, a powerful man, who was blessed with all the goods of fortune. A part of the surrounding country was his property; numerous herds fed on his pastures, and a great retinue and a crowd of servants adorned his mansion. He had an only daughter, called Aslog, [b] the fame of whose beauty spread far and wide. The greatest men of the country sought her, but all were alike unsuccessful in their suit, and he who had come full of confidence and joy, rode away home silent and melancholy. Her father, who thought his daughter delayed her choice only to select, forbore to interfere, and exulted in her prudence. But when, at length, the richest and noblest had tried their fortune with as little success as the rest, he grew angry, and called his daughter, and said to her," Hitherto I have left you to your free choice, but since I see that you reject all without any distinction, and the very best of your suitors seem not good enough for you, I will keep measures no longer with you. What! shall my family be extinct, and my inheritance pass away into the hands of strangers? I will break your stubborn spirit. I give you now till the festival of the great Winter-night; make your choice by that time, or prepare to accept him whom I shall fix on."

Aslog loved a youth called Orm, handsome as he was brave and noble. She loved him with her whole soul, and she would sooner die than bestow her hand on another. But Orm was poor, and poverty compelled him to serve in the mansion of her father. Aslog's partiality for him was kept a secret; for her father's pride of power and wealth was such that he would never have given his consent to an union with so humble a man.

When Aslog saw the darkness of his countenance, and heard his angry words, she turned pale as death, for she knew his temper, and doubted not but that he would put his threats into execution. Without uttering a word in reply, she retired to her silent chamber, and thought deeply but in vain how to avert the dark storm that hung over her. The great festival approached nearer and nearer, and her anguish increased every day.

At last the lovers resolved on flight. "I know," says Orm, "a secure place where we may remain undiscovered until we find an opportunity of quitting the country." At night, when all were asleep, Orm led the trembling Aslog over the snow and ice-fields away to the mountains. The moon and the stars sparkling still brighter in the cold winter's night lighted them on their way. They had under their arms a few articles of dress and some skins of animals, which were all they could carry. They ascended the mountains the whole night long till they reached a lonely spot inclosed with lofty rocks. Here Orm conducted the weary Aslog into a cave, the low and narrow entrance to which was hardly perceptible, but it soon enlarged to a great hall, reaching deep into the mountain. He kindled a fire, and they now, reposing on their skins, sat in the deepest solitude far away from all the world.

Orm was the first who had discovered this cave, which is shown to this very day, and as no one knew any thing of it, they were safe from the pursuit of Aslog's father. They passed the whole winter in this retirement. Orm used to go a hunting, and Aslog stayed at home in the cave, minded the fire, and prepared the necessary food. Frequently did she mount the points of the rocks, but her eyes wandered as far as they could reach only over glittering snow-fields.

The spring now came on—the woods were green—the meads put on their various colours, and Aslog could but rarely and with circumspection venture to leave the cave. One evening Orm came in with the intelligence that he had recognised her father's servants in the distance, and that he could hardly have been unobserved by them, whose eyes were as good as his own. "They will surround this place," continued he, "and never rest till they have found us; we must quit our retreat, then, without a moment's delay."

They accordingly descended on the other side of the mountain, and reached the strand, where they fortunately found a boat. Orm shoved off, and the boat drove into the open sea. They had escaped their pursuers, but they were now exposed to dangers of another kind: whither should they turn themselves? They could not venture to land, for Aslog's father was lord of the whole coast, and they would infallibly fall into his hands. Nothing then remained for them but to commit their bark to the wind and waves. They drove along the entire night. At break of day the coast had disappeared, and they saw nothing but the sky above, the sea beneath, and the waves that rose and fell. They had not brought one morsel of food with them, and thirst and hunger began now to torment them. Three days did they toss about in this state of misery, and Aslog, faint and exhausted, saw nothing but certain death before her.

At length, on the evening of the third day, they discovered an island of tolerable magnitude, and surrounded by a number of smaller ones. Orm immediately steered for it, but just as he came near it there suddenly rose a violent wind, and the sea rolled every moment higher and higher against him. He turned about with a view of approaching it on another side, but with no better success; his vessel, as oft as it approached the island, was driven back as if by an invisible power. "Lord God!" cried he, and blessed himself and looked on poor Aslog, who seemed to be dying of weakness before his eyes. But scarcely had the exclamation passed his lips when the storm ceased, the waves subsided, and the vessel came to the shore, without encountering any hindrance. Orm jumped out on the beach; some mussels that he found on the strand strengthened and revived the exhausted Aslog, so that she was soon able to leave the boat.

The island was overgrown with low dwarf shrubs, and seemed to be uninhabited; but when they had gotten about to the middle of it, they discovered a house reaching but a little above the ground, and appearing to be half under the surface of the earth. In the hope of meeting human beings and assistance, the wanderers approached it. They listened if they could hear any noise, but the most perfect silence reigned there. Orm at length opened the door, and with his companion walked in; but what was their surprise, to find everything regulated and arranged as if for inhabitants, yet not a single living creature visible. The fire was burning on the hearth, in the middle of the room, and a pot with fish hung on it apparently only waiting for some one to take it up and eat it. The beds were made and ready to receive their wearied tenants. Orm and Aslog stood for some time dubious, and looked on with a certain degree of awe, but at last, overcome by hunger, they took up the food and ate. When they had satisfied their appetites, and still in the last beams of the setting sun, which now streamed over the island far and wide, discovered no human being, they gave way to weariness, and laid themselves in the beds to which they had been so long strangers.

They had expected to be awakened in the night by the owners of the house on their return home, but their expectation was not fulfilled; they slept undisturbed till the morning sun shone in upon them. No one appeared on any of the following days, and it seemed as if some invisible power had made ready the house for their reception. They spent the whole summer in perfect happiness—they were, to be sure, solitary, yet they did not miss mankind. The wild birds' eggs, and the fish they caught, yielded them provisions in abundance.

When autumn came, Aslog brought forth a son. In the midst of their joy at his appearance, they were surprised by a wonderful apparition. The door opened on a sudden, and an old woman stepped in. She had on her a handsome blue dress: there was something proud, but at the same time something strange and surprising in her appearance.

"Do not be afraid," said she, "at my unexpected appearance—I am the owner of this house, and I thank you for the clean and neat state in which you have kept it, and for the good order in which I find everything with you. I would willingly have come sooner, but I had no power to do so till this little heathen (pointing to the new born-babe) was come to the light. Now I have free access. Only fetch no priest from the main-land to christen it, or I must depart again. If you will in this matter comply with my wishes, you may not only continue to live here, but all the good that ever you can wish for I will do you.

Whatever you take in hand shall prosper; good luck shall follow you wherever you go. But break this condition, and depend upon it that misfortune after misfortune will come on you, and even on this child will I avenge myself. If you want anything, or are in danger, you have only to pronounce my name three times and I will appear and lend you assistance. I am of the race of the old Giants, and my name is Guru. But beware of uttering in my presence the name of him whom no Giant may hear of, and never venture to make the sign of the cross, or to cut it on beam or board in the house. You may dwell in this house the whole year long, only be so good as to give it up to me on Yule evening, when the sun is at the lowest, as then we celebrate our great festival, and then only are we permitted to be merry. At least, if you should not be willing to go out of the house, keep your-selves up in the loft as quiet as possible the whole day long, and as you value your lives do not look down into the room until midnight is past. After that you may take possession of everything again."

When the old woman had thus spoken she vanished, and Aslog and Orm, now at ease respecting their situation, lived without any disturbance contented and happy. Orm never made a cast of his net without getting a plentiful draught; he never shot an arrow from his bow that it was not sure to hit; in short, whatever they took in hand, were it ever so trifling, evidently prospered.

When Christmas came, they cleaned up the house in the best manner, set everything in order, kindled a fire on the hearth, and as the twilight approached, they went up to the loft, where they remained quite still and quiet. At length it grew dark; they thought they heard a sound of whizzing and snorting in the air, such as the swans use to make in the winter tune. There was a hole in the roof over the fireplace which might be opened and shut either to let in the light from above, or to afford a free passage for the smoke. Orm lifted up the lid, which was covered with a skin, and put out his head. But what a wonderful sight then presented itself to his eyes. The little islands around were all lit up with countless blue lights, which moved about without ceasing, jumped up and down, then skipped down to the shore, assembled together, and came nearer and nearer to the large island where Orm and Aslog lived. At last they reached it, and arranged themselves in a circle around a large stone not far from the shore, and which Orm well knew. But what was his surprise, when he saw that the stone had flow completely assumed the form of a man, though of a monstrous and gigantic one! He could clearly perceive that the little blue lights were borne by Dwarfs, whose pale clay-coloured faces, with their huge noses and red eyes, disfigured too by birds' bills and owls' eyes, were supported by mis-shapen bodies; and they tottered and wabbled about here and there, so that they seemed to be at the same time merry and in pain. Suddenly, the circle opened; the little ones retired on each side, and Guru, who was now much enlarged and of as immense a size as the stone, advanced with gigantic steps. She threw both her arms round the stone image, which immediately began to receive life and motion. As soon as the first symptom of motion showed itself, the little ones began, with wonderful capers and grimaces, a song, or to speak more proper-ly, a howl, with which the whole island resounded and seemed to tremble at the noise. Orm, quite terrified, drew in his head, and he and Aslog remained in the dark, so still, that they hardly ventured to draw their breath.

The procession moved on toward the house, as might be clearly perceived by the nearer approach of the shouting and crying. They were now all come in, and, light and active, the Dwarfs jumped about on the benches; and heavy and loud sounded at intervals the steps of the giants. Orm and his wife heard them covering the table, and the clattering of the plates, and the shouts of joy with which they celebrated their banquet. When it was over and it drew near to midnight, they began to dance to that ravishing fairy-air which charms the mind into such sweet confusion, and which some have heard in the rocky glens, and learned by listening to the underground musicians. As soon as Aslog caught the sound of this air, she felt an irresistible longing to see the dance. Nor was Orm able to keep her back. "Let me look," said she, "or my heart will burst." She took her child and placed herself at the extreme end of the loft, whence, without being observed, she could see all that passed. Long did she gaze, without taking off her eyes for an instant, on the dance, on the bold and wonderful springs of the little creatures who seemed to float in the air, and not so much as to touch the ground, while the ravishing melody of the elves filled her whole soul. The child meanwhile, which lay in her arms, grew sleepy and drew its breath heavily, and without ever thinking on the promise she had given the old woman, she made, as is usual, the sign of the cross over the mouth of the child, and said, "Christ bless you, my babe!"

The instant she had spoken the word there was raised a horrible piercing cry. The spirits tumbled heads over heels out at the door with terrible crushing and crowding, their lights went out, and

in a few minutes the whole house was clear of them, and left deso-
late. Orm and Aslog frightened to death, hid themselves in the most
retired nook in the house. They did not venture to stir till daybreak,
and not till the sun shone through the hole in the roof down on the
fire-place did they feel courage enough to descend from the loft.

The table remained still covered as the underground-people
had left it; all their vessels, which were of silver, and manufactured
in the most beautiful manner, were upon it. In the middle of the
room, there stood upon the ground a huge copper vessel half full of
sweet mead, and by the side of it, a drinking-horn of pure gold. In
the corner lay against the wall a stringed instrument, not unlike a
dulcimer, which, as people believe, the Giantesses used to play on.
They gazed on what was before them, full of admiration, but without venturing to lay their hands on anything: but great and fearful
was their amazement, when, on turning about, they saw sitting at
the table an immense figure, which Orm instantly recognised as
the Giant whom Guru had animated by her embrace. He was now
a cold and hard stone. While they were standing gazing on it, Guru
herself entered the room in her giant-form. She wept so bitterly, that
her tears trickled down on the ground. It was long ere her sobbing
permitted her to utter a single word: at last she spoke:—

"Great affliction have you brought on me, and henceforth I
must weep while I live; yet as I know that you have not done this
with evil intentions, I forgive you, though it were a trifle for me to
crush the whole house like an egg-shell over your heads."

"Alas!" cried she, "my husband, whom I love more than myself there he sits, petrified for ever; never again will he open his

eyes! Three hundred years lived I with my father on the island of Kunnan, happy in the innocence of youth, as the fairest among the Giant-maidens. Mighty heroes sued for my hand; the sea around that island is still filled with the rocky fragments which they hurled against each other in their combats. Andfind won the victory, and I plighted myself to him. But ere I was married came the detestable Odin into the country, who overcame my father, and drove us all from the island. My father and sisters fled to the mountains, and since that time my eyes have beheld them no more. Andfind and I saved ourselves on this island, where we for a long time lived in peace and quiet, and thought it would never be interrupted. But destiny, which no one escapes, had determined it otherwise. Oluf [c] came from Britain. They called him the Holy, and Andfind instantly found that his voyage would be inauspicious to the giants. When he heard how Oluf's ship rushed through the waves, he went down to the strand and blew the sea against him with all his strength. The waves swelled up like mountains. But Oluf was still more mighty than he; his ship flew unchecked through the billows like an arrow from a bow. He steered direct for our island. When the ship was so near that Andfind thought he could reach it with his hands, he grasped at the forepart with his right hand, and was about to drag it down to the bottom, as he had often done with other ships. But Oluf the terrible Oluf, stepped forward, and crossing his hands over each other, he cried with a loud voice, 'Stand there as a stone, till the last day,' and in the same instant my unhappy husband became a mass of rock. The ship sailed on unimpeded, and ran direct against the mountain, which it cut through, and separated from it the little island which lies out yonder. [d]

"Ever since my happiness has been annihilated, and lonely and melancholy have I passed my life. On Yule-eve alone can petrified Giants receive back their life for the space of seven hours, if one of their race embraces them, and is, at the same time, willing to sacrifice a hundred years of their own life. But seldom does a Giant do that. I loved my husband too well not to bring him back cheerfully to life every time that I could do it, even at the highest price, and never would I reckon how often I had done it, that I might not know when the time came when I myself should share his fate, and at the moment that I threw my arms around him become one with him. But alas! even this comfort is taken from me; I can never more by any embrace awake him, since he has heard the name which I dare not utter; and never again will he see the light until the dawn of the last day shall bring it.

"I now go hence! You will never again behold me! All that is here in the house I give you! My dulcimer alone will I keep! But let no one venture to fix his habitation on the little islands that lie around here! There dwell the little underground ones whom you saw at the festival, and I will protect them as long as I live!"

With these words Guru vanished. The next spring Orin took the golden horn and the silver ware to Drontheim,where no one knew him. The value of these precious metals was so great, that he was able to purchase everything requisite for a wealthy man. He laded his ship with his purchases, and returned back to the island, where he spent many years in unalloyed happiness, and Aslog's father was soon reconciled to his wealthy son-in-law.

The stone image remained sitting in the house; no human power was able to move it. So hard was the stone, that hammer and axe flew in pieces without making the slightest impression upon it. The Giant sat there till a holy man came to the island, who with one single word removed him back to his former station, where he stands to this hour. The copper vessel, which the underground people left behind them, was preserved as a memorial upon the island, which bears the name of House Island to, the present day.

NOTES

[a] This tale was taken from oral recitation by Dr. Grimm, and inserted In Hauff's Märchenalmanach for 1827. Dr. Grimm's fidelity to tradition is too well known to leave any doubt of its genuineness.

[b] Aslög *(Light of the Aser)* is the name of the lovely daughter of Sigurd and Brynhilda, who became the wife of Ragnar Lodbrok. How beautiful and romantic is the account in the Volsunga Saga of old Heimer taking her, when an infant, and carrying her about with him in his harp, to save her from those who sought her life as the last of Sigurd's race; his retiring to remote streams and waterfalls to wash her, and his stilling her cries by the music of his harp!

[c] This is Saint Oluf or Olave, the warlike apostle of the North.

[d] A legend similar to this is told of Saint Oluf in various parts of Scandinavia. The following is an example:—As he was sailing by the high strand-hills in Honsherred, in which a giantess abode, she cried out to him,
Saint Oluf with the red beard hear!
My cellar-wall thou'rt sailing too near!
Oluf was incensed, and instead of guiding the ship through the rocks, he turned it toward the hill, replying:
Hearken thou witch with thy spindle and rock!
There shalt thou sit and be a stone-block!
and scarcely had he spoken when the hill burst and the giantess was turned Into stone. She is still seen sitting on the east side with her rock and spindle; out of the opposite mass sprang a holy well. Grimm. Deutsche Mythologie, p. 516.

NISSES [a]

Og Trolde, Hexer; Nisser i hver Vrase.
    —FINN MAGNUSSEN.

And Witches, Trolls, and Nisses In each nook.

The Nis is the same being that is called Kobold in Germany, Brownie in Scotland, and whom we shall meet in various other places under different appellations. He is in Denmark and Norway also called Nisse god-dreng *(Nissè good lad),* and in Sweden Tomtgubbe *(Old Man of the House),* or briefly Tomte.

He is evidently of the Dwarf family, as he resembles them in appearance, and, like them, has the command of money, and the same dislike to noise and tumult. He is of the size of a year-old child, but has the face of an old man. His usual dress is grey, with a pointed red cap; but on Michael-mas-day he wears a round hat like those of the peasants.

No farm-house goes on well unless there is a Nis in it, and well is it for the maids and the men when they are in favour with him. They may go to their beds and give themselves no trouble about their work, and yet in the morning the maids will find the kitchen swept up, and water brought; in, and the men will find the horses in the stable well cleaned and curried, and perhaps a supply of corn cribbed for them from the neighbours' barns. But he punishes them for any irregularity that takes place.

The Nisses of Norway, we are told, are fond of the moonlight, and in the winter time they may be seen jumping over the yard, or driving in sledges. They are also skilled in music and dancing, and will, it is said, give instructions on the fiddle for a *grey sheep*, like the Swedish Strömkarl. [b]

Every church, too, has its Nis, who looks to order, and chastises those who misbehave themselves. He is called the Kirkegrim.

NOTES

[a] Nisse, Grimm thinks (Deut. Mythol. p. 472) is Nicls, Niclsen, *i.e.* Nicolaus, Niclas, a common name in Germany and the North, which is also contracted to Klas, Claas.

[b] Wilse *ap* Grimm, Deut. Mythol., p. 479, 'who thinks he may have confounded the Nis with the Nöck.

The Nis Removing [a]

It is very difficult, they say, to get rid of a Nis when one wishes it. A man who lived in a house in which a Nis carried his pranks to great lengths resolved to quit the tenement, and leave him there alone. Several cart-loads of furniture and other articles were already gone, and the man was come to take away the last, which consisted chiefly of empty tubs, barrels, and things of that sort. The load was now all ready, and the man had just bidden farewell to his house and to the Nis, hoping for comfort in his new habitation, when happening, from some cause or other, to go to the back of the cart, there he saw the Nia sitting in one of the tubs in the cart, plainly with the intention of going along with him wherever he went. The good man was surprised and disconcerted beyond measure at seeing that all his labour was to no purpose; but the Nis began to laugh heartily, popped his head up out of the tub, and cried to the bewildered farmer, "Ha! we 're moving to-day, you see. " [b]

NOTES

[a] The places mentioned in the following stories are all in Jutland. It is remarkable that we seem to have scarcely any Nis stories from Sweden.
[b] This story is current in Germany, England, and Ireland. In the German story the farmer set fire to his barn to burn the Kobold in it. As he was driving oft', he tuned round to look at the blaze, and, to his no small mortification, saw the Kobold behind him in the cart, crying "It was time for us to come out—it was time for us to come out!"

The Penitent Nis

It is related of a Nis, who had established himself in a house in Jutland, that he used every evening, after the maid was gone to bed, to go into the kitchen to take his groute, which they used to leave for him in a wooden bowl.

One evening he sat down as usual to eat his supper with a good appetite, drew over the bowl to him, and was just beginning, as he thought, to make a comfortable meal, when he found that the maid had forgotten to put any butter into it for him. At this he fell into a furious rage, got up in the height of his passion, and went out into the cow-house, and twisted the neck of the best cow that was in it. But as he felt himself still very hungry, he stole back again to the kitchen to take some of the groute, such as it was, and when he had eaten a little of it be perceived that there was butter in it, but that it had sunk to the bottom under the groute. He was now so vexed at his injustice toward the maid, that, to make good the damage he had done, he went back to the cow-house and set a chest full of money by the side of the dead cow, where the family found it next morning, and by means of it got into flourishing circumstances.

The Nis and the Boy

There was a Nis in a house in Jutland; he every evening got his groute at the regular time, and he, in return, used to help both the men and the maids, and looked to the interest of the master of the house in every respect.

There came one time an arch mischievous boy to live at service in this house, and his great delight was, whenever he got an opportunity, to give the Nis all the annoyance in his power. One evening, late, when everything was quiet in the place, the Nis took his little wooden dish, and was just going to eat his supper, when he perceived that the boy had put the butter at the bottom, and concealed it, in hopes that he might eat the groute first, and then find the butter when all the groute was gone. He accordingly set about thinking how he might repay the boy in kind; so, after pondering a little, he went up to the loft, where the man and the boy were lying asleep in the same bed. When he had taken the bed-clothes off them, and saw the little boy by the side of the tall man, he said, "Short and long don't match;" and with this word he took the boy by the legs and dragged him down to the man's legs. He then went up to the head of the bed, and "Short and long don't match," said he again, and then he dragged the boy up once more. When, do what he would, he could not succeed in making the boy as long as the man, he still persisted in dragging him up and down in the bed, and continued at this work the whole night long, till it was broad daylight.

By this time he was well tired, so he crept up on the window-stool, and sat with his legs hanging down into the yard. But the house-dog—for all dogs have a great enmity to the Nis—as soon as he saw him, began to bark at him, which afforded such amusement to Nis, as the dog could not get up to him, that he put down first one leg and then the other to him, and teazed him, and kept saying, "Look at my little leg! look at my little leg!" In the meantime the boy had wakened, and had stolen up close behind him, and while Nis was least thinking of it, and was going on with his "Look at my little leg!" the boy tumbled him down into the yard to the dog, crying out at the same time, "Look at the whole of him now!"

The Nis stealing Corn

There lived a man at Thyrsting, in Jutland, who had a Nis in his barn. This Nis used to attend to the cattle, and at night he would steal fodder for them from the neighbours, so that this farmer had the best fed and most thriving cattle in the country.

One time the boy went along with the Nis to Fugleriis to steal corn. The Nis took as much as he thought he could well carry, but the boy was more covetous, and said, "Oh, take more; sure we can rest now and then?" "Rest!" said the Nis; "rest! and what is rest?" "Do what I tell you," replied the boy; "take more, and we shall find, rest when we get out of this."—The Nis then took more, and they went away with it. But when they were come to the lands of Thyrsting, the Nis grew tired, and then the boy said to him, "Here now is rest;" and they both sat down on the side of a little hill. "If I had known," said the Nis, as they were sitting there, "if I had known that rest was so good, I'd have carried, off all that was in the barn."

It happened some time after that the boy and the Nis were no longer friends, and as the Nis was sitting one day in the granary-window, with his legs hanging out into the yard, the boy ran at him and tumbled him back into the granary. But the Nis took his satisfaction of him that very same night; for when the boy was gone to bed, he stole down to where he was lying, and. carried him naked as he was out into the yard, and then laid two pieces of wood across the well, and put him lying on them, expecting that, when he awoke, he would fall from the fright down into the well and be drowned. But he was disappointed, for the boy came off without injury.

The Nis and the Mare

There was a man who lived in the town of Tirup, who had a very handsome white mare. This mare had for many years gone, like an heirloom, from father to son, because there was a Nis attached to her, which brought luck to the place.

This Nis was so fond of the mare, that he could hardly endure to let them put her to any kind of work, and he used to come himself every night and feed her of the best; and as for this purpose he usually brought a superfluity of corn, both threshed and in the straw, from the neighbours' barns, all the rest of the cattle enjoyed the advantage of it, and they were all kept in exceeding good case.

It happened at last that the farm-house passed into the hands of a new owner, who refused to put any faith in what they told him about the mare, so the luck speedily left the place, and went after the mare to his poor neighbour who bad bought her; and within five days after his purchase, the poor farmer who had bought the mare began to find his circumstances gradually improving, while the income of the other, day after day, fell away and diminished at such a rate, that be was hard set to make both ends meet.

If now the man who had gotten the mare had only known how to be quiet, and enjoy the good times that were come upon him, he and his children, and his children's children after him, would have been in flourishing circumstances till this very day. But when he saw the quantity of corn that came every night to his barn, he could not resist his desire to get a sight of the Nis. So he concealed himself one evening, at nightfall, in the stable; and as soon as it was midnight, he saw how the Nis came from his neighbour's barn and brought a sackful of corn with him. It was now unavoidable that the Nis should get a sight of the man who was watching; so he, with evident marks of grief, gave the mare her food for the last time, cleaned, and dressed her to the best of his abilities, and when he had done, turned round to where the man was lying and bid him farewell.

From that day forward the circumstances of both the neighbours were on an equality, for each now kept his own.

The Nis Riding

There was a Nis in a farm-house, who was for ever tormenting the maids, and playing all manner of roguish tricks on them, and they in return were continually planning how to be even with him. There came one time to the farm-house a Juttish drover and put up there for the night. Among his cattle, there was one very large Juttish ox; and when Nis saw him in the stable he took a prodigious fancy to get up and ride on his back. He accordingly mounted the ox, and immediately began to torment the beast in such a manner that he broke loose from his halter and ran out into the yard with the Nis on his back. Poor Nis was now terrified in earnest, and began to shout and bawl most lustily. His cries awakened the maids, but instead of coming to his assistance they laughed at him till they were ready to break their hearts. And when the ox ran against a piece of timber, so that the unfortunate Nis had his hood all torn by it, the maids shouted out and called him "Lame leg, Lame leg," and he made off with himself in most miserable plight. But the Nis did not forget it to the maids; for the following Sunday when they were going to the dance, he contrived, unknown to them, to smut their faces all over, so that when they got up to dance, every one that was there burst out a laughing at them.

The Nisses in Vosborg

There was once an exceeding great number of Nisses in Jutland. Those in Vosborg in particular were treated with so much liberality, that they were careful and solicitous beyond measure for 'their master's interest. They got every evening in their sweet-groute a large lump of butter, and in return for this, they once showed great zeal and gratitude.

One very severe winter, a lonely house in which there were six calves was so completely covered by the snow, that for the space of fourteen days no one, could get into it. When the snow was gone, the people naturally thought that the calves were all dead of hunger; but far from it, they found them all in excellent condition; the place cleaned up, and the cribs full of beautiful corn, so that it was quite evident the Nisses had attended to them.

But, the Nis, though thus grateful when well treated, is sure to avenge himself when any one does anything to annoy and vex him. As a Nis was one day amusing himself by running on the loft over the cow-house, one of the boards gave way and his leg went through. The boy happened to be in the cow-house when this happened, and when he saw the Nis's leg hanging down, he took up a dung fork, and gave him with it a smart rap on the leg. At noon; when the people were sitting round the table in the hall, the boy sat continually laughing to himself. The bailiff asked him what be was laughing at; and the boy replied, "Oh! a got such a blow at Nis to-day, and a gave him such a hell of a rap with my fork, when he put his leg down through the loft." "No," cried Nis, outside of the window, "it was not one, but three blows you gave me, for there were three prongs on the fork; but I shall pay you for it, my lad."

Next night, while the boy was lying fast asleep, Nis came and took him up and brought him out into the yard, then flung him over the house, and was so expeditious in getting to the other side of the house, that he caught him before he came to the ground, and instantly pitched him over again, and kept going on with this sport till the boy had been eight times backwards and forwards over the roof, and the ninth time he let him fall into a great pool of water, and then set up such a shout of laughter at him, that it wakened up all the people that were in the place.

In Sweden the Tomte is sometimes seen at noon, in summer, slowly and stealthily dragging a straw or an ear of corn. A farmer, seeing him thus engaged, laughed, and said, "What difference does it make if you bring away that or nothing?" The Tomte in displeasure left his farm, and went to that of his neighbour; and with him went all prosperity from him who had made light of him, and passed over to the other farmer. Any one who treated the industrious Tomte with respect, and set store by the smallest straw, became rich, and neatness and regularity prevailed in his household. [a]

NOTE

[a] Afzelius, Sago Häfdar., ii. 169. On Christmas-morning, he says, the peasantry gives the Tomte, his wages. i. e. a piece of grey cloth, tobacco, and a *shovelful of clay.*

NECKS, MERMEN AND MERMAIDS

El Necken mer i flodens vågor quäder,
Och ingen Hafsfru bleker sina kläder
Pas böljans rygg i milda solars glans.
    −STAGNELIUS.

The Neck no more upon the river sings,
And no Mermaid to bleach her linen flings
Upon the waves in the mild solar ray.

It is a prevalent opinion in the North that all the various beings of the popular creed were once worsted in a conflict with superior powers, and condemned to remain till doomsday in certain assigned abodes. The Dwarfs, or Hill *(Berg)* trolls, were appointed the hills; the Elves the groves and leafy trees; the Hill-people *(Högfolk* [a]*)* the caves and caverns; the Mermen, Mermaids, and Necks, the sea, lakes, and rivers; the River-man *(Strömkarl)* the small waterfalls. Both the Catholic and Protestant clergy have endeavoured to excite an aversion to these beings, but in vain. They are regarded as possessing considerable power over man and nature, and it is believed that though now unhappy, they will be eventually saved, or *faa förlossning* (get salvation), as it is expressed.

The NECK (in Danish Nökke [b]) is the river-spirit. The ideas respecting him are various. Sometimes he is represented as sitting, of summer nights, on the surface of the water, like a pretty little boy, with golden hair hanging in ringlets, and a red cap on his head; sometimes as above the water, like a handsome young man, but beneath like a horse; [c] at other times, as an old man with a long beard, out of which he wrings the water as he sits on the cliffs. In this last form, Odin, according to the Icelandic sagas, has sometimes revealed himself.

The Neck is very severe against any haughty maiden who makes an ill return to the love of her wooer; but should he himself fall in love with a maid of human kind, he is the most polite and attentive suitor in the world.

Though he is thus severe only against those who deserve it, yet country people when they are upon the water use certain precautions against his power. Metals, particularly steel, are believed *"to bind the Neck," (binda Necken);* and when going on the open sea, they usually put a knife in the bottom of the boat, or set a nail in a reed. In Norway the following charm is considered effectual against the Neck:—

> Nyk, nyk, naal i vatn!
> Jomfru Maria kastet staal i vatn
> Du sök, äk flyt!
> Neck, neck, nail in water!
> The virgin Mary casteth steel in water!
> Do you sink, I flit!

The Neck is a great musician. He sits on the water and plays on his gold harp, the harmony of which operates on all nature. To learn music of him, a person must present him with a black lamb, and also promise him resurrection and redemption.

The following story is told in all parts of Sweden:-

"Two boys were one time playing near a river that ran by their father's house. The Neck rose and sat on the surface of the water, and played on his harp; but one of the children said to him, 'What is the use, Neck, of your sitting there and playing? you will never be saved.' The Neck then began to weep bitterly, flung away his harp, and sank down to the bottom. The children went home, and told the whole story to their father, who was the parish priest. He said they were wrong to say so to the Neck, and desired them to go immediately back to the river, and console him with the promise of salvation. They did so; and when they came down to the river the Neck was sitting on the water, weeping and lamenting. They then said to him, 'Neck, do not grieve so; our father says that your Redeemer liveth also.' The Neck then took his harp and played most sweetly, until long after the sun was gone down."

This legend is also found in Denmark, but in a less agreeable form. A clergyman, it is said, was journeying one night to Roeskilde in Zealand. His way led by a hill in which there was music and dancing and great merriment going forward. Some dwarfs jumped suddenly out of it, stopped the carriage, and asked him whither he was going. He replied to the synod of the church. They asked him if he thought they could be saved. To that, he replied, he could not give an immediate answer. They then begged that he would give them a reply by next year. When he next passed, and they made the same demand, be replied, "No, you are all damned." Scarcely had be spoken the word, when the whole hill appeared in flames.

In another form of this legend, a priest says to the Neck, "Sooner will this cane which l hold in my hand grow green flowers than thou shalt attain salvation." The Neck in grief flung away his harp and wept, and the priest rode on. But soon his cane began to put forth leaves and blossoms, and he then went back to communicate the glad tidings to the Neck who now joyously played on all the entire night. [d]

NOTES

[a] *Berg* signifies a larger eminence, mountain, hill; *Hög,* a height, hillock. The *Hög-folk* are Elves and musicians.

[b] The Danish peasantry in Wormius' time described the Nökke (Nikke) as a monster with a human head, that dwells both in fresh and salt water. When any one was drowned, they said, *Nökken tog ham bort* (the Nökke took him away); and when any drowned person was found with the nose red, they said the Nikke has sucked him: *Nikken har suet ham.*—Magnusen, Eddalaere. Denmark being a country without any streams of magnitude, we meet in the Danske Folkesagn no legends of the Nökke; and in ballads, such as a The Power of the Harp," what in Sweden is ascribed to the Neck, is in Denmark imputed to the Havmand or Merman.

[c] The Neck is also believed to appear in the form of a complete horse, and can be made to work at the plough, if a bridle of a particular description be employed.—*Kalm's Vestgötha Resa.*

[d] Afzelius, Sago.bäfdar,ii. 156.

The Power of the Harp

Little Kerstin she weeps in her bower all the day;
Sir Peter in his courtyard is playing so gay.
My heart's own dear!
Tell me wherefore you grieve?
"Grieve you for saddle, or grieve you for steed?
Or grieve you for that I have you wed?"
My heart's, &c.
"And grieve do I not for saddle or for steed:
And grieve do I not for that I have you wed.
My heart's, &c.
"Much more do I grieve for my fair gold hair,
Which in the blue waves shall be stained to-day.
My heart's, &c.
"Much more do I grieve for Ringfalla flood,
In which have been drowned my two sisters proud.
My heart's, &c.
"It was laid out for me in my infancy,
That my wedding-day should prove heavy to me."
My heart's, &c.
"And I shall make them the horse round shoe,
He shall not stumble on his four gold shoes.
My heart's, &c.
"Twelve of my courtiers shall before thee ride,
Twelve of my courtiers upon each side."
My heart's, &c.
But when they were come to Ringfalla wood,
There sported a hart with gilded horns prowl.
My heart's, &c.
And all the courtiers after the hart are gone;
Little Kerstin, she must proceed alone.
My heart's, &c.
And when on Ringfalla bridge she goes,
Her steed he stumbled on his four gold shoes.
My heart's, &c.
Four gold shoes, and thirty gold nails,
And the maiden into the swift stream falls.

My heart's, &c.
Sir Peter he spake to his footpage so—
"Thou must for my gold harp instantly go."
My heart's, &c.
The first stroke on his gold harp he gave
The foul ugly Neck sat and laughed on the wave.
My heart's, &c.
The second time the gold harp he swept,
The foul ugly Neck on the wave sat and wept.
My heart's, &c.
The third stroke on the gold harp rang,
Little Kerstin reached up her snow-white arm.
My heart's, &c.
He played the bark from off the high trees;
He played Little Kerstin back on his knees.
My heart's, &c.
And the Neck he out of' the waves came there,
And a proud maiden on each arm be bare.
My heart's, &c.
Tell me wherefore you grieve? [a]

The STROMKARL, called in Norway Grim or Fosse-Grim [b] *(Waterfall-Grim)* is a musical genius like the Neck. Like him too, when properly propitiated, he communicates his art. The sacrifice also is a black lamb [c] which the offerer must present with averted head, and on Thursday evening. If it is poor the pupil gets no further than to the tuning of the instruments; if it is fat the Strömkarl seizes the votary by the right hand, and swings it backwards and forwards till the blood runs out at the finger-ends. The aspirant is then enabled to play in such a masterly manner that the trees dance and waterfalls stop at his music. [d]

The Havmand, or Merman, is described as of a handsome form, with green or black hair and beard. He dwells either in the bottom of the sea, or in the cliffs and hills near the sea shore, and is regarded as rather a good and beneficent kind of being. [e]

The Havfrue, or Mermaid, is represented in the popular tradition sometimes as a good, at other lames as an evil and treacherous being. She is beautiful in her appearance.

Fishermen sometimes see her in the bright summer's sun, when a thin mist hangs over the sea, sitting on the surface of the water, and combing her long golden hair with a golden comb, or driving up her snow-white cattle to feed on the strands and small islands. At other times she comes as a beautiful maiden, chilled and shivering with the cold of the night, to the fires the fishers have kindled, hoping by this means to entice them to her love. [f] Her appearance prognosticates both storm and ill success in their fishing. People that are drowned, and whose bodies are not found, are believed to be taken into the dwellings of the Mermaids. These beings are also supposed to have the power of foretelling future events. A Mermaid, we are told, prophesied the birth of Christian IV. of Denmark, and

En Havfrue op af Vandet steg,
Og spaade Herr Sinklar ilde.
SINCLAR'S VISA.
A mermaid from the water rose,
And spaed Sir Sinclar ill.

Fortune-telling has been in all countries a gift of the sea-people. We need hardly mention the prophecies of Nereus and Proteus.

A girl one time fell into the power of a Havfrue and passed fifteen years in her submarine abode without ever seeing the sun. At length her brother went down in quest of her, and succeeded in bringing her back to the upper world. The Havfrue waited for seven years expecting her return, but when she did not come back, she struck the water with her staff and made it boil up and cried—

Hade jag trott att du varit så falsk,
Så skulle jag kreckt dig din tiufvehals!
Had I but known thee so false to be,
Thy thieving neck I'd have cracked for thee. [g]

NOTES

[a] As sung in West Gothland and Vermland.

[b] *Fosse* is the North of England *force*.

[c] Or a white kid, Faye *ap*. Grimm, Deut. Mythol., p. 461.

[d] The Strömkarl has eleven different measures, to ten of which alone people may dance; the eleventh belongs to the night spirit his host. If any one plays it, tables and benches, cans and cups, old men and women, blind and lame, even the children in the cradle, begin to dance.—Arndt. *ut sup.*,

[e] In the Danske Viser and Folkesagn there are a few stories of Mermen, such as Rosmer Havmand arid Marstig's Daughter, both translated by Dr. Jamieson, and Agnete and the Merman, which resembles Proud Margaret. It was natural, says Afzelius, that what in Sweden was related of a Hill King, should, in Denmark, be ascribed to a Merman.

[f] The appearance of the Wood-woman *(Skogsfru)* or Elve-woman, is equally unlucky for hunters. She also approaches the fires, and seeks to seduce young men.

[g] Arvidsson, ii. 320, *ap*. Grimm, p. 463.

Duke Magnus and the Mermaid

DUKE MAGNUS looked out through the castle window,
How the stream ran so rapidly;
And there he saw how upon the stream sat
A woman most fair and lovelie,
Duke Magnus, Duke Magnus, plight thee to me,
I pray you still so freely;
Say me not nay, but yes, yes!
"O, to you I will give a travelling ship,
The best that a knight would guide;
It goeth as well on water as on firm land,
And through the fields all so wide.
Duke Magnus, &c.
"O, to you will I give a courser gray,
The best that a knight would ride;
He goeth as well on water as on firm land,
And through the groves all so wide."
Duke Magnus, &c.
"O, how should I plight me to you?
I never any quiet get;
I serve the king and my native land,
But with woman I match me not yet."
Duke Magnus, &c.
"To you will I give as much of gold
As for more than your life will endure;
And of pearls and precious stones handfuls;
And all shall be so pure."
Duke Magnus, &c.
"O gladly would I plight me to thee,
If thou wert of Christian kind;
But now thou art a vile sea-troll,
My love thou canst never win."
Duke Magnus, &c.
"Duke Magnus, Duke Magnus, bethink thee well,
And answer not so haughtily;
For if thou wilt not plight thee to me,
Thou shalt ever crazy be."

Duke Magnus, &c.
"I am a king's son so good,
How can I let you gain me?
You dwell not on land, but in the flood,
Which would not with me agree."
Duke Magnus, Duke Magnus, plight thee to me,
I offer you still so freely;
Say me not nay, but yes, yes! [a]

NOTE

[a] This is a ballad from Småland. Magnus was the youngest son of Gustavus Vass. He died out of his mind, It is well known that insanity pervaded the Vass family for centuries.

NORTHERN ISLANDS

Här Necken sin Harpa i Glasborgen slår,
Och Hafsfruar kamma sltt grönskande hår,
Och bleka den skinande drägten.
        –STAGNELIUS.

The Neck here his harp in the glass-castle plays,
And Mermaidens comb out their green hair always,
And bleach here their shining white clothes.

UNDER THE TITLE of Northern Islands we include all those lying in the ocean to the north of Scotland, to wit Iceland, the Feroes, Shetland, and the Orkneys.

These islands were all peopled from Norway and Denmark during the ninth century. Till that time many of them, particularly Iceland and the Feroes, though, perhaps, occasionally visited by stray Vikings, or by ships driven out of their course by tempests, had lain waste and desert from the creation, the abode alone of wild beasts and birds.

But at that period the proud nobles of Norway and Denmark, who scorned to be the vassals of Harold Fair-hair and Gorm the Old, the founders of the Norwegian and Danish monarchies, set forth in quest of new settlements, where, at a distance from these haughty potentates, they might live in the full enjoyment of their beloved independence. Followed by numerous vassals, they embarked on the wide Atlantic. A portion fixed themselves on the distant shores of Iceland; others took possession of the vacant Feroes; and more dispossessed the Peti and Papae, the ancient inhabitants of Shetland

and the Orkneys, and seized on their country.

As the Scandinavians were at that time still worshipers of Thor and Odin, the belief in Alfs and Dwarfs accompanied them to their new abodes, and there, as elsewhere, survived the introduction of Christianity. We now proceed to examine the vestiges of the old religion still to be traced.

ICELAND

It is in vain that we look into the works of travellers for information on the subject of popular belief in Iceland. Their attention was too much occupied by Geysers, volcanoes, agriculture, and religion, to allow them to devote any part of it to this, in their eyes, unimportant subject. So that, were it not for some short but curious notices given by natives of the island, we should be quite ignorant of the fate of the subordinate classes of the old religion in Iceland.

Torfaeus, who wrote in the latter end of the seventeenth century, gives, in his preface to his edition of Hrolf Krakas Saga, the opinion of a venerable Icelandic pastor, named Einar Gudmund, respecting the Dwarfs. This opinion Torfaeus heard when a boy from the lips of the old man.

"I believe, and am fully persuaded," said he, "that this people are the creatures of God, consisting of a body and a rational spirit; that they are of both sexes; marry, and have children; and that all human acts take place among them as with us: that they are possessed of cattle, and of many other kinds of property; have poverty and riches, weeping and laughter, sleep and wake, and have all other affections belonging to human nature; and that they enjoy a longer or a shorter term of life according to the will and pleasure of God. Their power of having children," he adds, "appears from this, that some of their women have had children by men, and were very anxious to have their offspring dipped in the sacred font, and initiated into Christianity; but they, in general, sought in vain. Thorkatla Mari, the wife of Karl, was pregnant by a Hill-man, but she did not bring the child Aresus into the world, as appears from the poems made on this fatal occasion.

"There was formerly on the lands of Haga a nobleman named Sigvard Fostre, who had to do with a Hill-woman. He promised her faithfully that he would take care to have the child received into the bosom of the church. In due time the woman came with her child and laid it on the churchyard wall, and along with it a gilded cup and a holy robe (presents she intended making to the church for the baptism of her child), and then retired a little way. The pastor inquired who acknowledged himself the father of the child. Sigvard, perhaps, out of shame, did not venture to acknowledge himself. The clerk now asked him if it should be baptised or not. Sigvard said 'No,' lest by assenting he should be proved to be the father. The infant then was left where it was, untouched and unbaptised. The mother, filled with rage, snatched up her babe and the cup, but left the vestment, the remains of which may still be seen in Haga. That woman foretold and inflicted a singular disease on Sigvard and his posterity till the ninth generation, and several of his descendants are to this day afflicted with it. Andrew Gudmund (from which I am the seventh in descent) had an affair of the same kind. He also refused to have the child baptised, and he and his posterity have suffered a remarkable disease, of which very many of them have died; but some, by the interposition of good men, have escaped the deserved punishment."

The fullest account we have of the Icelandic Elves or Dwarfs is contained in the following passage of the Ecclesiastical History of Iceland of the learned Finnus Johannaeus.

"As we have not as yet," says he, "spoken a single word about the very ancient, and I know not whether more ridiculous or perverse, persuasion of our forefathers about semigods, this seems the proper place for saying a few words about this so celebrated figment, as it was chiefly in this period it attained its acmè, and it was believed as a true and necessary article of faith, that there are genii or semi-gods, called in our language Alfa and Alfa-folk.

"Authors vary respecting their essence and origin. Some hold that they have been created by God immediately and without the intervention of parents, like some kinds of spirits: others maintain that they are sprung from Adam, but before the creation of Eve: [a] lastly, some refer them to another race of men, or to a stock of pre-Adamites. Some bestow on them not merely a human body, but an immortal soul: others assign them merely mortal breath *(spiritum)* instead of a soul, whence a certain blockhead, [b] in an essay written by him respecting them, calls them our half-kin *(half-kyn)*.

"According to the old wives' tales that are related about this race of genii who inhabit Iceland and its vicinity, they have a political form of government modelled after the same pattern as that which the inhabitants themselves are under. Two viceroys rule over them, who in turn every second year, attended by some of the subjects, sail to Norway, to present themselves before the monarch of the whole race, who resides there, and to give him a true report concerning the fidelity, good conduct, and obedience of the subjects; and those who accompany them are to accuse the government or viceroys if they have transgressed the bounds of justice or of good morals. If these are convicted of crime or injustice, they are forthwith stript of their office, and others are appointed in their place.

"This nation is reported to cultivate justice and equity above all other virtues, and hence, though they are very potent, especially with words and imprecations, they very rarely, unless provoked or injured, do any mischief to man; but when irritated they avenge themselves on their enemies with dreadful curses and punishments.

"The new-born infants of Christians are, before baptism, believed to be exposed to great peril of being stolen by them, and their own, which they foresee likely to be feeble in mind, in body, in beauty, or other gifts, being substituted for them. These supposititious children of the semigods are called Umskiptingar; whence nurses and midwives were strictly enjoined to watch constantly, and to hold the infant firmly in their arms, till it had had the benefit of baptism, lest they should furnish any opportunity for such a change. Hence it comes, that the vulgar use to call fools, deformed people, and those who act rudely and uncivilly, *Umskiptinga eins og hann sie ko minnaf Alfum, i.e.* changelings, and come of the Alfs.

"They use rocks, bills, and even the seas, for their habitations, which withinside are neat, and all their domestic utensils extremely clean and orderly. They sometimes invite men home, and take especial delight in the converse of Christians, some of whom have had intercourse with their daughters or sisters, who are no less wanton than beautiful, and have had children by them, who must by all means be washed in holy water, that they may receive an immortal soul, and one that can be saved. Nay, they have not been ashamed to feign that certain women of them have been joined in lawful marriage with men, and continued for a long time with them, happily at first, but, for the most part, with an ill or tragical conclusion.

"Their cattle, if not very numerous, are at least very profitable They are invisible as their owners are, unless when it pleases them to appear, which usually takes place when the weather is serene and the sun shining very bright; for as they do not see the sun within their dwellings, they frequently walk out in the sunshine that they may be cheered by his radiance. [c] Hence, even the coffins of dead kings and nobles, such as are the oblong stones which are to be seen here and there, in wildernesses and rough places, always lie in the open air and exposed to the sun.

"They change their abodes and habitations occasionally like mankind; this they do on new-year's night; whence certain dreamers and mountebanks used on that night to watch in the roads, that, by the means of various forms of conjurations appointed for that purpose, they might extort from them as they passed along the knowledge of future events. [d] But people in general, who were not acquainted with such things, especially the heads of families, used on this evening strictly to charge their children and servants to be sure to be serious and modest in their actions and language, lest their invisible guests, and mayhap future neighbours, should be aggrieved or any way offended. Hence, when going to bed they did not shut the outer doors of their houses, nor even the door of the sitting-room, but having kindled a light, and laid out a table, they desired the invisible personages who had arrived, or were to arrive, to partake, if it was their pleasure, of the food that was laid out for them; and hoped that if it pleased them to dwell within the limits of their lands, they would live safe and sound, and be propitious to them. As this superstitious belief is extremely ancient, so it long continued in full vigour, and was held by some even within the memory of our fathers." [e]

The Icelandic Neck, Kelpie, or Water-Spirit, is called Nickur, Ninnir, and Hnikur, one of the Eddaic names of Odin. He appears always in the form of a fine *apple-grey* horse on the sea-shore; but he may be distinguished from ordinary horses by the circumstance of his hoofs being reversed. If any one is so foolish as to mount him, he gallops off and plunges into the sea with his burden. He can, however, be caught in a particular manner, tamed, and made to work. [f]

The Icelanders have the same notions respecting the seals which we shall find in the Feroes and Shetland. It is a common opinion with them that King Pharaoh and his army were changed into these animals.

NOTE

[a] This was plainly a theory of the monks. It greatly resembles the Rabbinical account of the origin of the Mazckeen, which the reader will meet in the sequel.

Some Icelanders of the present day say, that one day, when Eve was washing her children at the running water, God suddenly called her. She was frightened, and thrust aside such of them as were not clean. God asked her if all her children were there, and she said, Yes; but got for answer, that what she tried to hide from God should be hidden from man. These children became instantly invisible and distinct from the rest. Before the flood came on, God put them into a cave and closed up the entrance. From them are descended all the underground-people.—Magnussen, *Eddalaere.*

[b] This was one Janus Gudmund, who wrote several treatises on this and similar subjects, particularly one "De Alfis et Alfheimum," which the learned bishop characterises as a work" nullius pretii, et meras nugas continens." We might, if we were to see it, be of a different opinion. Of Janus Gudmund Brynj Svenonius thus expresses himself to Wormius: *Janus Gudmundius, aere dirutus verius quam rude donatus, sibi et aliis inutiis in angulo consenuit.* Worm., Epist., 970.

[c] The Icelandlo dwarfs, it would appear, wore red clothes. In Nial's Saga (p. 70), a person gaily dressed *(i litkloedum)* is jocularly called Red-elf *(raud-álfr).*

[d] There was a book of prophecies called the *Kruckspá,* or Prophecy of Kruck, a man who was said to have lived in the 15th century. It treated of the change of religion and other matters said to have been revealed to him by the Dwarfs. Johannaeus says it was forged by Brynjalf Svenonius in or about the year 1660.

[e] Finni Johannaei Historia Ecclesiastica Islandiae, tom. ii. p. 368. Haviae, 1774. We believe we might safely add, is held at the present day, for the superstition is no more extinct in Iceland than elsewhere.

[f] Svenska Visor, iii. 128. Grimm, Deut. Mythol, p. 458. At Bahus, in Sweden a clever man contrived to throw on him an ingeniously made bridle so that he could not get away, and he ploughed all his land with him. One time the bridle fell off and the Neck, like a flash of fire, sprang into the lake and dragged the harrow down with him. Grimm, *ut sup.,* see p. 148.

FEROES

Sjurur touk tea besta svör
Sum Dvörgurin heji smuja.
—QVORFINS THAATTUR.

Sigurd took the very best sword
That the Dwarfs had ever smithed.

The people of the Feroes believe in the same classes of beings as the inhabitants of the countries whence their ancestors came.

They call the Trolls Underground-people, Hollow-men, Foddenskkmaend, and Huldefolk. These Trolls used frequently to carry people into their hills, and detain them there. Among several other instances, Debes [a] gives the following one of this practice:

"Whilst Mr. Taale was priest in Osteröe, it happened that one of his hearers was carried away and returned again. At last the said young man being to be married, and every thing prepared, and the priest being arrived the Saturday before at the parish, the bridegroom was carried away; wherefore they sent folks to look after him, but he could not be found. The priest desired his friends to have good courage, and that he would come again; which he did at last, and related that the spirit that led him away was in the shape of a most beautiful woman, and very richly dressed, who desired him to forsake her whom he was now to marry, and consider how ugly his mistress was in comparison of her, and what fine apparel she had. He said also that he saw the men that sought after him, and that they went close by him but could not see him, and that he heard their calling, and yet could not answer them; but that when he would not be persuaded he was again left at liberty."

The people of the Feroes call the Nisses or Brownies Niägru-isar, and describe them as little creatures with red caps on their heads, that bring luck to any place where they take up their abode.

It is the belief of the people of these islands that every ninth-night the seals put off their skins and assume the human form, and dance and sport about on the land. After some time, they resume their skins and return to the water. The following adventure, it is said, once occurred: [b]

"A man happening to pass by where a female seal was dis-porting herself in the form of a woman, found her skin, and took and hid it. When she could not find her skin to creep into, she was forced to remain in the human form; and as she was fair to look upon, that same man took her to wife, had children by her, and lived right happily with her. After a long time, the wife found the skin that had been stolen, and could not resist the temptation to creep into it, and so she became a seal again, and returned to the sea."

The Neck called Nikar is also an object of popular faith in the Feroes. He inhabits the streams and lakes, and takes a delight in drowning people.

NOTES
[a] Faeroae et Faeroa reserata. Lond. 1676.
[b] Thiele, lii. 51, from the MS. Travels of Svaboe in the Feroes.

SHETLAND

Well, since we are welcome to Yule,
Up wi 't Lightfoot, link it awa', boys!
Send for a fiddler, play up Foula reel,
The Shaalds will pay for a', boys.
SHETLAND SONG.

Dr. Hibbert's valuable work on the Shetland Islands [a] fortunately enables us to give a tolerably complete account of the fairy system of these islands.

The Shetlanders, he informs us, believe in two kinds of Trows, as they call the Scandinavian Trolls, those of the land and those of the sea.

The former, whom, like the Scots, they also term the *guid folk* and *guid neighbours,* they conceive to inhabit the interior of green hills. Persons who have been brought into their habitations have been dazzled with the splendour of what they saw there. All the interior walls are adorned with gold and silver, and the domestic utensils resemble the strange things that are found sometimes lying on the hills. These persons have always entered the hill on one side and gone out at the other.

They marry and have children, like their northern kindred. A woman of the island of Yell, who died not long since, at the advanced age of more than a hundred years, said, that she once met some fairy children, accompanied by a little dog, playing like other boys and girls, on the top of a hill. Another time she happened one night to raise herself up in the bed, when she saw a little boy with a white nightcap on his head, sitting at the fire. She asked him who he was. "I am Trippa's son," said he. When she heard this, she instantly *sained,* i. e. blessed herself, and Trippa's son vanished.

Saining is the grand protection against them; a Shetlander always sains himself when passing by their hills.

The Trows are of a diminutive stature, and they are usually dressed in gay green garments. When travelling from one place to another they may be seen mounted on bulrushes, and riding through the air. If a person should happen to meet them when on these journeys, he should, if be has not a bible in his pocket, draw a circle round him on the ground, and in God's name forbid their approach. They then generally disappear. [b]

They are fond of music and dancing, and it is their dancing that forms the fairy rings. A Shetlander lying awake in bed before day one morning, heard the noise of a party of Trows passing by his door. They were preceded by a piper, who was playing away lustily. The man happened to have a good ear for music, so he picked up the tune he heard played, and used often after to repeat it for his friends under the name of the Fairy-tune.

The Trows are not free from disease, but they are possessed of infallible remedies, which they sometimes bestow on their favourites. A man in the island of Unst had an earthen pot that contained an ointment of marvellous power. This he said he got from the hills, and, like the widow's cruise, its contents never failed.

They have all the picking and stealing propensities of the Scandinavian Trolls. The dairy-maid sometimes detects a Trow-woman secretly milking the cows in the byre. She sains herself; and the thief takes to flight so precipitately as to leave behind her a copper pan of a form never seen before

When they want beef or mutton on any festal occasion, they betake themselves to the Shetlanders' *scatholds* or town-mails, and with elf-arrows bring down their game. On these occasions they delude the eyes of the owner with the appearance of something exactly resembling the animal whom they have carried off, and by its apparent violent death by some accident. it is on this account that the flesh of such animals as have met a sudden or violent death is regarded as improper food.

A Shetlander, who is probably still alive, affirmed that he was once taken into a hill by the Trows. Here one of the first objects that met his view was one of his own cows, that was brought in to furnish materials for a banquet. He regarded himself as being in rather a ticklish situation if it were not for the protection of the Trow-women, by whose favour he had been admitted within the hill. On returning home, he learned, to his great surprise, that at the very moment he saw the cow brought into the hill, others had seen her falling over the rocks.

Lying-in-women and "unchristened bairns" they regard as lawful prize. The former they employ as wet-nurses, the latter they of course rear up as their own. Nothing will induce parents to show any attention to a child that they suspect of being a changeling. But there are persons who undertake to enter the hills and regain the lost child.

A tailor, not long since, related the following story. He was employed to work at a farm-house where there was a child that was an idiot, and who was supposed to have been left there by the Trows instead of some proper child, whom they had taken into the hills. One night, after he had retired to his bed, leaving the idiot asleep by the lire, he was suddenly waked out of his sleep by the sound of music, and on looking about him he saw the whole room full of fairies, who were dancing away their rounds most joyously. Suddenly the idiot jumped up and joined in the dance, and showed such a degree of acquaintance with the various steps and movements as plainly testified that it must have been a long time since be first went under the hands of the dancing-master. The tailor looked on for some time with admiration, but at last he grew alarmed and *sained* himself. On hearing this, the Trows all fled in the utmost disorder, but one of them, a woman, was so incensed at this interruption of their revels, that as she went out she touched the big toe of the tailor, and he lost the power of ever after moving it. [c]

In these cases of paralysis they believe that the Trows have taken away the sound member and left a log behind. They even sometimes sear the part, and from the want of sensation in it boast of the correctness of this opinion. [d]

With respect to the Sea-Trows, it is the belief of the Shetland-ers that they inhabit a region of their own at the bottom of the sea. [e] They here respire a peculiar atmosphere, and live in habitations con-structed of the choicest submarine productions. When they visit the upper world on occasions of business or curiosity, they are obliged to enter the skin of some animal capable of respiring in the water. One of the shapes they assume is that of what is commonly called a merman or mermaid, human from the waist upwards, terminating below in the tail of a fish. But their most favourite vehicle is the skin of the larger seal or Haaf fish, for as this animal is amphibious they can land on some rock, and there cast off their sea-dress and assume their own shape, and amuse themselves as they will in the upper world. They must, however, take especial care of their skins, as each has but one, and if that should be lost, the owner can never re-descend, but must become an inhabitant of the supramarine world.

The following Shetland tales will illustrate this.

NOTES

[a] Description of the Shetland Islands. Edinburgh, 1822.

[b] Edmonston's View, &c., of Zetland Islands. Edin. 1809.

[c] We need hardly to remind the reader that in what precedes Dr. Hibbert is to be regarded as the narrator in 1822.

[d] Edmonston, *ut supra*.

[e] Dr. Hibbert says he could get but little satisfaction from the Shetlanders respecting this submarine country.

Gioga's Son

A boat's-crew landed one time upon one of the stacks [a] with the intention of attacking the seals. They had considerable success; stunned several of them, and while they lay stupefied, stripped, them of their skins, with the fat attached to them. They left the naked carcases lying on the rocks, and were about to get into their boat with their spoils and return to Papa Stour, whence they had come. But just as they were embarking, there rose such a tremendous swell that they saw there was not a moment to be lost, and every one flew as quickly as he could to get on board the boat. They were all successful but one man, who had imprudently loitered behind. His companions were very unwilling to leave him on the skerries, perhaps to perish, but the surge increased so fast, that after many unsuccessful attempts to bring the boat in close to the stacks, they were obliged to depart, and leave the unfortunate man to his fate.

A dark stormy night came on, the sea dashed most furiously against the rocks, and the poor deserted Shetlander saw no prospect before him but that of dying of the cold and hunger, or of being washed into the sea by the breakers, which now threatened every moment to run over the stack.

At length he perceived several of the seals, who had escaped from the boatmen, approaching the skerry. When they landed they stripped off their seal-skin dresses and appeared in their proper forms of Sea-Trows. Their first object was to endeavour to recover their friends, who lay stunned and skinless. When they had succeeded in bringing them to themselves, they also resumed their proper form, and appeared in the shape of the sub-marine people. But in mournful tones, wildly accompanied by the raging storm, they lamented the loss of their sea-vestures, the want of which would for ever prevent them from returning to their native abodes beneath the deep waters of the Atlantic. Most of all did they lament for Ollavitinus, the son of Gioga, who, stripped of his seal-skin, must abide for ever in the upper world.

Their song was at length broken off by their perceiving the unfortunate boatman, who, with shivering limbs an despairing looks, was gazing on the furious waves that now dashed over the stack. Gioga, when she saw him, instantly conceived the design of rendering the perilous situation of the man of advantage to her son. She went up to him, and mildly addressed him, proposing to carry him on her back through the sea to Papa Stour, on condition of his getting her the seal-skin of her son.

The bargain was soon made, and Gioga equipped herself in her phocine garb; but when the Shetlander gazed on the stormy sea he was to ride through, his courage nearly failed him, and he begged of the old lady to have the kindness to allow him to cut a few holes in her shoulders and flanks, that he might obtain a better fastening for his hands between the skin and the flesh.

This, too, her maternal tenderness induced Gioga to consent to. The man, having prepared everything, now mounted, and she plunged into the waves with him, gallantly ploughed the deep, and landed him safe and sound at Acres Gio, in Papa Stour. He thence set out for Skeo, at Hamna Voe, where the skin was, and honourably fulfilled his agreement by restoring to Gioga the means of bringing back her son to his dear native land.

[a] *Stacks* or *skerries* are bare rocks out in the sea.

The Mermaid Wife

On a fine summer's evening, an inhabitant of Unst happened to be walking along the sandy margin of a voe. [a] The moon was risen, and by her light he discerned at some distance before him a number of the sea-people, who were dancing with great vigour on the smooth sand. Near them he saw lying on the ground several seal-skins.

As the man approached the dancers, all gave over their merriment, and flew like lightning to secure their garments; then clothing themselves, plunged in the form of seals into the sea. But the Shetlander, on coming up to the spot where they had been, and casting his eyes down on the ground, saw that they had left one skin behind them, which was lying just at his feet. He snatched it up, carried it swiftly away, and placed it in security.

On returning to the shore, he met the fairest maiden that eye ever gazed upon: she was walking backwards and forwards, lamenting m most piteous tones the loss of her seal-skin robe, without which she never could hope to rejoin her family and friends below the waters, but must remain an unwilling inhabitant of the region enlightened by the sun.

The man approached and endeavoured to console her, but she would not be comforted. She implored him in the most moving accents to restore her dress; but the view of her lovely face, more beautiful in tears, had steeled his heart. He represented to her the impossibility of her return, and that her friends would soon give her up;,and finally, made an offer to her of his heart, hand, and fortune.

The sea-maiden, finding she had no alternative, at length consented to beoome his wife. They were married, and lived together for many years, during which time they had several children, who retained no vestiges of their marine origin, saving a thin web between their fingers, and a bend of their hands, resembling that of the fore paws of a seal; distinctions which characterise the descendants of the family to the present day.

The Shetlander's love for his beautiful wife was unbounded, but she made but a cold return to his affection. Often would she steal out alone and hasten down to the lonely strand, and there at a given signal, a seal of large size would make his appearance, and they would converse for hours together in an unknown language; and she would return home from this meeting pensive and melancholy.

Thus glided away years, and her hopes of leaving the upper world had nearly vanished, when it chanced one day, that one of the children, playing behind a stack of corn, found a seal-skin. Delighted with his prize, he ran with breathless eagerness to display it before his mother. Her eyes glistened with delight at the view of it; for in it she saw her own dress, the loss of which had cost her so many tears. She now regarded herself as completely emancipated from thraldom; and in idea she was already with her friends beneath the waves. One thing alone was a drawback on her raptures. She loved her children, and she was now about to leave them for ever. Yet they weighed not against the pleasures she had in prospect: so after kissing and embracing them several times, she took up the skin, went out, and proceeded down to the beach.

In a few minutes after the husband came in, and the children told him what had occurred. The truth instantly flashed across his mind, and he hurried down to the shore with all the speed that love and anxiety could give. But he only arrived in time to see his wife take the form of a seal, and from the ledge of a rock plunge into the sea.

The large seal, with whom she used to hold her conversations, immediately joined her, and congratulated her on her escape, and they quitted the shore together. But ere she went she turned round to her husband, who stood in mute despair on the, rock, and whose misery excited feelings of compassion in her breast. "Farewell," said she to him, "and may all good fortune attend you. I loved you well while I was with you, but I always loved my first husband better." [b]

The water-spirit is in Shetland called Shoopiltee; he appears in the form of a pretty little horse, and endeavours to entice persons to ride on him, and then gallops with them into the sea.

NOTES
[a] A *voe* is a small bay.
[b] See below, *Germany.*

ORKNEYS

Harold was born where restless seas
Howl round the storm-swept Oreades.
SCOTT.

Of the Orcadian Fairies we have very little information. Brand [a] merely tells us, they were, in his time, frequently seen in several of the isles dancing and making merry; so that we may fairly conclude they differed little from their Scottish and Shetland neighbours. One thing he adds, which is of some importance, that they were frequently seen in armour.

Brownie seems to have been the principal Orkney Fairy, where he possessed a degree of importance rather beyond what was allotted to him in the neighbouring realm of Scotland.

"Not above forty or fifty years ago," says Brand, "almost every family had a Brownie, or evil spirit, so called, which served them, to whom they gave a sacrifice for its service; as, when they churned their milk, they took a part thereof and sprinkled every corner of the house with it for Brownie's use; likewise, when they brewed, they had a stone which they called Brownie's stone, wherein there was a little hole, into which they poured some wort for a sacrifice to Brownie. My informer, a minister of the country, told me that he had conversed with an old man, who, when young, used to brew and sometimes read upon his bible; to whom an old woman in the house said that Brownie was displeased with that book he read upon, which, if he continued to do, they would get no more service of Brownie. But he being better instructed from that book which was Brownie's eyesore, and the object of his wrath, when he brewed, he would not suffer any sacrifice to be given to Brownie; whereupon, the first and second brewings were spilt and for no use, though the wort wrought well, yet in a little time it left off working and grew cold; but of the third browst or brewing, he had ale very good, though he would not give any sacrifice to Brownie, with whom afterwards they were no more troubled. I had also from the same informer, that a lady in Unst, now deceased, told him that when she first took up house, she refused to give a sacrifice to Brownie, upon which, the first and second brewings misgave, but the third was good; and Brownie, not being regarded and rewarded as formerly he had been, abandoned his wonted service: which cleareth the Scripture, 'Resist the devil and he will flee from you.' They also had stacks of corn which they called Brownie's stacks, which, though they were not bound with straw ropes, or any way fenced as other stacks use to be, yet the greatest storm of wind was not able to blow anything off them."

A very important personage once, we are told, inhabited the Orkneys in the character of Brownie.

"Luridan," says Reginald Scot, "a familiar of this kind, did for many years inhabit the island of Pomonia, the largest of the Orkades in Scotland, supplying the place of manservant and maid-servant with wonderful diligence to those famifies whom he did haunt, sweeping their rooms and washing their dishes, and making their fires before any were up in the morning. This Luridan affirmed, that he was the *genius Astral* of that island; that his place or residence in the days of Solomon and David was at Jerusalem; that then he was called by the Jews Belelah; after that, he remained long in the dominion of Wales, instructing their bards in British poesy and prophecies, being called Wrthin, Wadd, Elgin; 'and now,' said he, 'I have removed hither, and, alas! my continuance is but short, for in seventy years I must resign my place to Balkin, lord of the Northern Mountains.'

"Many wonderful and incredible things did he also relate of this Balkin, affirming that he was shaped like a satyr, and fed upon the air, having wife and children to the number *of* twelve thousand, which were the brood of the Northern Fairies, inhabiting Southerland and Catenes, with the adjacent islands. And that these were the companies of spirits that hold continual wars with the fiery spirits in the mountain Heckla, that vomits fire in Islandia. That their speech was ancient Irish, and their dwelling the caverns of the rocks and mountains, which relation is recorded in the antiquities of Pomonia." [b]

Concerning Luridan, we are farther informed from the Book of Vanagastus, the Norwegian, that it is his nature to be always at enmity with fire; that he wages war with the fiery spirits of Hecla; and that in this contest they do often anticipate and destroy one another, killing and crushing when they meet in mighty and violent troops in the air upon the sea. And at such times, many of the fiery spirits are destroyed when the enemy hath brought them off the mountains to fight upon the water. On the contrary, when the battle is upon the mountain itself; the spirits of the air are often worsted, and then great moanings and doleful noises are heard in Iceland, and Russia, and Norway, for many days after. [c]

The Water-spirit called Tangle, from Tang, the seaweed with which he is covered, appears sometimes as a little horse, other times as a man.

NOTES

[a] Description of Orkney, Zetland, &c. Edin. 1703.
[b] Reg. Scot. Discoverie of Witchcraft, b. 2. c. 4. Lond. 1666.
[c] Quarterly Review, vol. xxii. p. 367

ISLE OF RUGEN

Des Tagscheins Blendung driickt,
Nur Finsternise beglückt;
Drum hausen wir so gem
Tief in des Erdballs Kern.
—MATTHISON.

Day's dazzling light annoys
Us, darkness only joys;
We therefore love to dwell
Deep underneath earth's shell.

We now return to the Baltic, to the Isle of Rügen, once a chief seat of the Vendish religion; but it's priests were massacred by the Scandinavians, and all traces of their system effaced. Its fairy mythology now agrees with that of its Gothic neighbours, and Mr. Arndt, [a] a native of the island, has enabled us to give the following tolerably full account of it:-

The inhabitants of Rügen believe in three kinds of Dwarfs, or underground people, the White, the Brown, and the Black; so named from the colour of their several habiliments.

The White are the most delicate and beautiful of all, and are of an innocent and gentle disposition. During the winter, when the face of nature is cold, raw, and cheerless, they remain still and quiet in their hills, solely engaged in the fashioning of the finest works in silver and gold, of too delicate a texture for mortal eyes to discern. Thus they pass the winter; but no sooner does the spring return than they abandon their recesses, and live through all the summer above ground, in sunshine and starlight, in uninterrupted revelry and enjoyment. The moment the trees and flowers begin to sprout and bud in the early days of spring, they emerge from their bills, and get among the stalks and branches, and thence to the blossoms and flowers, where they sit and gaze around them. In the night, when mortals sleep, the White Dwarfs come forth, and dance their joyous roundels in the green grass, about the hills, and brooks, and springs, making the sweetest and most delicate music, bewildering travellers, who hear and wonder at the strains of the invisible musicians. They may, if they will, go out by day, but never in company; these daylight rambles being allowed them only when alone and under some assumed form. They therefore frequently fly about in the shape of party-coloured little birds, or butterflies, or snow-white doves, showing kindness and benevolence to the good who merit their favour.

The Brown Dwarfs, the next in order, are less than eighteen inches high. They wear little brown coats and jackets, and a brown cap on their head, with a little silver bell in it. Some of them wear black shoes with red strings in them; in general, however, they wear fine glass ones; at their dances none of them wear any other. They are very handsome in their persons, with clear light-coloured eyes, and small and most beautiful hands and feet. They are on the whole of a cheerful, good-natured disposition, mingled with some roguish traits. Like the White Dwarfs, they are great artists in gold and silver, working so curiously as to astonish those who happen to see their performances. At night they come out of their hills and dance by the light of the moon and stars. They also glide invisibly into people's houses, their caps rendering them imperceptible by all who have not similar caps. They are said to play all kinds of tricks, to change the children in the cradles, and take them away. This charge is perhaps unfounded, but certainly, children who fall into their hands must serve them for fifty years. They possess an unlimited power of transformation, and can pass through the smallest keyholes. Frequently they bring with them presents for children, or lay gold rings and ducats, and the like, in their way, and often are invisibly present, and save them from the perils of fire and water. They plague and annoy lazy men-servants and untidy maids with frightful dreams; oppress them as the nightmare; bite them as fleas; and scratch and tear them like cats and dogs; and often in the night frighten, in the shape of owls, thieves and lovers, or, like Will-'o-the-wisps, lead them astray into bogs and marshes, and perhaps up to those who are in pursuit of them.

The Black Dwarfs wear black jackets and caps, are not handsome like the others, but on the contrary are horridly ugly, with weeping eyes, like blacksmiths and colliers. They are most expert workmen, especially in steel, to which the can give a degree at once of hardness and flexibility wine no human smith can imitate; for the swords they make will bend like rushes, and are as hard as diamonds. In old times arms and armour made by them were in great request: shirts of mail manufactured by them were as fine as cobwebs, and yet no bullet would penetrate them, and no helm or corslet could resist the swords they fashioned; but all these things are now gone out of use.

These Dwarfs are of a malicious, ill disposition, and delight in doing mischief to mankind; they are unsocial, and there are seldom more than two or three of them seen together; they keep mostly in their hills, and seldom come out in the daytime, nor do they ever go far from home. People say that in the summer they are fond of sitting under the elder trees, the smell of which is very grateful to them, and that any one that wants anything of them must go there and call them. Some say they have no music and dancing, only howling and whimpering; and that when a screaming is heard in the woods and marshes, like that of crying children, and a mewing and screeching like that of a multitude of cats or owls, the sounds proceed from their midnight assemblies, and are made by the vociferous Dwarfs.

The principal residence of the two first classes of the underground-people in Rügen is what are called the Nine-hills, near Rambin. These hills lie on the west point of the island, about a quarter of a mile from the village of Rambin in the open country. They are small mounds, or Giants' graves (*Hünengräber*), as such are called, and are the subject of many a tale and legend among the people. The account of their origin is as follows:-

"A long, long time ago there lived in Rügen a mighty Giant named Balderich. He was vexed that the country was an island, and that he had always to wade through the sea when he wanted to go to Pomerania and the main land. He accordingly got an immense apron made, and he tied it round his waist and filled it with earth, for he wanted to make a dam of earth for himself from the island to the mainland. As he was going with his load over Rodenkirchen, a hole tore in the apron, and the clay that fell out formed the Nine-hills. He stopped the hole and went on; but when he he had gotten to Gustau, another hole tore in the apron, and thirteen little hills fell out. He proceeded to the sea with what he had now remaining, and pouring the earth into the waters, formed the hook of Prosnitz, and the pretty little peninsula of Drigge. But there still remained a small space between Rügen and Pomerania, which so incensed the Giant that he fell down in a fit and died, from which unfortunate accident his dam was never finished." [b]

A Giant-maiden commenced a similar operation on the Pomeranian side "in order," said she, "that l may be able to go over the bit of water without wetting my little slippers." So she filled her apron with sand and hurried down to the sea-side. But there was a hole in the apron and just behind Sagard a part of the sand ran out and formed a little hill named Dubbleworth. "Ah!" said she, "now my mother will scold me." She stopped the hole with her hand and ran on as fast as she could. But her mother looked over the wood and cried, "You nasty child, what are you about? Come here and you shall get a good whipping." The daughter in a fright let go the apron, and all the sand ran out and formed the barren hifis near Litzow. [c]

The Dwarfs took up their abode in the Nine-hills. The White ones own two of them, and the Brown ones seven, for there are no Black ones there. These dwell chiefly on the coast-hills, along the shore between the Ahlbeck and Mönchgut, where they hold their assemblies, and plunder the ships that are wrecked on the coast.

The Neck is called in Rügen Nickel. Some fishers once launched their boat on a lonely lake. Next day when they came they saw it in a high beech-tree. "Who the devil has put the boat in the tree?" cried one. A voice replied, but they saw no one, "'Twas no devil at all, but l and my brother Nickel." [d]

The following stories Mr. Arndt, who, as we have observed, is a native of Rügen, says he heard in his boyhood from Hinrich Vieck, the Statthalter or Bailiff of Grabitz, who abounded in these legends; "so that it is, properly speaking," says he, "Hinrich Vieck, and not I, that relates." We therefore see no reason to doubt of their genuineness, though they may be a little embellished. [e]

NOTES

[a] Arndt, Märchen und Jugenderinnerungen. Berlin, 1818.

[b] A Danish legend (Thiele, 1. 79) tells the same of the sand-hills of Nestved in Zealand. A Troll who dwelt near it wished to destroy it, and for that purpose he went down to the sea-shore and filled his wallet with sand and threw it on his back. Fortunately there was a hole in the wallet, and so many sand-hills fell out of it, that when he came to Nestved there only remained enough to form one hill more. Another Troll, to punish a farmer, filled one of his gloves with sand, which sufficed to cover his victim's house completely. With what remained in the fingers he formed a row of hillocks near it.

[c] Grimm, Dent. Myth., p. 502

[d] Grimm, Deutsche Sagen, i, p. 70.

[e] Grimm also appears to regard them as genuine.

Adventures of John Dietrich

There once lived in Rambin an honest, industrious man, named James Dietrich. He had several children, all of a good disposition, especially the youngest, whose name was John. John Dietrich was a handsome, smart boy, diligent at school, and obedient at home. His great passion was for hearing stories, and whenever he met any one who was well stored, he never let them go till he had heard them all.

When John was about eight years old he was sent to spend a summer with his uncle, a farmer in Rodenkirchen.

Here John had to keep cows with other boys, and they used to drive them to graze about the Nine-hills. There was an old cow-herd, one Klas (*i.e.* Nick) Starkwolt, who used frequently to join the boys, and then they would sit down together and tell stories. Klas abounded in these, and he became John Dietrich's dearest friend. In particular, he knew a number of stories of the Nine-hills and the undergroundpeople in the old times, when the Giants disappeared from the country, and the little ones came into the hills. These tales John swallowed so eagerly that he thought of nothing else, and was for ever talking of golden cups, and crowns, and glass shoes, and pockets full of ducats, and gold rings, and diamond coronets, and snow-white brides, and such like. Old Klas used often to shake his head at him and say, "John! John! what are you about? The spade and sithe will be your sceptre and crown, and your bride will wear a garland of rosemary and a gown of striped drill." Still John almost longed to get into the Nine-hills; for Klas had told him that any one who by luck or cunning should get the cap of one of the little ones might go down with safety, and, instead of their making a servant of him, he would be their master. The person whose cap he got would be his servant, and obey all his commands. [a]

St. John's day, when the days are longest and the nights short-est, was now come. Old and young kept the holiday, had all sorts of plays, and told all kinds of stories. John could now no longer contain himself but the day after the festival he slipt away to the Nine-hills, and when it grew dark laid himself down on the top of the highest of them, where Klas had told him the undergroundpeople had their principal dance-place. John lay quite still from ten till twelve at night. At last it struck twelve. Immediately there was a ringing and a singing in the hills, and then a whispering and a lisping and a whiz and a buzz all about him; for the little people were now some whirling round and round in the dance, and others sporting and tumbling about in the moonshine, and playing a thousand merry pranks and tricks. He felt a secret dread come over him at this whispering and buzzing, for he could see nothing of them, as the caps they wore made them invisible; but he lay quite still, with his face in the grass and his eyes fast shut, snoring a little, just as if he was asleep. Yet now and then he ventured to open his eyes a little and peep out, but not the slightest trace of them could he see, though it was bright moonlight.

It was not long before three of the undergroundpeople came jumping up to where he was lying; but they took no heed of him, and flung their brown caps up into the air, and caught them from one another. At length one snatched the cap out of the hand of another and flung it away. It flew direct, and fell upon John's head. The mo-ment he felt it he caught hold of it, and, standing up, bid farewell to sleep. He swung his cap about for joy, and made the little silver bell of it tingle, and then set it upon his head, and—O wonderful!—that instant he saw the countless and merry swarm of the little people.

The three little men came slily up to him, and thought by their nimbleness to get back the cap; but he held his prize fast, and they saw clearly that nothing was to be done in this way with him; for in size and strength John was a giant in comparison of these little fellows, who hardly came up to his knee. The owner of the cap now came up very humbly to the finder, and begged, in as supplicating a tone as if his life depended upon it, that he would give him back his cap. But "No," said John, "you sly little rogue, you'll get the cap no more. That's not the sort of thing that one gives away for buttered cake: I should be in a nice way with you if I had not something of yours; but now you have no power over me, but must do what I please. And I will go down with you, and see how you live below, and you shall be my servant—Nay, no grumbling, you know you must. I know that just as well as you do, for Klas Starkwolt told it to me often and often."

The little man looked as if he had not heard or understood one word of all this; he began all his crying and whining over again, and wept, and screamed, and howled most piteously for his little cap. But John cut the matter short by saying to him, "Have done; you are my servant, and I intend to take a trip with you." So he gave up, especially as the others told him that there was no remedy.

John now flung away his old hat, and put on the cap, and set it firm on his head, lest it should slip off or fly away, for all his power lay in the cap. He lost no time in trying its virtues, and commanded his new servant to fetch him food and drink. And the servant ran away like the wind, and in a second was there again with bottles of wine, and bread, and rich fruits. So John ate and drank, and looked on at the sports and the dancing of the little ones, and it pleased him right well, and he behaved himself stoutly and wisely, as if he was a born master.

When the cock had now crowed for the third time, and the little larks had made their first twirl in the sky, and the infant light appeared in solitary white streaks in the east, then it went hush, hush, hush, through the bushes, and flowers, and stalks; and the hills rang again, and opened up, and the little men went down. John gave close attention to everything, and found that it was exactly as he had been told. And behold! on the top of the hill, where they had just been dancing, and where all was full of grass and flowers, as people see it by day, there rose of a sudden, when the retreat was sounded, a bright glass point. Whoever wanted to go in stepped upon this; it opened, and he glided gently in, the glass closing again after him; and when they had all entered it vanished, and there was no farther trace of it to be seen. Those who descended through the glass point sank quite gently into a wide silver tun, which held them all, and could have easily harboured a thousand such little people. John and his man went down into such a one along with several others, all of whom screamed out and prayed him not to tread on them, for if his weight came on them they were dead men. He was, however, careful, and acted in a very friendly way toward them. Several tuns of this kind went up and down after each other, until all were in. They hung by long silver chains, which were drawn and held below.

In his descent John was amazed at the wonderful brilliancy of the walls between which the tun glided down. They were all, as it were, beset with pearls and diamonds, glittering and sparkling brightly, and below him he heard the most beautiful music tinkling at a distance, so that he did not know what was become of him, and from excess of pleasure he fell fast asleep.

He slept a long time, and when he awoke he found himself in the most beautiful bed that could be, such as he had never seen the like of in his father's house, and it was in the prettiest little chamber in the world, and his servant was beside him with a fan to keep away the flies and gnats. He had hardly opened his eyes when his little servant brought him a basin and towel, and held him the nicest new clothes of brown silk to put on, most beautifully made; with these was a pair of new black shoes with red ribbons, such as John had never beheld in Rambin or in Rodenkirchen either. There were also there several pairs of beautiful shining glass shoes, such as are only used on great occasions. John was, we may well suppose, delighted to have such clothes to wear, and he put them upon him joyfully. His servant then flew like lightning and returned with a fine breakfast of wine and milk, and beautiful white bread and fruits, and such other things as little boys are fond of. He now perceived, every moment, more and more, that Klas Starkwolt, the old cowherd, knew what he was talking about, for the splendour and magnificence he saw here surpassed anything he had ever dreamt of. His servant, too, was the most obedient one possible: a nod or a sign was enough for him, for he was as wise as a bee, as all these little people are by nature.

John's bed-chamber was all covered with emeralds and other precious stones, and in the ceiling was a diamond as big as a nine-pin bowl, that gave light to the whole chamber. In this place they have neither sun, nor moon, nor stars to give them light; neither do they use lamps or candles of any kind; but they live in the midst of precious stones, and have the purest of gold and silver in abundance, and the skill to make it light both by day and by night, though, indeed, properly speaking, as there is no sun here, there is no distinction of day and night, and they reckon only by weeks. They set the brightest and clearest precious stones in their dwellings, and in the ways and passages leading under the ground, and in the places where they have their large halls, and their dances and feasts, where they sparkle so as to make it eternal day.

When John had finished his breakfast, his servant opened a. little door in the wall, where was a closet with the most beautiful silver and gold cups and dishes and other vessels, and baskets filled with ducats, and boxes of jewels and precious stones. There were also charming pictures, and the most delightful story-books he had seen in the whole course of his life.

John spent the morning looking at these things; and, when it was mid-day, a bell rang, and his servant said, "Will you dine alone, sir, or with the large company?"—"With the large company, to be sure," replied John. So his servant led him out. John, however, saw nothing but solitary halls, lighted up with precious stones, and here and there little men and women, who appeared to him to glide out of the clefts and fissures of the rocks. Wondering what it was the bells rang for, he said to his servant, "But where is the company?" And scarcely had he spoken when the hail they were in opened out to a great extent, and a canopy set with diamonds and precious stones was drawn over it. At the same moment he saw an immense throng of nicely-dressed little men and women pouring in through several open doors: the floor opened in several places, and tables, covered with the most beautiful ware, and the most luscious meats, and fruits, and wines, placed themselves beside each other, and the chairs arranged themselves along the tables, and then the men and women took their seats.

The principal persons now came forward, bowed to John, and led him to their table, where they placed him among. their most beautiful maidens,—a distinction which pleased John well. The party, too, was very merry, for the underground people are extremely lively and cheerful, and can never stay long quiet. Then the most charming music sounded over their heads; and beautiful birds, flying about, sung most sweetly; and these were not real birds but artificial ones, which the little men make so ingeniously that they can fly about and sing like natural ones.

The servants, of both sexes, who waited at table, and handed about the gold cups, and the silver and crystal baskets with fruit, were children belonging to this world, whom some casualty or other had thrown among the undergroundpeople, and who, having come down without securing any pledge, were fallen into the power of the little ones. These were differently clad from them. The boys and girls were dressed in snow-white coats and jackets, and wore glass shoes, so fine that their steps could never be heard, with blue caps on their heads, and silver belts round their waists.

John at first pitied them, seeing how they were forced to run about and wait on the little people; but as they looked cheerful and happy, and were handsomely dressed, and had such rosy cheeks, he said to himself; "After all, they are not so badly off, and I was myself much worse when I had to be running after the cows and bullocks. To be sure, I am now a master here, and they are servants; but there is no help for it: why were they so foolish as to let themselves be taken and not get some pledge beforehand? At any rate, the time must come when they shall be set at liberty, and they will certainly not be longer than fifty years here." With these thoughts he consoled himself, and sported and played away with his little play-fellows, and ate, and drank, and made his servant and the others tell him stories, for he would know every thing exactly.

They sat at table about two hours; the principal person then rang a little bell, and the tables and chairs all vanished in a whiff, leaving the company all on their feet. The birds now struck up a most lively air, and the little people danced their rounds most merrily. When they were done, the joyous sets jumped, and leaped, and whirled themselves round and round, as if the world was grown dizzy. And the pretty little girls that sat next John caught hold of him and whirled him about; and, without making any resistance, he danced round and round with them for two good hours. Every afternoon while he remained there, he used to dance thus merrily with them; and, to the last hour of his life, he used to speak of it with the greatest glee. His language was—that the joys of heaven, and the songs and music of the angels, which the righteous hoped to enjoy there, might be excessively beautiful, but that he could conceive nothing to equal the music and the dancing under the earth, the beautiful and. lively little men, the wonderful birds in the branches, and the tinkling silver bells on their caps. "No one," said he, "who has not seen and heard it, can form any idea whatever of it."

When the music and dancing were over, it might be about four o'clock. The little people then disappeared, and went each about their work or their pleasure. After supper they sported and danced in the same way; and at midnight, especially on starlight nights, they slipped out of their hifis to dance in the open air. John used then, like a good boy, to say his prayers and go to sleep, a duty he never neglected either in the evening or in the morning.

For the first week that John was in the glass-hill, he only went from his chamber to the great hall and back again. After the first week, however, he began to walk about, making his servant show and explain everything to him. He found that there were in that place the most beautiful walks, in which he might ramble along for miles, in all directions, without ever finding an end of them, so immensely large was the hill that the little people lived in, and yet outwardly it seemed but a little hill, with a few bushes and trees growing on it.

It was extraordinary that, between the meads and fields, which were thick sown with hills, and lakes, and islands, and ornamented with trees and flowers in the greatest variety, there ran, as it were, small lanes, through which, as through crystal rocks, one was obliged to pass to come to any new place; and the single meads and fields were often a mile long, and the flowers were so brilliant and so fragrant, and the song of the numerous birds so sweet, that John had never seen anything on earth at all like it. There was a breeze, and yet one did not feel the wind; it was quite clear and bright, and yet there was no heat; the waves were dashing, still there was no danger; and the most beautiful little barks and canoes came, like white swans, when one wanted to cross the water, and went backwards and forwards of themselves. Whence all this came no one knew, nor could his servant tell anything about it; but one thing John saw plainly, which was, that the large carbuncles and diamonds that were set in the roof and walls gave light instead of the sun, moon, and stars.

These lovely meads and plains were, for the most part, quite lonesome. Few of the undergroundpeople were to be seen upon them, and those that were, just glided across them, as if in the greatest hurry. It very rarely happened that any of them danced out here in the open air; sometimes about three of them did so; at the most half a dozen: John never saw a greater number together. The meads were never cheerful, except when the corps of servants, of whom there might be some hundreds, were let out to walk. This, however, happened but twice a-week, for they were mostly kept employed in the great hall and adjoining apartments, or at school.

For John soon found they had schools there also; he had been there about ten months, when one day he saw something snow-white gliding into a rock, and disappearing. "What!" said he to his servant, "are there some of you too that wear white, like the servants?" He was informed that there were; but they were few in number, and. never appeared at the large tables or the dances, except once a year, an the birthday of the great Hill-king, who dwelt many thousand miles below in the great deep. These were the oldest men among them, some of them many thousand years old, who knew all things, and could tell of the beginning of the world, and were called the Wise. They lived all alone, and only left their chambers to instruct the underground children and the attendants of both sexes, for whom there was a great school.

John was greatly pleased with this intelligence, and he determined to take advantage of it: so next morning he made his servant conduct him to the school, and was so well pleased with it that he never missed a day going there. They were taught there reading, writing, and accounts, to compose and relate histories and stories, and many elegant kinds of work; so that many came out of the hills, both men and women, very prudent and knowing people, in consequence of what they were taught there. The biggest, and those of best capacity, received instruction in natural science and astronomy, and in poetry and riddle-making, arts highly esteemed by the little people. John was very diligent, and soon became extremely clever at painting and drawing; he wrought, too, most ingeniously in gold, and silver, and stones, and in verse and riddle-making he had no fellow.

John had spent many a happy year here without ever thinking of the upper world, or of those he had left behind, so pleasantly passed the time—so many an agreeable play-fellow he had among the children.

Of all his playfellows there was none of whom he was so fond as of a little fair-haired girl, named Elizabeth Krabbin, She was from his own village, and was the daughter of Frederick Krabbe, the minister of Rambin. She was but four years old when she was taken away, and John had often heard tell of her. She was not, however, stolen by the little people, but came into their power in this manner. One day in summer, she, with other children, ran out into the fields: in their rambles they went to the Nine-hills, where little Elizabeth fell asleep, and was forgotten by the rest. At night, when she awoke, she found herself under the ground among the little people. It was not merely because she was from his own village that John was so fond of Elizabeth, but she was a most beautiful child, with clear blue eyes and ringlets of fair hair, and a most angelic smile.

Time flew away unperceived: John was now eighteen, and Elizabeth sixteen. Their childish fondness had become love, and the little people were pleased to see it, thinking that by means of her they might get John to renounce his power, and become their servant; for they were fond of him, and would willingly have had him to wait upon them; for the love of dominion is their vice. But they were mistaken. John had learned too much from his servant to be caught in that way.

John's chief delight was in walking about alone with Elizabeth; for he now knew every place so well that he could dispense with the attendance of his servant. In these rambles he was always gay and lively, but his companion was frequently sad and melancholy, thinking on the land above, where men lived, and where the sun, moon, and stars, shine. Now it happened in one of their walks, that as they talked of their love, and it was after midnight, they passed under the place where the tops of the glass-hills used to open and let the underground-people in and out. As they went along they heard of a sudden the crowing of several cocks above. At this sound, which she had not heard for twelve years, little Elizabeth felt her heart so affected that she could contain herself no longer, but throwing her arms about John's neck, she bathed his cheeks with her tears. At length she spake—

"Dearest John," said she, "everything down here is very beautiful, and the little people are kind, and do nothing to injure me, but still I have always been uneasy, nor ever felt any pleasure till I began to love you; and yet that is not pure pleasure, for this is not a right way of living, such as it should be for human beings. Every night I dream of my dear father and mother, and of our church-yard, where the people stand so piously at the church-door waiting for my father, and I could weep tears of blood that I cannot go into the church with them, and worship God as a human being should; for this is no Christian life we lead down here, but a delusive half heathen one. And only think, dear John, that we can never marry, as there is no priest to join us. Do, then, plan some way for us to leave this place; for I cannot tell you how I long to get once more to my father, and among pious Christians."

John, too, had not been unaffected by the crowing of the cocks, and he felt what he had never felt here before, a longing after the land where the sun shines, and he replied, "Dear Elizabeth, all you say is true, and I now feel that it is a sin for Christians to stay here; and it seems to me as if our Lord said to us in that cry of the cocks,' Come up, ye Christian children, out of those abodes of illusion and magic; come to the light of the stars, and act as children of light.' I now feel that it was a great sin for me to come down here, but I trust I shall be forgiven on account of my youth; for I was a child and knew not what I did. But now I will not stay a day longer. They cannot keep *me* here."

At these last words, Elizabeth turned pale, for she recollected that she was a servant, and must serve her fifty years. "And what will it avail me," cried she, "that I shall continue young and be but as of twenty years when I go out, for my father and mother will be dead, and all my companions will be old and gray; and you, dearest John, will be old and gray also," cried she, throwing herself on his bosom.

John was thunderstruck at this, for it had never before occurred to him; he, however, comforted her as well as he could, and declared he would never leave the place without her. He spent the whole night in forming various plans; at last he fixed on one, and in the morning he despatched his servant to summon to his apartment six of the principal of the little people. When they came, John thus mildly addressed them:

"My friends, you know how I came here, not as a prisoner or servant, but as a lord and master over one of you, and consequently, over all. You have now for the ten years I have been with you treated me with respect and attention, and for that I am your debtor. But you are still more my debtors, for I might have given you every sort of annoyance and vexation, and you must have submitted to it. I have, however, not done so, but have behaved as your equal, and have sported and played with you rather than ruled over you. I now have one request to make. There is a girl among your servants whom I love, Elizabeth Krabbin, of Rambin, where I was born, Give her to me, and let us depart. For I will return to where the sun shines and the plough goes through the land. I ask to take nothing with me but her, and the ornaments and furniture of my chamber."

He spoke in a determined tone, and they hesitated and cast their eyes to the ground; at last the oldest of them replied:

"Sir, you ask what we cannot grant. It is a fixed law, that no servant shall leave this place before the appointed time. Were we to break through this law, our whole subterranean empire would fall. Anything else you desire, for we love and respect you, but we cannot give up Elizabeth."

"You can and you shall give her up," cried John in a rage; "go think of it till to-morrow. Return here at this hour. I will show you whether or not I can triumph over your hypocritical and cunning stratagems."

The six retired. Next morning, on their return, John addressed them in the kindest manner, but to no purpose; they persisted in their refusal. He gave them till the next day, threatening them severely in case of their still proving refractory.

Next day, when the six little people appeared before him, John looked at them sternly, and made no return to their salutations, but said to them shortly, "Yes, or No?" And they answered with one voice, "No." He then ordered his servant to summon twenty-four more of the principal persons with their wives and children. When they came, they were in all five hundred, men, women, and children. John ordered them forthwith to go and fetch pickaxes, spades, and bars, which they did in a second.

He now led them out to a rock in one of the fields, and ordered them to fall to work at blasting, hewing, and dragging stones. They toiled patiently, and. made as if it were only sport to them. From morning till night their task-master made them labour without ceasing, standing over them constantly, to prevent their resting. Still their obstinacy was inflexible; and at the end. of some weeks his pity for them was so great, that he was obliged to give over.

He now thought of a new species of punishment for them. He ordered them to appear before him next morning, each provided with a new whip. They obeyed, and John commanded them to strip and lash one another till the blood should run down on the ground, and. he stood looking on as grim and cruel as an eastern tyrant. Still the little people cut and slashed. themselves, and mocked at John, and refused to comply with his wishes. This he did for three or four days.

Several other courses did he try, but all in vain; his temper was too gentle to struggle with their obstinacy, and he began now to despair of ever accomplishing his dearest wish. He began even to hate the little people whom he was before so fond of; he kept away from their banquets and dances, and associated alone with Elizabeth, and ate and drank quite solitary in his chamber. In short, he became almost a perfect hermit, and sank into moodiness and melancholy.

While in this temper, as he was taking a solitary walk in the evening, and, to divert his melancholy, was flinging the stones that lay in his path against each other, he happened to break a tolerably large one, and out of it jumped a toad. The moment John saw the ugly animal, he caught him up in ecstasy, and put him into his pocket and ran home, crying, "Now I have her! I have my Elizabeth! Now you shall get it, you little mischievous rascals!" And on getting home he put the toad into a costly silver casket, as if it was the greatest treasure.

To account for John's joy you must know that Klas Starkwolt had often told him that the underground people could not endure any ill smell, and that the sight or even the smell of a toad made them faint and suffer the most dreadful tortures, and that by means of stench and. these odious ugly animals, one could compel them to anything. Hence there are no bad smells to be found in the whole glass empire, and a toad is a thing unheard of there; this toad must therefore have been inclosed in the stone from the creation, as it were for the sake of John and Elizabeth.

Resolved to try the effect of his toad, John took the casket under his arm and went out, and on the way he met two of the little people in a lonesome place. The moment he approached them they fell to the ground, and whimpered and howled most lamentably, as long as he was near them.

Satisfied now of his power, he next morning summoned the fifty principal persons, with their wives and children, to his apartment. When they came, he addressed them, reminding them once again of his kindness and. gentleness toward them, and of the good terms on which they bad hitherto lived. He reproached them with their ingratitude in refusing him the only favour he had ever asked of them, but firmly declared he would not give way to their obstinacy. "Wherefore," said he, "for the last time, think for a minute, and if you then say No, you shall feel that pain which is to you and your children the most terrible of all pains."

They did not take long to deliberate, but unanimously replied "No;" and they thought to themselves what new scheme has the youth hit on, with which he thinks to frighten wise ones like us, and they smiled as they said No. Their smiling enraged John above all, and he ran back a few hundred paces, to where he had laid the casket with the toad, under a bush.

He was hardly come within a hundred paces of them when they all fell to the ground as if struck with a thunderbolt, and began to howl and whimper, and to writhe, as if suffering the most excruciating pain. They stretched out their hands, and cried, "Have mercy! have mercy! we feel you have a toad, and there is no escape for us. Take the odious beast away, and we will do all you require." He let them kick a few seconds longer, and. then took the toad away. They then stood up and felt no more pain. John let all depart but the six chief persons, to whom he said:—

"This night between twelve and one Elizabeth and. I will depart. Load then for me three waggons, with gold, and silver, and precious stones. I might, you know, take all that is in the hill, and you deserve it, but I will be merciful. Farther, you must put all the furniture of my chamber in two waggons, and. get ready for me the handsomest travelling-carriage that is in the hill, with six black horses. Moreover, you must set at liberty all the servants who have been so long here that on earth they would be twenty years old and upwards, and you must give them as much silver and gold as will make them rich for life, and make a law that no one shall be detained here longer than his twentieth year."

The six took the oath, and went away quite melancholy, and John buried his toad deep in the ground. The little people laboured hard and prepared everything. At midnight everything was out of the hill, and John and Elizabeth got into the silver tun, and were drawn up.

It was then one o'clock, and it was midsummer, the very time that twelve years before John had gone down into the hill. Music sounded around them, and. they saw the glass hill open, and the rays of the light of heaven shine on them after so many years; and when they got out they saw the first streaks of dawn already in the east. Crowds of the undergroundpeople were around them busied about the waggons. John bid them a last farewell, waved. his brown cap three times in the air, and then flung it among them. And at the same moment he ceased to see them; he beheld nothing but a green hill, and the well-known bushes and fields, and heard the church clock of Rambin strike two. When all was still, save a few larks, who were tuning their morning songs, they all fell on their knees and worshiped God, resolving henceforth to lead a pious and a Christian life. When the sun rose, John arranged the procession, and they set out for Rambin. Every well-known object that they saw awaked. pleasing recollections in the bosom of John and his bride; and as they passed by Rodenkirchen, John recognised, among the people that gazed at and followed them, his old friend Klas Starkwolt, the cowherd, and his dog Speed. It was about four in the morning when they entered Rambin, and they halted in the middle of the village, about twenty paces from the house where John was born. The whole village poured out to gaze on these Asiatic princes, for such the old sexton, who had in his youth been at Moscow and Constantinople, said they were. There John saw his father and mother, and his brother Andrew, and his sister Trine. The old minister, Krabbe, stood there too, in his black slippers and white night cap, gaping and staring with the rest.

John discovered himself to his parents, and Elizabeth to hers, and the wedding-day was soon fixed, and such a wedding was never seen before or since in the island of Rügen; for John sent to Stralsund and Greifswald for whole boatloads of wine, and sugar, and coffee, and whole herds of oxen, sheep, and pigs were driven to the wedding. The quantity of harts, and. roes, and hares that were shot on the occasion, it were vain to attempt to tell, or to count the fish that was caught. There was not a musician in Rügen and Pomerania that was not engaged, for John was immensely rich, and he wished to display his wealth.

John did not neglect his old friend Klas Starkwolt, the cowherd. He gave him enough to make him comfortable the rest of his days, and insisted on his coming and staying with him as often and as long as he wished.

After his marriage, John made a progress through the country with his beautiful Elizabeth, and they purchased towns, and villages, and lands, until he became master of nearly half Rügen, and a very considerable count in the country. His father, old James Dietrich, was made a nobleman, and his brothers and sisters gentlemen and ladies—for what cannot money do?

John and his wife spent their days in doing acts of piety and charity. They built several churches, and they had the blessing of every one that knew them, and died universally lamented. It was Count John Dietrich that built and richly endowed the present church of Rambin. He built it on the site of his father's house, and presented to it several of the cups and plates made by the underground people, and his own and Elizabeth's glass shoes, in memory of what had befallen them in their youth. But they were all taken away in the time of the great Charles the Twelfth of Sweden, when the Russians came on the island, and the Cossacks plundered even the churches, and took away everything.

NOTE

[a] The population of Lusatia (Lausatz) is like that of Pomerania and Rügen, Vendish. Hence, perhaps, it is that in the Lusatian tale of the Fairy-sabbath, we meet with caps with bells, and a descent into the interior of a mountain in a kind of boat as in this tale Wilcomm, Sagen und Märchen aus der Oberlausitz. Hanov. 1843. Blackwood's Magazine for June, 1844.

The Little Glass Shoe

A peasant, named John Wilde, who lived in Rodenkirchen, found one time a glass shoe on one of the hills where the little people used to dance. He clapped it instantly into his pocket and ran away with it, keeping his hand as close on his pocket as if he had a dove in it; for he knew that he had found a treasure which the underground people must redeem at any price.

Others say that John Wilde lay in ambush one night for the underground people, and gained an opportunity of pulling off one of their shoes, by stretching himself there with a brandy-bottle beside him, and acting like one that was dead drunk; for he was a very cunning man, not over scrupulous in his morals, and had taken in many a one by his craftiness, and, on this account, his name was in no good repute among his neighbours, who, to say the truth, were willing to have as little to do with him as possible. Many hold, too, that he was acquainted with forbidden arts, and used to carry on an intercourse with the fiends and old women that raised storms, and such like.

However, be this as it may, when John had gotten the shoe, he lost no time in letting the folk that dwell under the ground know that he had it. So at midnight he went to the Nine-hills, and cried with all his might, "John Wilde, of Rodenkirchen, has got a beautiful glass shoe. Who will buy it? Who will buy it?" For he knew that the little one who had lost the shoe must go barefoot till he got it again, and that is no trifle, for the little people have generally to walk upon very hard and stony ground.

John's advertisement was speedily attended to. The little fellow who had lost the shoe made no delay in setting about redeeming it. The first free day he got, that he might come out into the daylight, he came as a respectable merchant, and knocked at John Wilde's door, and asked if John had not a glass shoe to sell? "For," says he, "they are an article now in great demand, and are sought for in every market." John replied that it was true he had a very little little, nice, pretty little glass shoe, but it was so small that even a Dwarf's foot would be squeezed in it; and that God Almighty must make people on purpose for it before it could be of any use; but that, for all that, it was an extraordinary shoe, and, a valuable shoe, and a dear shoe, and it was not every merchant that could afford to pay for it.

The merchant asked to see it, and when be had examined it, "Glass shoes," said he, "are not by any means such rare articles, my good friend, as you think here in Rodenkirchen, because you do not happen to go much into the world. However," said he, after hemming a little, "I will give you a good price for it, because I happen to have the very fellow of it." And he bid the countryman a thousand dollars for it.

"A thousand dollars are money, my father used to say when he drove fat oxen to market," replied John Wilde, in' a mocking tone; "but it will not leave my hands for that shabby price; and, for my own part, it may ornament the foot of my daughter's doll. Harkye, friend: I have heard a sort of little song sung about the glass shoe, and it is not for a parcel of dirt that it will go out of my hands. Tell me now, my good fellow, should you happen to know the knack of it, that in every furrow I make when I am ploughing I should find a ducat? If not, the shoe is still mine, and you may inquire for glass shoes at those other markets."

The merchant made still a great many attempts, and twisted and turned in every direction to get the shoe; but when he found the farmer inflexible, be agreed to what John desired, and swore to the performance of it. Cunning John believed him, and gave him up the glass shoe, for he knew right well with whom he had to do. So the business being ended, away went the merchant with his glass shoe.

Without a moment's delay, John repaired to his stable, got ready his horses and his plough, and drove out to the field. He selected a piece of ground where he would have the shortest turns possible, and began to plough. Hardly had the plough turned up the first sod, when up sprang a ducat out of the ground, and it was the same with every fresh furrow he made. There was now no end of his ploughing, and John Wilde soon bought eight new horses, and put them into the stable to the eight he already had—and their mangers were never without plenty of oats in them—that he might be every two hours to yoke two fresh horses, and so be enabled to drive them the faster.

John was now insatiable in ploughing; every morning he went out before sunrise, and many a time he ploughed on till after midnight. Summer and winter it was plough, plough with him evermore, except when the ground was frozen as hard as a stone. But he always ploughed by himself, and never suffered any one to go out with him, or to come to him when he was at work, for John understood too well the nature of his crop to let people see what it was he ploughed so constantly for.

But it fared worse with himself than his horses, who ate good oats and were regularly changed and relieved, while he grew pale and meagre by reason of his continual working and toiling. His wife and children had no longer any comfort of him; he never went to the alehouse or the club; he withdrew from every one, and scarcely ever spoke a single word, but went about silent and wrapped up in his own thoughts. All the day long he toiled for his ducats, and at night he had to count them and to plan and meditate how he might find out a still swifter kind of plough.

His wife and neighbours lamented over his strange conduct, his dullness and melancholy, and began to think that he was grown foolish. Everybody pitied his wife and children, for they imagined that the numerous horses he kept in his stable, and the preposterous mode of agriculture that he pursued, with his unnecessary and superfluous ploughing, must soon leave him without house or land.

But their anticipations were not fulfilled. True it is, the poor man never enjoyed a happy or contented hour since he began to plough the ducats up out of the ground. The old saying held good in his case, that he who gives himself up to the pursuit of gold is half way in the claws of the evil one. Flesh and blood cannot bear perpetual labour, and John Wilde did not long hold out against this running through the furrows day and night. He got through the first spring, but one day in the second, he dropped down at the tail of the plough like an exhausted November fly. Out of the pure thirst after gold he was wasted away and dried up to nothing; whereas he had been a very strong and hearty man the day the shoe of the little underground man fell into his hands.

His wife, however, found after him a considerable treasure, two great nailed up chests full of good new ducats, and his sons purchased large estates for themselves, and became lords and noblemen. But what good did all that do poor John Wilde?

The Wonderful Plough

There was once a farmer who was master of one of the little black ones, that are the blacksmiths and armourers; and he got him in a very curious way. On the road leading to this farmer's ground there stood a stone cross, and every morning as he went to his work he used to stop and kneel down before this cross, and pray for some minutes.

On one of these occasions he noticed on the cross a pretty bright insect, of such a brilliant hue that he could not recollect having ever before seen the like with an insect. He wondered greatly at this, yet still he did not disturb it; but the insect did not remain long quiet, but ran without ceasing backwards and forwards on the cross, as if it was in pain, and wanted to get away. Next morning the farmer again saw the very same insect, and again it was running to and fro, in the same state of uneasiness. The farmer began now to have some suspicions about it, and thought to himself, "Would this now be one of the little black enchanters? For certain, all is not right with that insect; it runs about just like one that bad an evil conscience, as one that would, yet cannot, go away:" and a variety of thoughts and conjectures passed through his mind; and he called to mind what he had often heard from his father, and other old people, that when the under groundpeople chance to touch anything holy, they are held fast and cannot quit the spot, and are therefore extremely careful to avoid all such things. But he also thought it may as well be something else; and you would perhaps be committing a sin in disturbing and taking away the little animal; so he let it stay as it was.

But when he had found it twice more in the same place, and

still running about with the same marks of uneasiness, he said, "No, it is not all right with it. So now, in the name of God!" and he made a grasp at the insect, that resisted and clung fast to the stone; but he held it tight, and tore it away by main force, and lo! then he found he had, by the top of the head, a little ugly black chap, about six inches long, screeching and. kicking at a most furious rate.

The farmer was greatly astounded at this sudden transformation; still he held his prize fast and kept calling to him, while he administered to him a few smart slaps on the buttocks: "Be quiet, be quiet, my little man! if crying was to do the business, we might look for heroes in swaddling clothes. We'll just take you with us a bit, and see what you are good for."

The little fellow trembled and shook in every limb, and then began to whimper most piteously, and to beg hard of the farmer to let him go. But "No, my lad," replied the farmer, "I will not let you go till you tell me who you are, and how you came here, and what trade you know, that enables you to earn your bread in the world." At this the little man grinned and shook his head, but said not a word in reply, only begged and prayed the more to get loose; and the farmer found that he must now begin to entreat him if he would coax any information out of him. But it was all to no purpose. He then adopted the contrary method, and whipped and slashed him till the blood run down, but just to as little purpose; the little black thing remained as dumb as the grave, for this species is the most malicious and obstinate of all the underground race.

The farmer now got angry, and he said, "Do but be quiet, my child; I should be a fool to put myself into a passion with such a little brat. Never fear, I shall soon make you tame enough."

So saying, he ran home with him, and clapped him into a black, sooty, iron pot, and put the iron lid upon it, and laid on the top of the lid a great heavy stone, and set the pot in a dark cold room, and as he was going out he said to him, "Stay there, now, and freeze till you are black! I 'll engage that at last you will answer me civilly."

Twice a-week the farmer went regularly into the room and asked his little black captive if he would answer him now; but the little one still obstinately persisted in his silence. The farmer had now, without success, pursued this course for six weeks, at the end of which time his prisoner at last gave up. One day as the farmer was opening the room door, he, of his own accord, called out to him to come and take him out of his dirty stinking dungeon, promising that he would now cheerfully do all that was wanted of him.

The farmer first ordered him to give him his history. The black one replied, "My dear friend you know it just as well as I, or else you never had had me here. You see I happened by chance to come too near the cross, a thing we little people may not do, and there I was held fast and obliged instantly to let my body become visible; so, then, that people might not recognise me, I turned myself into an insect. But you found me out. For when we get fastened to holy or consecrated things, we never can get away from them unless a man takes us off. That, however, does not happen without plague and annoyance to us, though, indeed, to say the truth, the staying fastened there is not over pleasant. And so I struggled against you, too, for we have a natural aversion to let ourselves be taken into a man's hand." "Ho, ho! is that the tune with you?" cried the farmer: "you have a natural aversion, have you? Believe me, my sooty friend, I have just the same for you; and so you shall be away without a moment's delay, and we will lose no time in making our bargain with each other. But you must first make me some present." "What you will, you have only to ask," said the little one: "silver and gold, and precious stones, and costly furniture—all shall be thine in less than an instant."—"Silver and gold, and precious stones, and all such glittering fine things will I none," said the farmer; "they have turned the heart and broken the neck of many a one before now, and few are they whose lives they make happy. I know that you are handy smiths, and have many a strange thing with you that other smiths know nothing about. So come, now, swear to me that you will make me an iron plough, such that the smallest foal may be able to draw it without being tired, and then run off with you as fast as your legs can carry you." So the black swore, and the farmer then cried out, "Now, in the name of God; there, you are at liberty," and the little one vanished like lightning.

Next morning, before the sun was up, there stood in the farmer's yard a new iron plough, and he yoked his dog Water to it, and though it was of the size of an ordinary plough, Water drew it with ease through the heaviest clay-land, and it tore up prodigious furrows. The farmer used this plough for many years, and the smallest foal or the leanest little horse could draw it through the ground, to the amazement of every one who beheld it, without turning a single hair. And this plough made a rich man of the.. farmer, for it cost him no horse-flesh, and he led a cheerful and contented life by means of it. Hereby we may see that moderation holds out the longest, and that it is not good to covet too much.

The Lost Bell

A shepherd's boy belonging to Patzig, about half a mile from Bergen, where there are great numbers of the underground people in the hills, found one morning a little silver bell on the green heath, among the Giants'-graves, and fastened it on him. It happened to be the bell belonging to the cap of one of the little Brown ones, who had lost it while he was dancing, and did not immediately miss it, or observe that it was no longer tinkling in his cap. He had gone down into the hill without his bell, and having discovered his loss, was filled with melancholy. For the worst thing that can befall the underground people is to lose their cap, then their shoes; but even to lose the bell from their caps, or the buckle from their belts, is no trifle to them. Whoever loses his bell must pass some sleepless nights, for not a wink of sleep can he get till he has recovered it.

The little fellow was in the greatest trouble, and searched and looked about everywhere; but how could he learn who had the bell? For only on a very few days in the year may they come up to the daylight; nor can they then appear in their true form. He had turned himself into every form of birds, beasts, and men; and he had sung and rung, and groaned and moaned, and lamented and inquired about his bell, but not the slightest tidings, or trace of tidings, had he been able to get. For what was worst of all, the shepherd's boy had left Patzig the very day he found the little bell, and was now keeping sheep at Unruh, near Gingst: so it was not till many a day after, and then by mere chance, that the little underground fellow recovered his bell, and with it his peace of mind.

He had thought it not unlikely that a raven, or a crow, or a jackdaw, or a magpie, had found his bell, and from his thievish disposition, which is caught with anything bright and shining, had carried it into his nest; with this thought he had turned himself into a beautiful little bird, and searched all the nests in the island, and had sung before all kinds of birds, to see if they had found what he had lost, and could restore him his sleep; but nothing had he been able to learn from the birds. As he now, one evening, was flying over the waters of Baby and the fields of Unruh, the shepherd's boy, whose name was Fritz Schlagenteufel *(Smite-devil)*, happened to be keeping his sheep there at the very time. Several of the sheep had bells about their necks, and they tinkled merrily, when the boy's dog set them trotting. The little bird, who was flying over them thought of his bell, and sung, in a melancholy tone,

> Little bell, little bell,
> Little ram as well,
> You, too, little sheep,
> If you've my Tingletoo,
> No sheep's so rich as you,
> My rest you keep.

The boy looked up and listened to this strange song which came out of the sky, and saw the pretty bird, which seemed to him still more strange:—"Odds bodikins!" said he to himself, "if one but had that bird that's singing up there, so plain that one of us would hardly match him! What can he mean by that wonderful song? The whole of it is, it must be a feathered witch. My rams have only pinchbeck bells, he calls them rich cattle; but I have a silver bell, and he sings nothing about me." And with these words he began to fumble in his pocket, took out his bell, and rang it.

The bird in the air instantly saw what it was, and was rejoiced beyond measure. He vanished in a second—flew behind the nearest bush—alighted and drew off his speckled feather-dress, and turned himself into an old woman dressed in tattered clothes. The old dame, well supplied with sighs and groans, tottered across the field to the shepherd's boy, who was still ringing his bell, and wondering what was become of the beautiful bird. She cleared her throat, and coughing up from the bottom of her chest, bid him a kind good evening, and asked him which was the way to Bergen. Pretending then that she had just seen the little bell, she exclaimed, "Good Lord! what a charming pretty little bell! Well! in all my life I never beheld anything more beautiful! Harkye, my son, will you sell me that bell? And what may be the price of it? I have a little grandson at home, and such a nice plaything as it would make for him!" "No," replied the boy, quite short, "the bell is not for sale. It is a bell, that there is not such another bell in the whole world. I have only to give it a little tinkle, and my sheep run of themselves wherever I would have them go. And what a delightful sound it has! Only listen, mother!" said he, ringing it: "is there any weariness in the world that can hold out against this bell? I can ring with it away the longest time, so that it will be gone in a second."

The old woman thought to herself, "We will see if he can hold out against bright shining money." And she took out no less than three silver dollars, and offered them to him: but he still replied, "No, I will not sell my bell." She then offered him five dollars. "The bell is still mine," said he. She stretched out her hand full of ducats: he replied, this third time, "Gold is dirt and does not ring." The old dame then shifted her ground, and turned the discourse another way. She grew mysterious, and began to entice him by talking of secret arts, and of charms by which his cattle might be made to thrive prodigiously, relating to him all kinds of wonders of them. It was then the young shepherd began to long, and he now lent a willing ear to her tales.

The end of the matter was, that she said to him, "Harkye, my child! give me the bell and see! here is a white stick for you," said she, taking out a little white stick which had Adam and Eve very ingeniously cut on it, as they were feeding the herds of Paradise, with the fattest sheep and lambs dancing before them; and there was the shepherd David too, as he stood with his sling against the giant Goliath. "I will give you," said the old woman, "this stick for the bell, and as long as you drive the cattle with it they will be sure to thrive. With this you will become a rich shepherd: your wethers will always be fat a month sooner than the wethers of other shepherds, and every one of your sheep will have two pounds of wool more than others, and yet no one will be ever able to see it on them."

The old woman handed him the stick. So mysterious was her gesture, and so strange and bewitching her smile, that the lad was at once in her power. He grasped eagerly at the stick, gave her his hand, and cried, "Done! Strike hands! The bell for the stick!" And cheerfully the old woman struck hands, and took the bell, and went like a light breeze over the field and the heath. He saw her vanish, and she seemed to float away before his eyes like a mist, and to go off with a slight whiz and whistle that made the shepherd's hair stand on end.

The underground one, however, who, in the shape of an old woman, had wheedled him out of his bell, had not deceived him. For the under groundpeople dare not lie, but must ever keep their word; a breach of it being followed by their sudden change into the shape of toads, snakes, dunghill-beetles, wolves and apes; forms in which they wander about, objects of fear and aversion for a long course of years before they are freed. They, therefore, have naturally a great dread of lying. Fritz Schlagenteufel gave close attention and made trial of his new shepherd's-staff and he soon found that the old woman had told him the truth, for his flocks, and his work, and all the labour of his hands prospered with him and had wonderful luck, so that there was not a sheep-owner or head shepherd but was desirous of having Fritz Schlagenteufel in his employment.

It was not long, however, that he remained an underling. Before he was eighteen years of age, he had gotten his own flocks, and in the course of a few years was the richest sheep-master in the whole island of Rügen; until at last, he was able to purchase a knight's estate for himself, and that estate was Grabitz, close by Rambin, which now belongs to the lords of Sunde. My father [a] knew him there, and how from a shepherd's boy he was become a nobleman, and, he always conducted himself like a prudent, honest and pious man, who had a good word from every one. He brought up his sons like gentlemen, and his daughters like ladies, some of whom are still alive and accounted people of great consequence. And well may people who hear such stories wish that they had met with such an adventure, and had found a little silver bell which the underground people had lost.

NOTE
[a] Hinrich Vick's of course, for he is the narrator.

The Black Dwarfs of Granitz

Not far from the Ahlbeck lies a little mansion called Granitz, just under the great wood on the sea-coast called the wood of Granitz. In this little seat lived, not many years ago, a nobleman named Von Scheele. Toward the close of his life he sank into a state of melancholy, though hitherto a very cheerful and social man, and a great sports-man. People said that the old man took to his lonesome way of living from the loss of his three beautiful daughters, who were called the three fair-haired maidens, and who grew up here in the solitude of the woods, among the herds and the birds, and who had all three gone off in the same night and never returned. The old man took this greatly to heart, and withdrew himself from the world and all cheerful society. He had great intercourse with the little black people, and he was many a night out of the house, and no one knew where he had been; but when he came home in the gray of the morning, he would whisper his housekeeper, and say to her, "Ha, ha! I was at a grand table last night."

This old gentleman used to relate to his friends, and confirm it with many a stout trooper's and sportsman's oath, that the underground people swarmed among the fir-trees of Granitz, about the Ahlbeck, and along the whole shore. He used often, also, to show to those whom he took to walk there, a great number of little foot-prints, like those of very small children, in the sand, and he has suddenly called out to his companions, "Hush! Listen how they are, buzzing and whispering!"

Going once with some friends along the sea-shore, he all of a sudden stood still, as if in amazement, pointed to the sea, and cried out, "My soul! there they are again at full work, and there are several thousands of them employed about a few sunken casks of wine that they are rolling to the shore; oh! what a jovial carouse there will be to-night!" He then told his companions that he could see them both by day and by night, and that they did nothing to him; nay, they were his most particular friends, and one of them had once saved his house from being burnt by waking him in the night out of a profound sleep, when a firebrand, that had fallen out on the floor, was just on the point of setting fire to some wood and straw that lay there. He said that almost every day some of them were to be seen on the sea-shore, but that during high storms, when the sea was uncommonly rough, almost all of them were there looking after amber and shipwrecks, and for certain no ship ever went to pieces but they got the best part of the cargo, and hid it safe under the ground. And how grand a thing, he added, it is to live under the sand-hills with them, and bow beautiful their crystal palaces are, no one can have any conception who has not been there.

GERMANY

Von wilden getwergen han ich gehöret sagen
Si sin in holren bergen; unt daz si ze scherme tragen
Einez heizet tarnkappen, von wunderlicher art—
Swerz hat an sime libe, der sol vil wohl sin bewart
Vor slegen unt vor stichen.
—NIBELUNGEN, LIED st. 342.

Of wild dwarfs I oft have heard men declare
They dwell In hollow mountains; and for defence they wear
A thing called a Tarn-cloke, of wonderful nature—
Who has It on his body will ever be secure
'Gainst cutting and 'gainst thrusting.

THE RELIGION of the ancient Germans, probably the same with that of the Scandinavians, contained, like it, Alfs, Dwarfs, and Giants. The Alfs have fallen from the popular creed, [a] but the Dwarfs still retain their former dominion. Unlike those of the North, they have put off their heathen character, and, with their human neighbours, have embraced a purer faith. With the creed they seem to have adopted the spirit of their new religion also. In most of the traditions respecting them we recognise benevolence as one of the principal traits of their character.

The oldest monuments of German popular belief are the poems of the Heldenbuch *(Hero-book)* and the spirit-stirring Nibelungen Lied. [b] In these poems the Dwarfs are actors of importance.

In this last-named celebrated poem the Dwarf Albrich appears as the guardian of the celebrated Hoard which Sifrit (Siegfried) won from the Nibelungen. The Dwarf is twice vanquished by the hero who gains his Tarn-kappe, or Mantle of Invisibility. [c]

In the Heldenbuch we meet with the Dwarf-king Laurin, whose garden Dietrich of Bern and his warriors broke into and laid waste. To repel the invader the Dwarf appears in magnificent array: twenty-three stanzas are occupied with the description of his banner, helmet, shield, and other accoutrements. A furious combat ensues, in which the Dwarf has long the advantage, as his magic ring and girdle endow him with the strength of twenty-four men, and his Hel Keplein [d] (Tarnkappe) renders him invisible at pleasure. At length, by the advice of Hildebrand, Dietrich strikes off the Dwarfs finger, breaks his girdle, and pulls off his Hel Keplein, and thus succeeds in vanquishing his enemy. Laurin is afterwards reconciled to the heroes, and prevails on them to enter the mountain in which he dwelt, and partake of a banquet. Having them now in his power, he treacherously makes them all his prisoners. His queen, however, Ditlaub's sister, whom he had stolen away from under a linden, releases them: their liberation is followed by a terrific engagement between them and Laurin, backed by a numerous host of Dwarfs. Laurin is again overcome; he loses his queen; his hill is plundered of its treasures, and himself led to Bern, and there reduced to the extremity of earning his bread by becoming a buffoon.

In the poem named Húrnen Sifrit [e] the Dwarf Eugel [f] with invisibility. renders the hero good service in his combat with the enchanted Dragon who had carried off the fair Chrimhild from Worms, and enclosed her in the Drachenstein. When *Sifrit* is treacherously attacked by the Giant Kuperan, the ally of the Dragon, the Dwarf flings his Nebelkappe over him to protect him.

But the most celebrated of Dwarfs is Elberich, [g] who aided the emperor Otnit or Ortnit to gain the daughter of the Paynim Soldan of Syria.

Otnit ruled over Lombardy, and had subdued all the neighbouring nations. His subjects wishing him to marry, he held a council to consider the affair. No maiden mentioned was deemed noble enough to share his bed. At last his uncle Elias, king of the "wild Russians," says:-

"I know of a maiden, noble and high-born,
Her no man yet hath wooed, his life who hath not lorn.
"She shineth like the roses and the gold ruddy,
She fair is in her person, thou must credit me;
She shines o'er other women, as bright roses do,
So fair a child was never; they say she good is too."

The monarch's imagination is inflamed, and, regardless of the remonstrances of his council, he determines to brave all dangers, to sail with a powerful army to Syria, where the maiden dwelt, and to win her or to die. He regulates his kingdom, and says to his uncle:-

As soon as May appeareth, with her days so clear,
Then pray thou of thy friends all, their warriors to cheer,
To hold themselves all ready; go things as they may,
We will, with the birds' singing, sail o'er the sea away.

The queen now endeavours to dissuade her son, but finding her efforts vain, resolves to aid him as far as she can. She gives him a ring, and desires him to ride toward Rome till he comes to where a linden stands before a hill, from which runs a brook, and there he will meet with an adventure. She farther tells him to keep the ring uncovered, and the stone of it will direct him.

Obeying his directions, Otnit rides alone from his palace at Garda, continually looking at his ring:

> Unto a heath he came then, close by the Garda lake,
> Where everywhere the flowers and clover out did break;
> The birds were gaily singing, their notes did loudly ring,
> He all the night had waked, he was weary with riding.
> The sun over the mountains and through the welkin shone,
> Then looked he full oft on the gold and on the stone;
> Then saw he o'er the meadow, down trodden the green grass,
> And a pathway narrow, where small feet used to pass.
> Then followed he downwards, the rocky wall boldly,
> Till he had found the fountain, and the green linden-tree,
> And saw the heath wide spreading, and the linden branching high.
> It had upon its boughs full many a guest worthy.
> The birds were loudly singing, each other rivalling,
> "I have the right way ridden," spake Otnit the king;
> Then much his heart rejoiced, when he saw the linden spread;
> He sprang down from his courser, he held him by the head.
> And when the Lombarder had looked on the linden
> He began to laugh loud; now list what he said then:
> "There never yet from tree came so sweet breathing a wind."
> Then saw he how an infant was laid beneath the lind,
> Who had himself full firmly rolled in the grass;
> Then little the Lombarder knew who he was:
> He bore upon his body so rich and noble a dress,
> No king's child upon earth e'er did the like possess.
> His dress was rich adorned with gold and precious stone;
> When he beneath the linden the child found all alone:
> "Where now is thy mother?" king Otnit he cries;
> "Thy body unprotected beneath this tree here lies."

This child was Elberich, whom the ring rendered visible. After a hard struggle, Otnit overcomes him. As a ransom, Elberich promises him a magnificent suit of armour—

"I'll give thee for my ransom the very best harnéss
That either young or old in the world doth possess.
"Full eighty thousand marks the harness is worth well,
A sword too I will give thee, with the shirt of mail,
That every corselet cuts through as if steel it were not;
There ne'er was helm so strong yet could injure it a jot.
"I ween in the whole world no better sword there be,
I brought it from a mountain is called Almari;
It is with gold adorned, and clearer is than glass;
I wrought it in a mountain is called Gűickelsass.
"The sword I will name to thee, it is bright of hue,
Whate'er thou with it strikest no gap will ensue,
It is Rossè called, I tell to thee its name;
Wherever swords are drawing it never will thee shame.
"With all the other harness I give thee leg armour,
In which there no ring is, my own hand wrought it sure;
And when thou hast the harness thou must it precious hold,
There's nothing false within it, it all is of pure gold.
"With all the armour rich I give thee a helmet,
Upon an emperor's head none a better e'er saw yet;
Full happy is the man who doth this helmet bear,
His head is recognised, a mile off though he were.
"And with the helmet bright I will give to thee a shield,
So strong and so good too, if to me thanks thou 'It yield;
It never yet was cut through by any sword so keen,
No sort of weapon ever may that buckler win."

Elberich persuades the king to lend him his ring; when he gets it he becomes invisible, and amuses himself by telling him of the whipping he will get from his mother for having lost it. At last when Otnit is on the point of going away, Elberich returns the ring, and, to his no small surprise, informs him that he is his father, promising him, at the same time, if he is kind to his mother, to stand his friend, and assist him to gain the heathen maid.

When May arrives Otnit sails from Messina with his troops. As

they approach Sunders, probably Saida, eg. Sidon] they are a little
in dread of the quantity of shipping they see in the port, and the
king regrets and bewails having proceeded without his dwarf-sire.
But Elberich has, unseen, been sitting on the mast. He appears, and
gives his advice, accompanied by a stone, which, by being put into
the mouth, endows its possessor with the gift of all languages. On
the heathens coming alongside the vessel, Otnit assumes the character of a merchant, and is admitted to enter the port. He forthwith
proposes to murder the inhabitants in the night, an act of treachery
which is prevented by the strong and indignant rebukes of the Dwarf.

Elberich sets off to Muntabur, [Mount Tabor] the royal residence, to demand the princess. The Soldan, enraged at the insolence
of the invisible envoy, in vain orders his men to put him to death;
the "little man" returns unscathed to Otnit, and bids him prepare for
war. By the aid of Elberich, Otnit wins, after great slaughter on both
sides, the city of Sunders. He then, under the Dwarf's advice, follows
up his conquest by marching for Muntabur, the capital. Elberich, still
invisible, except to the possessor of the ring, offers to act as guide.

"Give me now the horse here they lead by the hand,
And I will guide thine army unto the heathens' land;
If any one should ask thee, who on the horse doth ride?
Thou shalt say nothing else, but—an angel is thy guide."

The army, on seeing the horse and banner advancing as it
were of themselves, blessed themselves, and asked Otnit why he
did not likewise.

"It is God's messenger!" Otnit then cried:
"Who unto Muntabur will be our trusty guide;

Him ye should believe in, who like Christians debate,
Who in the fight them spare not, he leads to heaven straight."

Thus encouraged, the troops cheerfully follow the invisible standard-bearer, and soon appear before Muntabur, where Elberich delivers the banner to king Elias, and directs them to encamp. He meanwhile enters the city, flings down the artillery from the walls, and when the Soldan again refuses to give his daughter, plucks out some of his majesty's beard [h] and hair, in the midst of his courtiers and guards, who in vain cut and thrust at the viewless tormentor. A furious battle ensues. The queen and princess resort to prayers to their gods Apollo and Mahomet for the safety of the Soldan, The princess is thus described:

Her mouth flamed like a rose, and like the ruby stone,
And equal to the full moon her lovely eyes they shone.
With roses she bedecked had well her head,
And with pearls precious,—no one comforted the maid:
She was of exact stature, slender in the waist,
And turned like a taper was her body chaste.
Her hands and her arms, you nought in them could blame,
Her nails they so clear were, people saw themselves in them;
And her hair ribbons were of silk costly,
Which she left down hanging, the maiden fair and free.
She set upon her head high a crown of gold red,—
Elberich the little, he grieved for the maid;—
In front of the crown lay a carbuncle stone,
That in the royal palace like a taper shone.

Elberich endeavours to persuade her to become a Christian, and espouse Otnit; and to convince her of the incapacity of her gods, he tumbles their images into the fosse. Overcome by his representations and her father's danger, the princess, with her mother's consent, agrees to wed the monarch whom Elberich points out to her in the battle, and she gives her ring to be conveyed to him. The Dwarf unperceived, leads her out of the city, and delivers her to her future husband, strictly forbidding all intercourse between them, previous to the maiden's baptism. [1] When the old heathen misses his daughter he orders out his troops to recover her. Elberich hastens to king Elias, and brings up the Christians. A battle ensues: the latter are victorious, and the princess is brought to Sunders;—ere they embark Elberich and Elias baptise her, and ere they reached Messina. "the noble maiden was a wife."

As yet not intimately acquainted with Christianity, the young empress asks Otnit about his god, giving him to understand that she knew his deity, who had come to her father's to demand her for him. Otnit corrects her mistake, telling her that the envoy was Elberich, whom she then desires to see. At the request of Otnit the Dwarf reveals himself to the queen and court.

> Long time he refused,—he showed him then a stone,
> That like unto the sun, with the gold shone;
> Ruby and -carbuncle was the crown so rich,
> Which upon his head bare the little Elberich.
> The Dwarf let the people all see him then,
> They began to look upon him, both women and men;
> Many a fair woman with rosy mouth then said,
> "I ween a fairer person no eye imth e'er survey'd."

* * *

> Then Elberich the little a harp laid hold upon;
> Full rapidly he touched the strings every one
> In so sweet a measure that the hall did resound;
> All that him beheld then, they felt a joy profound.

After giving Otnit abundance of riches, and counselling him to remunerate those who had lost their relatives in his expedition, Elberich takes leave of the king. He then vanishes, and appears no more.

Otnit is the most pleasing poem in the Heldenbuch. Nothing can he more amiable than the character of the Dwarf, who is evidently the model of Oberon. We say this, because the probability is much greater that a French writer should have taken a Dwarf from a German poet, than that the reverse should have occurred. The connexion between the two works appears indubitable.

An attempt has already been made to trace the origin of Dwarfs, and the historical theory respecting those of the North rejected. A similar theory has been given of those of Germany, as being a people subdued between the fifth and tenth centuries by a nation of greater power and size. The vanquished fled to the mountains, and concealed themselves in caverns, only occasionally venturing to appear; and hence, according to this theory, the origin of Dwarf stories. As we regard them as an integrant part of Gotho-German religion, we must reject this hypothesis in the case of Germany also.

Beside the Dwarfs, we meet in the Nibelungen Lied with beings answering to the Nixes or Water-spirits. When [i] the Burgundians on their fatal journey to the court of Ezel (Attila) reached the banks of the Danube, they found that it could not be crossed without the aid of boats. Hagene then proceeded along the bank in search of a ferry. Suddenly he heard a plashing in the water, and on lookmg more closely he saw some females who were bathing. He tried to steal on them, but they escaped him and went hovering over the river. He succeeded, however, in securing their clothes, and in exchange for them the females, who were Watermaids *(Merewiper)* promised to tell him the result of the visit to the court of the Hunnish monarch. One of them then named Hadeburch assured him of a prosperous issue, on which he restored the garments. But then another, named Sigelint told him that Hadeburch had lied for the sake of the clothes; for that in reality the event of the visit would be most disastrous, as only one of the party would return alive. She also informed him where the ferry was, and told him how they might outwit the ferry-man and get over.

We cannot refrain from suspecting that in the original legend these were Valkyrias and not Water-nymphs, for these last would hardly strip to go into the water, their native element. In the prose introduction to the Eddaic poem of Völundr we are told that he and his two elder brothers went to Wolfdale and built themselves a house by the water named Wolfsea or lake, and one morning early they found on the shore of the lake three women who were spinning flax: beside them were lying their *swan-dresses.* They were "Valkyrias, and king's daughters." The three brothers took them home and made them their wives, but after seven years they flew away and returned no more. It is remarkable, that in the poem there is not the slightest allusion to the swan-dresses, though it relates the coming and the departure of the maidens. We are then to suppose either that there were other poems on the subject, or that these dresses were so well known a vehicle that it was deemed needless to mention them. We are to suppose also that it was by securing these dresses that the brothers prevented the departure of the maidens, and that it was by recovering them that they were enabled to effect their escape. In effect in the German legend of Wielant (Völundr), the hero sees three *doves* flying to a spring, and as soon as they touch the ground. they become maidens. He then secures their clothes, and will not return them till one of them consents to become his wife. [k]

This legend resembles the tale of the Stolen Veil in Musaeus, and those of the Peri-wife and the Mermaid-wife related above. [l] In the Breton tale of Bisclavaret, or the Warwolf, we learn that no one who became a wolf could resume his human form, unless he could recover the clothes which he had put off previous to undergoing the transformation [m].

Our readers may like to see how the preface to the old editions of the Heldenbuch accounts for the origin of the Dwarfs.

"God," says it," gave the Dwarfs being, because the land and the mountains were altogether waste and uncultivated, and there was much store of silver and gold, and precious stones and pearls still in the mountains. Wherefore God made the Dwarfs very artful and. wise, that they might know good and evil right well, and, for what everything was good. They knew also for what stones were good. Some stones give great strength; some make those who carry them about them invisible, that is called a mist-cloke *(nebelkap);* and therefore did God give the Dwarfs skill and wisdom. Therefore they built handsome hollow bills, and God gave them riches, etc.

"God created the Giants, that they might kill the wild beasts, and the great dragons *(würm),* that the Dwarfs might thereby be more secure. But in a few years the Giants would too much oppress the Dwarfs, and the Giants became altogether wicked and, faithless.

"God then created the Heroes; 'and be it known that the Heroes were for many years right true and worthy, and they then came to the aid of the Dwarfs against the faithless Giants; '—God made them strong, and their thoughts were of manhood, according to honour, and of combats and war."

We will divide the objects of German popular belief at the present day, into four classes:—

1. Dwarfs;

2. Wild-women;

3. Kobolds;

4. Nixes.

NOTES

[a] The only remnant is *Alp,* the nightmare; the *elfon* of modern writers is merely an adoption of the English *elves.*

[b] The edition of this poem which we have used, is that by Shönhuth, Leipzig, 1841.

[c] Tarn from *taren,* to dare, says Dobenek, because it gave courage along with invisibility. It comes more probably we think from the old German *ternen,* to hide. Kappe is properly a cloak, though the Tarnkappe or Nebelkappe Is generally represented as a cap, or hat.

[d] From *hehlen,* to conceal.

[e] *Horny Siegfred;* for when he slew the dragon, he bathed himself in his blood, and became horny and invulnerable everywhere except in one spot between his shoulders, where a linden leaf stuck. In the Nibelungen Lied, *(st.* 100), Hagene says,

Yet still more know I of him—this to me is certain,
A terrible Lind-dragon the herds hand hath slain;
He in the blood him bathed, and horny grew his skin;
Hence woundeth him no weapon, full oft it hath been seen.

[f] MM. Grimm thought at one time that this name was properly Engel, and that it was connected with the changes of Alp, Alf, to Engel (see above). They query at what time the dim.*Engelein* first came into use, and when the angels were first represented under the form of children—a practice evidently derived from the idea of the Elves. In Otfried and other writers of the ninth and tenth centuries, they say, the angels are depicted as young men; but in the latter half of the thirteenth, a popular preacher named Berthold, says: *Ir sehet woldaz si allesamt sint juncliche gemälet; als ein kint daz dá vûnf jár alt ist swá man sie málet.*

[g] Elberich, (the Albrich of the Nibelungen Lied,) as we have said (above), is Oberon. From the usual change of *l* into *u* (as *al, au, col, cou,* etc.), in the French language, Elberich or Albrich (derived from Alp, Alf) becomes Auberich; and *ich* not being a French termination, the diminutive *on* was substituted, and so it became Auberon, or Oberon; a much more likely origin than the usual one from *L'aube dujour.* For this derivation of Oberon we are indebted to Dr. Grimm.

[h] This may have suggested the well-known circumstance in Huon de Bordeaux.

[i] So Oberon in Huon de Bordeaux.

[j] Str. 1564,*seq*

[k] Grimm, Deut. Mythol., p. 398, *seq.*

[l] See above; below, *Ireland;* and Grimm, *ut sup.* p. 1216. The swan-dresses also occur in the Arabian tales of Jahanshah and Hassan of Bassora in Trebutien's Arabian Nights.

[m] Poésies de Marie de France, i. 177, *seq*

DWARFS

Fort, fort! Mich schau' die Sonne nicht,
Ich darf nicht langer harren;
Mich Elfenkind vor ihren Licht
Sähst du zum Fels erstarren.
–La Motte Fouque.

Away! let not the sun view me,
I dare no longer stay;
An Elfin-child thou wouldst me see,
To atone turn at his ray.

These beings are called Zwerge *(Dwarfs),* Berg- and Erdmänlein *(Hill
and Ground-mannikins),* the Stille Volk *(Still-people),* and the Kleine
Yolk *(Little-people).* [a] The following account of the Still-people at
Plesse will give the popular idea respecting them. [b]

At Plesse, a castle in the mountains in Hesse, are various
springs, wells, clefts and holes in the rocks, in which, according to
popular tradition, the Dwarfs, called the Still-people, dwell. They
are silent and beneficent, and willingly serve those who have the
good fortune to please them, if injured they vent their anger, not
on mankind, but on the cattle, which they plague and torment. This
subterranean race has no proper communication with mankind,
but pass their lives within the earth, where their apartments and
chambers are filled with gold and precious stones. Should occasion
require their visit to the surface of the earth, they accomplish the
business in the night, and not by day. This Hill-people are of flesh
and bone, like mankind, they bear children and die, but in addition to
the ordinary faculties of humanity, they have the power of making

themselves invisible, and of passing through rocks and walls, with the same facility as through the air. They sometimes appear to men, lead them with them into clifts, and if the strangers prove agreeable to them, present them with valuable gifts. [c]

NOTES

[a] Another term is Wicht and its dim. Wichtlein, answering to the Scandinavian Vattr and the Anglo-Saxon *wiht*, English *wight*, all of which signify a being, a person, and also a thing in general. Thus our words *aught* and *naught* were *anwiht* and *nawiht*.

[b] See Grimm's Deutsche Sagen, vol. i. p. 38. As this work is our chief authority for the Fairy Mythology of Germany, our materials are to be considered as taken from it, unless when otherwise expressed.

[c] In Lusatia (Lausatz) if not in the rest of Germany, the same idea of the Dwarfs being fallen angels, prevails as in other countries: see the tale of the Fairies'-sabbath in the work quoted above.

The Hill-Man at the Dance

Old people have positively asserted that some years ago, at the celebration of a wedding in the village of Glass, a couple of miles from the Wunderberg, and the same distance from the city of Saltzburg, there came toward evening a little Hill-man out of the Wunderberg. He desired all the guests to be merry and cheerful, and begged to be permitted to join in their dance, which request was not refused. He accordingly danced three dances with some of the maidens of good repute, and with a gracefulness that inspired all present with admiration and delight. After the dance he returned them his thanks, accompanied by a present to each of the bridal party of three pieces of money of an unknown coin, each of which they estimated to be worth four creutzers. Moreover, he recommended them to dwell in peace and concord, to live like Christians, and, by a pious education, to bring up their children in goodness. He told them to lay up these coins with their money, and constantly to think of him, and so they would rarely come to distress; but warned them against becoming proud, and advised them, on the contrary, to relieve their neighbours with their superfluities.

The Hill-man remained with them till night, and took some meat and drink from each as they offered it to him, but only very little. He then renewed his thanks, and concluded by begging of one of the company to put him over the river Satzach, opposite the mountain. There was at the wedding a boatman, named John Ständl, who got ready to comply with the dwarf's request, and they went together to the water's-edge. As they were crossing, the man asked for his payment, and the Hill-man humbly presented him three-pence. The boatman utterly rejected this paltry payment; but the little man gave him for answer, that he should not let that annoy him, but keep the three-pence safe and he would never suffer want, provided he put a restraint on arrogance. He gave him at the same time, a little stone with these words: "Hang this on your neck, and you will never be drowned in the water." And of this he had a proof that very year. Finally, the Hill-man exhorted him to lead a pious and humble life, and being landed on the opposite bank, departed speedily from the place. [a]

NOTE
[a] This tale is given by MM. Grimm, from the Brixener Volksbuch. 1782.

The Dwarf's Feast

There appeared in the night to one of the Counts von Hoya, an extremely small little man. The count was utterly amazed at him, but he bid him not to be frightened; said he had a request to make of him, and entreated that he might not be refused. The count gave a willing assent, qualified with the provision, that the thing requested should be a matter which lay in his power, and would not be injurious to him or his. The little man then said, "There will come tomorrow night some people to thy house, and make a feast, if thou will lend, them thy kitchen, and hall for as long as they want them, and order thy servants to go to sleep, and no one to look at what they are doing or are about; and also let no one know of it but thyself; only do this and we shall be grateful to thee for thy courtesy: thou and thy family will be the better of it; nor will it be in any way hurtful to thee or thine." The count readily gave his consent, and on the following night there came, as if they were a travelling party, over the bridge into the house a great crowd of little people, exactly such as the Hill-mannikins are described to be. They cooked, cut up wood, and laid out the dishes in the kitchen, and had every appearance of being about preparing a great entertainment.

When it drew near the morning, and they were about to take their departure, the little man came again up to the count, and with many thanks, presented him a sword, a salamander-cloth, and a golden ring, in which there was inserted a red-lion, with directions for himself and his descendants to keep these three articles safe; and so long as they kept them together all would be at unity and well in the county, but as soon as they were separated from each other it would be a token that there was evil coming on the county: the red lion too would always become pale when one of the family was to die.

They were long preserved in the family; but in the time when count Jobst and his brothers were in their minority, and Francis von Halle was governor of the land, two of the articles, the sword and the salamander-cloth, were taken away, but the ring remained with the family until they became extinct. What has become of it since is unknown. [a]

NOTE
[a] Related by Hammelmanm in the Oldenburg Chronicle, by Praetorius Bräuner, and others.

The Friendly Dwarfs

Close to the little town of Dardesheim, between Halberstadt and Brunswick, is a spring of the finest water called the Smansborn, and which flows out of a hill in which in old. times the dwarfs dwelt. When the former inhabitants of the country were in want of a holi-day-dress, or, at a family festival, of any rare utensils, they went and stood before this Dwarf-hill, knocked three times, and pronounced their petition in a distinct and. audible tone, adding,

> Before the sun is up to-morrow.
> At the hill shall be the things we borrow.

The Dwarfs thought themselves sufficiently compensated if there was only some of the festive victuals set down before the hill.

Wedding Feast of the Little People

The little people of the Eilenburg in Saxony had occasion to celebrate a wedding, and. with that intent passed one night through the key-hole and the window-slits into the castle-hall, and jumped down on the smooth level floor like peas on a barn floor. The noise awoke the old count, who was sleeping in the hall in his high four-post bed, and on opening his eyes, he wondered not a little at the sight of such a number of the little fellows.

One of them appareled as a herald came up to him, and addressing him with the utmost courtesy and in very polite terms invited him to share in their festivity. "We, however," added he, "have one request to make, which is, that you alone should be present, and that none of your people should presume to look on with you, or to cast so much as one glance." The old count answered in a friendly tone, "Since you have disturbed my sleep, I will join your company." A little small woman was now introduced to him; little torch-bearers took their places; and cricket-music struck up. The count found great difficulty to keep from losing the little woman in the dance, she jumped away from him so lightly, and at last whirled him about at such a rave that he could with difficulty recover his breath.

But in the very middle of their spritely dance, suddenly all became still, the music ceased, and the whole company hurried to the slits of the doors, mouse-holes, and everywhere else where there was a corner to slip into. The bride-pair, the heralds, and dancers, looked upwards to a hole that was in the ceiling of the hall, and there discovered the face of the old countess, who overflowing with curiosity, was looking down on the joyous assembly. They then bowed themselves before the count, and the person who had invited him stept forward again and thanked him for the hospitality he had shown them: "But," said he, "since our wedding and our festivity has been thus disturbed by another eye gazing on it, your race shall henceforward never count more than seven Eilenburgs." They then pressed out after one another with great speed, and soon all was silent, and the old count alone in the dark ball. The curse has lasted till the present time, and one of six living knights of Eilenburg has always died before the seventh was born. [a]

NOTE

[a] This tale was orally related to MM. Grimm in Saxony. They do not mention the narrator's rank in life.

Smith Riechert

On the east side of the Dwarf-hill of Dardesheim there is a piece of arable land. A smith named Riechert had sown this field with peas; but he observed that when they were just in perfection they were pulled in great quantities. Riechert built himself a little hut on his ground, there to lie in wait for the thief; and there he watched day and night. In the daytime he could see no alteration, but every morning he found that, notwithstanding all his watchfulness, the field had been plundered during the night. Vexed to the heart at seeing that all his labour was in vain, he determined to thresh out on the ground what remained of the peas. So with the daybreak Smith Riechert commenced his work. Hardly was one half of his peas threshed when he heard a piteous wailing, and on going to look for the cause, be found on the ground under the peas one of the dwarfs whose skull he had rapped with his flail, and who was now visible, having lost his mist-cap with the blow. The Dwarf ran back into the hill as fast as his legs could carry him.

However, little tiffs like this disturbed but for a very short time the good understanding of the Dwarf-people and the inhabitants. But the Dwarfs emigrated at last, because the tricks and scoffs of several of the inhabitants were become no longer bearable, as well as their ingratitude for several services they had rendered them. Since that time no one has ever heard or seen anything of the Dwarfs in the neighbourhood.

Dwarfs stealing Corn

'Tis not very long since there were Dwarfs at Jüne near Göttingen, who used to go into the fields and steal the sheaves of corn. This they were able to do the more easily by means of a cap they wore, which made them invisible. They did much injury to one man in particular who had a great deal of corn. At length he hit on a plan to catch them. At noon one day he put a rope round the field, and when the Dwarfs went to creep under it, it knocked off their caps. Being now visible, they were caught. They gave him many fair words, promising if he would take away the rope to give him a peck *(mette)* of money if he came to that same place *before sunrise.* He agreed, but a friend whom he consulted told him to go not at sunrise but a little before twelve at night, as it was at that hour that the day really began. He did as directed, and there he found the Dwarfs, who did not expect him, with the peck of money. The name of the family that got it is Mettens.

A farmer in another part of the country being annoyed in a similar manner, was told to get willow-rods and beat the air with them, and he thus would knock of some of their caps and discover them. He and his people did so, and they captured one of the Dwarfs, who told the farmer that if he would let him go, he would give him a waggon-load of money, but he must come for it before sunrise. At the same time he informed him where his abode was. The farmer having enquired when the sun really rose, and being told at twelve o'clock, yoked his waggon and drove off, but when he came to the Dwarfs' hole, he heard them shouting and singing within:

It is good that the bumpkin doth not know

That up at twelve the sun doth go.

When he asked for something, they showed him a dead horse, and bade him take it with him, as they could give him nothing else. He was very angry at this, but as he wanted food for his dogs, he cut off a large piece and laid it on his waggon. But when he came home, lo! it was all pure gold. Others then went to the place, but both hole and horse had vanished. [a]

NOTE

[a] Grimm, Deut. Mythol., p. 434. Both legends are in the Low-Saxon dialect.

Journey of Dwarfs over the Mountain

On the north side of the Hartz there dwelt several thousand Dwarfs in the clefts of the rocks, and in the Dwarf-caves that still remain. It was, however, but rarely that they appeared to the inhabitants in a visible form; they generally went about among them protected by their mist-caps; unseen and unnoticed.

Many of these Dwarfs were good-natured, and, on particular occasions, very obliging to the inhabitants, who used, for instance, in case of a wedding or a christening, to borrow various articles for the table out of the caves of the Dwarfs, It was, however, highly imprudent to provoke their resentment; as when injured or offended, they were malicious and wicked, and did every possible injury to the offender.

A baker, who lived in the valley between Blenkenburg and Quedlinburg, used to remark that a part of the loaves he baked was always missing, though he never could find out the thief. This continual secret theft was gradually reducing him to poverty. At last he began to suspect the Dwarfs of being the cause of his misfortune. He accordingly got a bunch of little twigs, and beating the air with them in all directions, at length struck the mist-caps off some Dwarfs, who could now conceal themselves no longer. There was a great noise made about it; several other Dwarfs were caught in the act of committing theft, and at last the whole of the Dwarf-people were forced to quit the country. In order, in some degree, to indemnify the inhabitants for what had been stolen, and at the same time to be able to estimate the number of those that departed, a large cask was set up on what is now called Kirchberg, near the village of Thele, into which each Dwarf was to cast a piece of money. This cask was found, after the departure of the Dwarfs, to be quite filled with ancient coins, so great was their number.

The Dwarf-people went by Warnstadt, a village not far from Quedinburg, still going toward the east. Since that time the Dwarfs have disappeared out of this country; and it is only now and then that a solitary one may be seen.

The Dwarfs on the south side of the Hartz were, in a similar manner, detected plundering the corn-fields. They also agreed to quit the country, and. it was settled that they should pass over a small bridge near Neuhof, and that each, by way of transit-duty, should cast a certain portion of his property into a cask to be set there. The peasants, on their part, covenanted not to appear or look at them. Some, however, had the curiosity to conceal themselves under the bridge, that they might at least hear them departing. They succeeded in their design, and heard during several hours, the trampling of the little men, sounding exactly as if a large flock of sheep was going over the bridge.

Other accounts of the departure of the Dwarfs relate as follows:—

The Dosenberg is a mountain in Hesse on the Schwalm, in which, not far from the bank of the stream, are two holes by which the Dwarfs [a] used to go in and out. One of them. came frequently in a friendly way to the grandfather of Tobi in Singlis, when he was out in his fields. As he was one day cutting his corn he asked him if he would the next night, for a good sum of money, take a freight over the river. The farmer agreed, and in the evening the Dwarf brought him a sack of wheat as an earnest. Four horses were then put to the waggon, and the farmer drove to the Dosenberg, out of the holes of which the Dwarf brought heavy, but invisible loads to the waggon, which the farmer then drove through the water over to the other side. He thus kept going backwards and forwards from ten at night till four in the morning, by which time the horses were quite tired. Then said the Dwarf; "It is enough, now you shall see what you have been carrying!" He bade him look over his right shoulder, and then he saw the country far and near filled with the Dwarfs. "These thousand years," then said the Dwarf, "have we dwelt in the Dosenberg; our time is now up, and we must go to another land. But the hill is still so full of money that it would suffice for the whole country." He then loaded Tobi's waggon with money and departed. The farmer had difficulty in bringing home so heavy a load, but he became a rich man. His posterity are still wealthy people, but the Dwarfs have disappeared out of the country for ever.

At Offensen on the Aller in Lower Saxony, lived a great farmer, whose name was Hövermann. He had a boat on the river; and one day two little people came to him and asked him to put them over the water. They went twice over the Aller to a great tract of land that is called. the Allerô, which is an uncultivated plain extending so wide and far that one can hardly see over it. When the farmer had crossed the second time one of the Dwarfs said to him, "Will you have now a sum of money or so much a head?" "I'd rather have a sum of money," said the farmer. One of them took off his hat and put it on the farmer's head, and said, "You'd have done better to have taken so much a head." The farmer, who had as yet seen nothing and whose boat had gone as if there was nothing in it, now beheld the whole Allerô swarming *(krimmeln un wimmeln)* with little men. These were the Dwarfs that he had brought over. From that time forward the Hövermanns had the greatest plenty of money, but they are all now dead and gone, and the place is sold. But when was this? Oh! in the old time when the Dwarfs were in the world, but now there 's no more of them, thirty or forty years ago. [b]

NOTES
[a] The terms used in the original are *Wichtelmänner, Wichtelmännerchen,* and *Wichtel.*
[b] Grimm, Deut. Mythol, p. 428. The latter story is in the Low-Saxon dialect.

The Dwarfs borrowing Bread

Albert Steffel, aged seventy years, who died in the year 1680, and Hans Kohmann, aged thirty-six, who died in 1679, two honest, veracious men, frequently declared that as one time Kohmann's grandfather was working in his ground which lay in the neighbourhood of the place called the Dwarfs' hole, and his wife had brought out to the field to him for his breakfast some fresh baked bread, and had laid it, tied up in a napkin, at the end of the field, there came up soon after a little Dwarf-woman, who spoke to him about his bread, saying, that her own was in the oven, and that her children were hungry and could not wait for it, but that if he would give her his, she would be certain to replace it by noon. The man consented, and at noon she returned, spread out a very white little cloth, and laid on it a smoking hot loaf, and with many thanks and entreaties told him he might eat the bread without any apprehension, and that she would return for the cloth. He did as she desired, and when she returned she told him that there had been so many forges erected that she was quite annoyed, and would be obliged to depart and abandon her favourite dwelling. She also said that the shocking cursing and swearing of the people drove her away, as also the profanation of Sunday, as the country people, instead of going to church, used to go look at their fields, which was altogether sinful. [a]

NOTE

[a] In Scandinavia the Dwarfs used to borrow beer, even a barrel at a time, which one of them would carry off on his shoulders, Thiele i. 121. In the Highlands of Scotland, a firlot of meal. In all cases they paid honestly. On one occasion, a dwarf came to a lady named Fru *(Mrs.)* Mettè of Overgaard, in Jutland, and asked her to lend her silk gown to Fru Mettè of Undergaard, for her wedding. She gave it, but as it was not returned as soon as she expected, she went to the hill and demanded it aloud. The hill-man brought it out to her all spotted with wax, and told her that if she had not been so impatient. every spot on it would have been a diamend. Thiele iii. 48.

The Vends of Lüneburg, we are told, called the underground folk Görzoni (from *gora,* hill), and the hills are still shown in which they dwelt. They used to borrow bread from people; they intimated their desire invisibly, and people used to lay it for them outside of the door. In the evening they returned it, knocking at the window, and leaving an additional cake to express their thankfulness, Grimm, Deut, Mythol., p. 423.

The Changeling

It was the belief, in some parts of Germany, that if a child that was not thriving were taken to a place named Cyriac's Mead, near Neuhausen, and left lying there and given to drink out of Cyriac's Well, at the end of nine days it would either die or recover.

The butler and cook of one of the spiritual lords of Germany, without being married, had a child, which kept crying day and night, and evermore craving for food and yet it never grew nor throve. It was finally resolved to try on it the effect of Cyriac's Mead, and the mother set out for that place with the child on her back, whose weight was so great that she hardly could endure it. As she was toiling along under her burden, she met a travelling student, who said to her, "My good woman, what sort of a wild creature is that you are carrying? I should not wonder if it were to crush in your neck." She replied that it was her dear child which would not grow nor thrive, and that she was taking it to Neuhausen to be rocked. "But," said he, "that is not your child; it is the devil. Fling it into the stream." But she refused, and maintained that it *was* her child, and kissed it. Then said he, "Your child is at home in the inner bedroom in a new cradle behind the ark. Throw, I tell you, this monster into the stream." With many tears and, groans the poor woman at length did as he required and immediately there was heard under the bridge on which they were standing a howling and a growling as if wolves and bears were in the place. When the woman reached home she found her own child healthy and lively and laughing in its new cradle.

A Hessian legend tells that as a woman was reaping corn at the Dosenberg, with her little child lying near her on the ground, a Dwarf-woman *(wichtelweib)* came and took it and left her own lying in its stead. When the mother came to look after her dear babe a great ugly jolterhead was there gaping at her. She cried out and roared Murder! so lustily that the thief came back with the child. But she did not restore it till the mother had put the changeling to her breast and given it some ennobling human milk. [a]

There was, it is said, in Prussian Samland, an inn-keeper whom the underground folk had done many good turns. It grieved him to see what bad clothes they had, and he desired his wife to leave new little coats for them. They took the new clothes, but cried out, "Paid off! Paid off!" and went all away.

Another time they gave great help to a poor smith, and every night they made bran-new pots, pans, kettles and plates for him. His wife used to leave some milk for them, on which they fell like wolves, and drained the vessel to the bottom, and then cleaned it and went to their work. When the smith had. grown rich by means of them, his wife made for each of them a pretty httle red coat and cap, and left them in their way. "Paid off! Paid off!" cried they, slipped on the new clothes, and went away without working the iron that was left for them, and never returned.

There was a being named a Scrat or Schrat, Schretel, Schretlein. [b] This name is used in old German to translate *pilosus* in the narratives of those who wrote in Latin, and it seems sometimes to denote a House- sometimes a Wood-spirit. Terms similar to it are to be found in the cognate languages, and it is perhaps the origin of Old Scratch, a popular English name of the devil.

There is, chiefly in Southern Germany, a species of beings that greatly resemble the Dwarfs. They are called Wichtlein *(Little Wights)*, and are about three quarters of an ell high. Their appearance is that of old men with long beards. They haunt the mines, and are dressed like miners, with a white hood to their shirts and leather aprons, and are provided with lanterns, mallets, and hammers. They amuse themselves with pelting the workmen with small stones, but do them no injury, except when they are abused and cursed by them.

They show themselves most especially in places where there is an abundance of ore, and the miners are always glad to see them; they flit about in the pits and shafts, and appear to work very hard, though they in reality do nothing. Sometimes they seem as if working a vein, at other times putting the ore into buckets, at other times working at the windlass, but all is mere show. They frequently call, and when one comes there is no one to be seen.

At Kuttenburg, in Bohemia, the Wichtlein have been seen in great numbers. They announce the death of a miner by knocking three times, and when any misfortune is about to happen they are heard digging, pounding, and imitating all other kinds of work. At times they make a noise, as if they were smiths labouring very hard at the anvil, hence the Bohemians call them Haus-Schmiedlein *(Little House-Smiths)*.

In Istria the miners set, every day, in a particular place, a little pot with food in it for them. They also at certain times in each year buy a little red coat, the size of a small boy's, and make the Wichtlein a present of it. If they neglect this, the little people grow very angry. [c]

In Southern Germany they believe in a species of beings somewhat like the Dwarfs, called Wild, Wood, Timber, and Moss-people. These generally live together in society, but they sometimes appear singly. They are small in stature, yet somewhat larger than the Elf, being the size of children of three years, grey and old-looking, hairy and clad in moss. The women are of a more amiable temper than the men, which last live further back in the woods; they wear green clothes faced with red, and cocked-hats. The women come to the wood-cutters and ask them for something to eat; they also take it away of themselves out of the pots; but they always make a return in some way or other, often by giving good advice. Sometimes they help people in their cooking or washing and haymaking, and they feed the cattle. They are fond of coming where people are baking, and beg of them to bake for them also a piece of dough the size of half a mill-stone, and to leave it in a certain place. They sometimes, in return, bring some of their own baking to the ploughman, which they lay in the furrow or on the plough, and they are greatly offended if it is rejected. The wood-woman sometimes comes with a broken wheel-barrow, and begs to have the wheel repaired, and she pays by the chips which turn into gold, or she gives to knitters a ball of thread which is never ended. A woman who good-naturedly gave her breast to a crying Wood-child, was rewarded by its mother by a gift of the bark on which it was lying. She broke a splinter off it and threw it into her faggot, and on reaching home she found it was pure gold. Their lives are attached, like those of the Hamadryads, to the trees, and if any one causes by friction the inner bark to loosen a Wood-woman dies.

Their great enemy is the Wild-Huntsman, who driving invisibly through the air pursues and kills them. A peasant one time hearing the usual baying and cheering in a wood, would join in the cry. Next morning he found hanging at his stable-door a quarter of a green Moss-woman as his share of the game. When the woodmen are felling timber they cut three crosses in a spot of the tree that is to be hewn, and the Moss-women sit in the middle of these and so are safe from the Wild-Huntsman. [d]

The following account of the popular belief in the parts of Germany adjacent to Jutland has been given by a late writer. [e]

In Friesland the Dwarfs are named Oennereeske, in some of the islands Oennerbänske, and in Holstein Unnerorske. [f] The same stories are told of them as of the Dwarfs and Fairies elsewhere. They take away, and keep for long periods, girls with whom they have fallen in love; they steal children and leave changelings in their stead, the remedy against which is to lay a bible under the child's pillow; they lend and borrow pots, plates, and such like, sometimes lending money with or even without interest; they aid to build houses and churches; help the peasant when his cart has stuck in the mire, and will bring him water and pancakes to refresh him when at work in the fields.

NOTES

[a] Grimm, Dent. Mythol., p. 437.

[b] See Grimm, *utt sup., p.* 447 *seq.*

[c] Deutsche Sagen, from Praetorius., Agricola, and others.

[d] Grimm, Deut. Mythol., pp. 451, 881.

[e] Kohl, Die Marschen und Inseln der Herzogthûmer Schleswig und Holstein.

[f] These terms all signify *Underground folk.*

The Dwarf-Husband

A poor girl went out one day and as she was passing by a hill she heard a Dwarf hammering away inside of it, for they are handy smiths, and singing at his work. She was so pleased with the song, that she could not refrain from wishing aloud that she could sing like him, and live like him under the round. Scarcely had she expressed the wish when the singing ceased, and a voice came out of the hill, saying, "Should you like to live with us?"' "To be sure I should," replied the girl, who probably had no very happy life of it above ground. Instantly the Dwarf came out of the hill and made a declaration of love, and a proffer of his hand and a share in his subterranean wealth. She accepted the offer and lived very comfortably with him, as he proved an excellent little husband.

Inge of Rantum

The Friesland girls are, however, rather shy of these matches, and if they have unwarily been drawn into an engagement they try to get out of it if they possibly can.

A girl named Inge of Rantum had some way or other got into an engagement with one of the Underground people. The wedding-day was actually fixed, and she could only be released from her bond on one condition—that of being able, before it came, to tell the real name of her lover. All her efforts to that effect were in vain, the dreaded day was fast approaching and she fell into deep melancholy. On the morning of her wedding-day she went out and strolled in sorrowful mood through the fields, saying to herself as she plucked some flowers, "Far happier are these flowers than I." As she was stooping to gather them, she thought she heard a noise under the ground. She listened and recognised it as the voice of her lover, who, in the excess of his joy at the arrival of his wedding-day, was frolicking and singing, "To-day I must bake and boil and roast and broil and wash and brew; for this is my wedding-day. My bride is the fair Inge of Rantum, and my name is Ekke Nekkepem. Hurrah! Nobody knows *that* but myself!" "Aye, but *I* know it too!" said Inge softly to herself and she placed her nosegay in her bosom and went home. Toward evening came the Dwarf to claim his bride. "Many thanks, dear Ekke Nekkepem," said she, "but if you please I would rather stay where I am." The smiling face of the bridegroom grew dark as thunder, but he recollected how he had divulged his secret, and saw that the affair was past remedy.

The Nis of Sutland is called Puk [a] in Friesland. Like him he wears a pointed red cap, with a long grey or green jacket, and slippers on his feet. His usual abode is under the roof, and he goes in and out either through a broken window, which is never mended, or through some other aperture left on purpose for him. A bowl of groute must be left on the floor for him every evening, and he is very angry if there should be no butter in it. When well treated he makes himself very useful by cleaning up the house, and tending the cattle. He sometimes amuses himself by playing tricks on the servants, tickling, for example, their noses when they are asleep, or pulling off the bedclothes. Stories are told of the Puk, similar to some above related of the Juttish Nis.

NOTE

[a] The Puk is also called Niss-Puk, Huis-Puk, Niske, Niske-Puk, Nise-Bok, Niss-Kuk——all compounds or corruptions of Nisse and Puk. He is also named from his racketing and noise Pulter-Clsss, *i. e.* Nick Knocker, (the German Poltergeist,) Class being the abbreviation of Nicolaus, Niclas.

The Wild-Women

Ein Mägdlein kam tin Abendglanz,
Wie ich's noch me gefunden.
—SCHRIEBER.

A maiden came in Evening's glow,
Such as I ne'er have met.

The Wilde Frauen or Wild-women of Germany bear a very strong resemblance to the Elle-maids of Scandinavia. Like them they are beautiful, have fine flowing hair, live within hills, and only appear singly or in the society of each other. They partake of the piety of character we find among the German Dwarfs.

The celebrated Wunderberg, or Underberg, on the great moor near Salzburg, is the chief haunt of the Wild-women. The Wunderberg is said to be quite hollow, and supplied with stately palaces, churches, monasteries, gardens, and springs of gold and silver. Its inhabitants, beside the Wild-women, are little men, who have charge of the treasures it contains, and who at midnight repair to Salzburg to perform their devotions in the cathedral; giants, who used to come to the church of Grödich and exhort the people to lead a godly and pious life; and the great emperor Charles V., with golden crown and sceptre, attended by knights and lords. His grey beard has twice encompassed the table at which he sits, and when it has the third time grown round it, the end of the world and the appearance of the Antichrist will take place. [a]

The following is the only account we have of the Wild-women.

The inhabitants of the village of Grödich and the peasantry of

333

the neighbourhood assert that frequently, about the year 1753, the Wild-women used to come out of the Wunderberg to the boys and girls that were keeping the cattle near the hole within Glanegg, and give them bread to eat.

The Wild-women used frequently to come to where the people were reaping. They came down early in the morning, and in the evening, when the people left off work, they went back into the Wunderberg without partaking of the supper.

It happened once near this hill, that a little boy was sitting on a horse which his father had tethered on the headland of the field. Then came the Wild-women out of the hill and wanted to take away the boy by force. But the father, who was well acquainted with the secrets of this hill, and what used to occur there, without any dread hasted up to the women and took the boy from them, with these words': "What makes you presume to come so often out of the hill, and now to take away my child with you? What do you want to do with him?" The Wild-women answered:

"He will be better with us, and have better care taken of him than at home. We shall be very fond of the boy, and he will meet with no injury." But the father would not let the boy out of his hands, and the Wild-women went away weeping bitterly.

One time the Wild-women came out of the Wunderberg, near the place called the Kugelmill, which is prettily situated on the side of this hill, and took away a boy who was keeping cattle. This boy, whom every one knew, was seen about a year after by some wood-cutters, in a green dress, and sitting on a block of this hill. Next day they took his parents with them, intending to search the hill for him, but they all went about it to no purpose, for the boy never appeared any more.

It frequently has happened that a Wild-woman out of the Wunderberg has gone toward the village of Anif, which is better than a mile from the hill. She used to make holes and beds for herself in the ground. She had uncommonly long and beautiful hair, which reached nearly to the soles of her feet. A peasant belonging to the village often saw this woman going and coming, and he fell deeply in love with he; especially on account of her beautiful hair. He could not refrain from going up to he; and he gazed on her with delight; and at last, in his simplicity, he laid himself without any repugnance, down by her side. The second night the Wild-woman asked him if he had not a wife already? The peasant however denied his wife, and said he had not.

His wife meanwhile was greatly puzzled to think where it was that her husband went every evening, and slept every night. She therefore watched him and found him in the field sleeping near the Wild-woman:—"Oh, God preserve thy beautiful hair!" said she to the Wild-woman; "what are you doing there?" [b] With these words the peasant's wife retired and left them, and her husband was greatly frightened at it. But the Wild-woman upbraided him with his false denial, and said to him, "Had your wife manifested hatred and spite against me, you would now be unfortunate, and would never leave this place; but since your wife was not malicious, love her from henceforth, and dwell with her faithfully, and never venture more to come here, for it is written, 'Let every one live faithfully with his wedded wife;' though the force of this commandment will greatly decrease, and with it all the temporal prosperity of married people. Take this shoefull of money from me: go home, and look no more about you."

As the fair maiden who originally possessed the famed Old-enburg Horn was probably a Wild-woman, we will place the story of it here.

NOTES
[a] All relating to the Wild-women and the Wunderberg is given by MM. Grimm from the Brixener Volksbuch, 1782. For an account of the various *Bergentrückte Helden,* see the Deutsche Mythologie, ch. xxxii.
[b] In a similar tradition (Strack, Beschr. von Eilsen, p. 120) the wife cuts off one of her fair long tresses, and is afterwards most earnestly conjured by her to restore it.

336

The Oldenburg Horn

In the time of count Otto of Oldenburg, who succeeded his father Ulrich in the year 967, a wonderful transaction occurred. For as he, being a good sportsman, and one who took great delight in the chase, had set out early one day with his nobles and attendants, and had hunted in the wood of Bernefeuer, and. the count himself had put up a roe, and followed him alone from the wood of Bernefeuer to the Osenberg, and with his white horse stood on the top of the hill, and endeavoured to trace the game, be said to himself for it was an excessively hot day, "Oh God! if one had now but a cool drink!"

No sooner had the count spoken the word than the Osenberg opened, and out of the cleft there came a beautiful maiden, fairly adorned and handsomely dressed, and with her beautiful hair divided on her shoulders, and a garland on her head. And she had a rich silver vessel, that was gilded and shaped like a hunter's horn, well and ingeniously made, granulated, and fairly ornamented. It was adorned with various kinds of arms that are now but little known, and with strange unknown inscriptions and ingenious figures, and it was soldered together and adorned in the same manner as the old antiques, and it was beautifully and ingeniously wrought. This horn the maiden held in her hand, and it was full, and she gave it into the hand of the count, and prayed that the count would drink out of it to refresh himself therewith.

When the count had received and taken this gilded silver horn from the maiden, and had opened it and looked into it, the drink, or whatever it was that was in it, when he shook it, did not please him, and he therefore refused to drink for the maiden. Whereupon the maiden said, "My dear lord, drink of it upon my faith, for it will do you no harm, but will be of advantage;" adding farther, that if the count would drink out of it, it would go well with him, count Otto, and his, and also with the whole house of Oldenburg after him, and that the whole country would improve and flourish. But if the count would place no faith in her, and would not drink of it, then for the future, in the succeeding family of Oldenburg, there would remain no unity. But when the count gave no heed to what she said, but, as was not without reason, considered with himself a long time whether be should drink or not, he held the silver gilded horn in his hand and swung it behind him, and poured it out, and some of its contents sprinkled the white horse, and where it fell and wetted him the hair all came off.

When the maiden saw this, she desired to have her horn back again, but the count made speed down the hill with the horn, which he held in his hand, and when be looked round he observed that the maiden was gone into the hill again. And when terror seized on the count on account of this, he laid spurs to his horse, and at full speed hasted to join his attendants, and informed them of what had befallen him. He moreover showed them the silver gilded horn, and took it with him to Oldenburg, and the same horn, as it was obtained in so wonderful a manner, was preserved as a costly jewel by him, and by all the succeeding reigning princes of the house of Oldenburg. [a]

NOTE

[a] Given by Büsching (Volks-sagen Märchen und Legenden. Leipzig, 1820), from Hammelmann's Oldenburg Chronicle, *1599*. Mme. Naubert has, in the second volume of her Volksmärchen, wrought it up into a tale of 130 pages.
The Oldenburg horn, or what is called such, is now in the King of Denmark's collection.

THE KOBOLDS [a]

Von Kobolt sang die Amme mir
Von Kobolt sing' ich winder.
   –VON HALEM.

Of Kobold sang my nurse to me;
   Of Kobold I too sing.

The Kobold is exactly the same being as the Danish Nis, and Scottish Brownie, and English Hobgoblin. [b] He performs the very same services for the family to whom he attaches himself.

When the Kobold is about coming into any place, he first makes trial of the disposition of the family in this way. He brings chips and saw-dust into the house, and throws dirt into the milk vessels. If the master of the house takes care that the chips are not scattered about, and that the dirt is left in the vessels, and the milk drunk out of them, the Kobold comes and stays in the house as long as there is one of the family alive.

The change of servants does not affect the Kobold, who still remains. The maid who is going away must recommend her successor to take care of him, and treat him well. If she does not so, things go ill with her till she is also obliged to leave the place.

The history of the celebrated Hinzelmann will give most full and satisfactory information respecting the nature and properties of Kobolds; for such he was, though he used constantly to deny it. His history was written at considerable length by a pious minister, named Feldmann. MM. Grimm gives us the following abridgement of it. [c]

_____

NOTES

[a] This word is usually derived from the Greek κόβαλος, a knave, which is found in Aristophanes. According to Grimm (p. 468) the German Kobold is not mentioned by any writer anterior to the thirteenth century; we find the French Gobelin in the eleventh; see *France*.

[b] In Hanover the Will-o'the-wisp is called the Tückebold, s. e. Tücke-Kobold, and is, as his name denotes, a malicious being. Voss. Lyr. Ged., ii. p. 315.

[c] Deutsche Sagen, i. p. 103. Feldmann's work is a l2mo vol. of 379 pages.

Hinzelmann [a]

A wonderful house-spirit haunted for a long time the old castle of Hudemühlen, situated in the country of Lüneburg, not far from the Aller, and of which there is nothing remaining but the walls. It was in the year 1584 that he first notified his presence, by knocking and making various noises. Soon after he began to converse with the servants in the daylight. They were at first terrified at hearing a voice and seeing nothing, but by degrees they became accustomed to it and thought no more of it. At last he became quite courageous, and began to speak to the master of the house himself; and used, in the middle of the day and in the evening, to carry on conversations of various kinds; and at meal-times he discoursed. with those who were present, whether strangers or belonging to the family. When all fear of him was gone he became quite friendly and intimate: he sang, laughed, and went on with every kind of sport, so long as no one vexed him: and his voice was on these occasions soft and tender like that of a boy or maiden. When he was asked whence he came, and what he had to do in that place, he said he was come from the Bohemian mountains, and that his companions were in the Bohemian forest—that they would not tolerate him, and that he was in consequence obliged to retire and take refuge with good people till his affairs should be in a better condition. He added that his name was Hinzelmann, but that he was also called Lüring; and that be had a wife whose name was Hille Bingels. When the time for it was come he would let himself he seen in his real shape, but that at present it was not convenient for him to do so. In all other respects he was, he said, as good and honest a fellow as need be.

The master of the house, when he saw that the spirit attached himself more and more to him, began to get frightened, and knew not how he should get rid of him. By the advice of his friends he determined at last to leave his castle for some time, and set out for Hanover. On the road they observed a white feather that flew beside the carriage, but no one knew what it signified. When he arrived at Hanover he missed a valuable gold chain that he wore about his neck, and his suspicions fell upon the servants of the house. But the innkeeper took the part of his servants, and demanded satisfaction for the discreditable charge. The nobleman, who could prove nothing against them, sat in his chamber in bad spirits, thinking how be should manage to get himself out of this unpleasant affair, when all of a sudden he heard Hinzelmann's voice beside him, saying, "Why are you so sad? If there is anything gone wrong with you tell it to me, and I shall perhaps know bow to assist you. If I were to make a guess, I should say that you are fretting on account of a chain you have lost." "What are you doing here?" replied the terrified nobleman; "why have you followed me? Do you know anything about the chain?" "Yes, indeed," said Hinzelmann, "I have followed you, and I kept you company on the road, and was always present: did you not see me? why, I was the white feather that flew beside the carriage. And now I 'll tell you where the chain is:—Search under the pillow of your bed, and there you 'll find it." The chain was found where he said; but the mind of the nobleman became still more uneasy, and he asked him in an angry tone why be had brought him into a quarrel with the landlord on account of the chain, since he was the cause of his leaving his own house. Hinzelmann replied, "Why do you retire from me? I can easily follow you anywhere, and be where you are. It is much better for you to return to your own estate, and not be quitting it on my account. You see well that if I wished it I could take away all you have, but I am not inclined to do so." The nobleman thought some time of it, and at last came to the resolution of returning home, and trusting in God not to retreat a step from the spirit.

At home in Hudemühlen, Hinzelmann now showed himself extremely obliging, and active and industrious at every kind of work. He used to toil every night in the kitchen; and if the cook, in the evening after supper, left the plates and dishes lying in a heap without being washed, next morning they were all nice and clean, shining like lookingglasses, and put up in proper order. She therefore might depend upon him, and go to bed in the evening after supper without giving herself any concern about them. In like manner nothing was ever lost in the kitchen; and if anything was astray Hinzelmann knew immediately where to find it, in whatever corner it was hid, and gave it into the hands of the owner. If strangers were expected, the spirit let himself be heard in a particular manner, and his labours were continued the whole night long: he scoured the pots and kettles, washed the dishes, cleaned the pails and tubs. The cook was grateful to him for all this, and not only did what he desired, but cheerfully got ready his sweet milk for his breakfast. He took also the charge of superintending the other men and maids. He noticed how they got through their business; and when they were at work he encouraged them with good words to be industrious. But if any one was inattentive to what he said, he caught up a stick and communicated his instructions by laying on heartily with it. He frequently warned the maids of their mistress's displeasure, and reminded them of some piece of work which they should set about doing. He was equally busy in the stable: he attended to the horses, and curried them carefully, so that they were as smooth in their coats as an eel; they also throve and improved so much, in next to no time, that everybody wondered at it.

His chamber was in the upper story on the right hand side, and his furniture consisted of only three articles. Imprimis, of a settle or arm-chair, which he plaited very neatly for himself of straw af different colours, full of handsome figures and crosses, which no one looked upon without admiration. Secondly, of a little round table, which was on his repeated entreaties made and put there. Thirdly, of a bed and bedstead, which he had also expressed a wish for. There never was any trace found as if a man had lain in it; there could only be perceived a very small depression, as if a cat had been there. The servants, especially the cook, were obliged every day to prepare a dish full of sweet milk, with crums of wheaten bread, and place it upon his little table; and it was soon after eaten up clean. He sometimes used to come to the table of the master of the house, and they were obliged to put a chair and a plate for him at a particular place. Whoever was helping, put his food on his plate, and if that was forgotten he fell into a great passion. What was put on his plate vanished, and a glass full of wine was taken away for some time, and was then set again in its place empty. But the food was afterwards found lying under the benches, or in a corner of the room.

In the society of young people Hinzelmann was extremely

cheerful. He sang and made verses: one of his most usual ones was,

> If thou here wilt let me stay,
> Good luck shalt thou have alway;
> But if hence thou wilt me chase,
> Luck will ne'er come near the place.

He used also to repeat the songs and sayings of other people by way of amusement or to attract their attention. The minister Feldmann was once invited to Hudemühlen, and when he came to the door he heard some one above in the hall singing, shouting, and making every sort of noise, which made him think that some strangers had come the evening before, and were lodged above, and making themselves merry. He therefore said to the steward, who was standing in the court after having cut up some wood, "John, what guests have you above there?" The steward answered, "We have no strangers;. it is only our Hinzelmann who is amusing himself; there is not a living soul else in the hall." When the minister went up into the hall, Hinzelmann sang out to him

> My thumb, my thumb,
> And my elbow are two.

The minister wondered at this unusual kind. ef song, and he said to Hinzelmann, "What sort of music is that you come to meet me with?" "Why," replied Hinzehnann, "it was from yourself l learned the song, for you have often sing it, and it is only a few days since l heard it from you, when you were in a certain place at a christening."

Hinzelmann was fond of playing tricks, but he never hurt any one by them. He used to set servants and workmen by the ears as they sat drinking in the evening, and took great delight then in looking at the sport. When any one of them was well warmed with liquor, and let anything fall under the table and stooped to take it up, Hinzelmann would give him a good box on the ear from behind, and at the same time pinch his neighbour's leg. Then the two attacked each other, first with words and then with blows; the rest joined in the scuffle, and they dealt about their blows, and were repaid in kind; and next morning black eyes and swelled faces bore testimony of the fray. But Hinzelmann's very heart was delighted at it, and he used afterwards to tell how it was he that began it, on purpose to set them fighting. He however always took care so to order matters that no one should run any risk of his life.

There came one time to Hudemühlen a nobleman who undertook to banish Hinzelmann. Accordingly, when he remarked that he was in a certain room, of which all the doors and windows were shut fast, he had this chamber and the whole house also beset with armed men, and went himself with his drawn sword into the room, accompanied by some others. They however saw nothing, so they began to cut and thrust left and right in all directions, thinking that if Hinzelmann had a body some blow or other must certainly reach him and kill him; still they could not perceive that their hangers met anything but mere air. When they thought they must have accomplished their task, and were going out of the room tired with their long fencing, just as they opened the door, they saw a figure like that of a black marten, and heard these words, "Ha, ha! how well you caught me!" But Hinzelmann afterwards expressed himself very bitterly for this insult, and declared, that he would have easily had an opportunity of revenging himself, were it not that he wished to spare the two ladies of the house any uneasiness. When this same nobleman not long after went into an empty room in the house, he saw a large snake lying coiled up on an unoccupied bed. It instantly vanished, and he heard the words of the spirit—"You were near catching me."

Another nobleman had heard a great deal about Hinzelmann, and he was curious to get some personal knowledge of him. He came accordingly to Hudemühlen, and his wish was not long ungratified, for the spirit let himself be heard from a corner of the room where there was a large cupboard, in which were standing some empty wine-jugs with long necks. As the voice was soft and delicate, and somewhat hoarse, as if it came out of a hollow vessel, the nobleman thought it likely that he was sitting in one of these jugs, so he got up and ran and caught them up, and went to stop them, thinking in this way to catch the spirit. While he was thus engaged, Hinzelmann began to laugh aloud, and cried out, "If I had not heard long ago from other people that you were a fool, I might now have known it of myself; since you thought I was sitting in an empty jug, and went to cover it up with your hand, as if you had me caught. I don't think you worth the trouble, or I would have given you, long since, such a lesson, that you should remember me long enough. But before long you will get a slight ducking." He then became silent, and did not let himself be heard any more so long as the nobleman stayed. Whether he fell into the water, as Hinzelmann threatened him, is not said, but it is probable he did.

There came, too, an exorcist to banish him. When he began his conjuration with his magic words, Hinzelmann was at first quite quiet, and did not let himself be heard at all, but when he was going to read the most powerful sentences against him, he snatched the book out of his hand, tore it to pieces, so that the leaves flew about the room, caught hold of the exorcist himself, and squeezed and scratched him till he ran away frightened out of his wits. He complained greatly of this treatment, and said, "I am a Christian, like any other man, and I hope to be saved." When he was asked if he knew the Kobolds and Knocking-spirits *(Polter Geister),* he answered, "What have these to do with me? They are the Devil's spectres, and I do not belong to them. No one has any evil, but rather good, to expect from me. Let me alone and you will have luck in everything; the cattle will thrive, your substance will increase, and everything will go on well."

Profligacy and vice were quite displeasing to him; he used frequently to scold severely one of the family for his stinginess, and told the rest that he could not endure him on account of it. Another he upbraided with his pride, which he said he hated from his heart. When some one once said to him that if he would be a good Christian, he should call upon God, and say Christian prayers, he began the Lord's Prayer, and went through it till he came to the last petition, when he murmured "Deliver us from the Evil one" quite low. He also repeated the Creed, but in a broken and stammering manner, for when he came to the words, "I believe in the forgiveness of sins, the resurrection of the body, and life everlasting," he pronounced them in so hoarse and indistinct a voice that no one could rightly hear and understand him. The minister of Eicheloke, Mr. Feldmann, said that his father was invited to dinner to Hudemühlen at Whitsuntide, where he heard Hinzelmann go through the whole of the beautiful hymn, *"Nun bitten wir den heiligen Geist,"* in a very high but not unpleasant voice, like that of a girl or a young boy. Nay, he sang not merely this, but several other spiritual songs also when requested, especially by those whom he regarded as his friends, and with whom he was on terms of intimacy.

On the other hand, he was extremely angry when he was not treated with respect and as a Christian. A nobleman of the family of Mandelsloh once came to Hudemühlen. This nobleman was highly respected for his learning; he was a canon of the cathedral of Verden, and had been ambassador to the Elector of Brandenburg and the King of Denmark. When he heard of the house-spirit, and that he expected to be treated as a Christian, he said he could not believe that all was right with him: he was far more inclined to regard him as the Enemy and the Devil, for that God had never made men of that kind and form, that angels praised God their Lord, and guarded and protected men, with which the knocking and pounding and strange proceedings of the House-spirit did not accord. Hinzelmann, who had not let himself be heard since his arrival, now made a noise and cried out, "What say you Barthold? (that was the nobleman's name) am I the Enemy? I advise you not to say too much, or I will show you another trick, and teach you to deliver a better judgment of me another time." The nobleman was frightened when he heard a voice without seeing any one, broke off the discourse, and would hear nothing more of him, but left him in possession of his dignity.

Another time a nobleman came there, who, when he saw a chair and plate laid for Hinzelmann at dinner, refused to pledge him. At this the spirit was offended, and he said, "I am as honest and good a fellow as he is; why then does he not drink to me?" To this the nobleman replied, "Depart hence, and go drink with thy infernal companions; thou hast nothing to do here." When Hinzelmann heard that, he became so highly exasperated, that he seized him by the strap with which, according to the custom of those days, his cloak was fastened under his chin, dragged him to the ground. and choked and pressed him in such a manner that all that were present were in pain lest he should kill him; and the gentleman did not come to himself for some hours after the spirit had left him.

Another time an esteemed friend of the master of Hudemühlen was travelling that way, but he hesitated to come in on account of the House-spirit, of whose mischievous turn he had heard a great deal, and sent his servant to inform the family that he could not call upon them. The master of the house sent out and pressed him very much to come in and dine there, but the stranger politely excused himself, by saying that it was not in his power to stop; he, however, added, that he was too much terrified at the idea of sitting at the same table eating and drinking with a devil. Hinzelmann, it appears, was present at this conversation out in the road; for when the stranger had thus refused they heard these words, "Wait, my good fellow, you shall be well paid for this talk." Accordingly, when the traveller went on and came to the bridge over the Meisse, the horses took fright, entangled themselves in the harness, and horses, carriage and all, were within an ace of tumbling down into the water. When everything had been set to rights, and the carriage had got on about a gun-shot, it was turned over in the sand on the level ground, without, however, those who were in it receiving any farther injury.

Hinzelmann was fond of society, but the society he chiefly delighted in was that of females, and he was to them very friendly and affable. There were two young ladies at Hudemühlen, named Anne and Catherine, to whom he was particularly attached; he used to make his complaint to them whenever he was angry at anything, and held, besides, conversations of every kind with them. Whenever they travelled he would not quit them, but accompanied them everywhere in the shape of a white feather. When they went to sleep at night, he lay beneath, at their feet, outside the clothes, and in the morning there was a little hole to be seen, as if a little dog had lain there.

Neither of these ladies ever married; for Hinzelmann frightened away their wooers. Matters had frequently gone so far as the engagement, but the spirit always contrived to have it broken off. One lover he would make all bewildered and confused when he was about to address the lady, so that he did not know what he should say. In another he would excite such fear as to make him quiver and tremble. But his usual way was to make a writing appear before their eyes on the opposite white wall, with these words in golden letters: "Take maid Anne, and leave me maid Catherine." But if any one came to court lady Anne, the golden writing changed all at once, and became "Take maid Catherine, and leave me maid Anne." If anyone did not change his course for this, but persisted in his purpose, and happened to spend the night in the house, he terrified and tormented him so in the dark with knocking and flinging and pounding, that he laid aside all wedding-thoughts, and was right glad to get away with a whole skin. Some, when they were on their way back, he tumbled, themselves and their horses, over and over, that they thought their necks and legs would be broken, and yet knew not how it had happened to them. In consequence of this, the two ladies remained unmarried; they arrived to a great age, and died within a week of each other.

One of these ladies once sent a servant from Hudemühlen to Rethem to buy different articles; while he was away Hinzelmann began suddenly to clapper in the ladies' chamber like a stork, and then said, "Maid Anne, you must go look for your things to-day in the mill-stream." She did not know what this meant; but the servant soon came in, and related, that as he was on his way home, he had seen a stork sitting at no great distance from him, which he shot at, and it seemed to him as if he had hit it, but that the stork had remained sitting, and at last began to clap its wings aloud and then flew away. It was now plain that Hinzelmann knew this, and his prophecy also soon came to pass. For the servant, who was a little intoxicated, wanted to wash his horse, who was covered with sweat and dirt, and he rode him into the mill-stream in front of the castle; but owing to his drunkenness he missed the right place, and got into a deep hole, where, not being able to keep his seat on the horse, he fell off and was drowned. He had not delivered the things he had brought with him; so they and the body together were fished up out of the stream.

Hinzelmann also informed and warned others of the future. There came to Hudemühlen a colonel, who was greatly esteemed by Christian III King of Denmark, and who had done good service in the wars with the town of Lübeck. He was a good shot and passionately fond of the chase, and used to spend many hours in the neighbouring woods after the harts and the wild sows. As he was getting ready one day to go to the chase as usual, Hinzelmann came and said, "Thomas (that was his name), I warn you to be cautious how you shoot, or you will before long meet with a mishap." The colonel took no notice of this, and thought it meant nothing. But a few days after, as he was firing at a roe, his gun burst, and took the thumb off his left hand. When this occurred, Hinzelmann was instantly by his side, and said, "See, now, you have got what I warned you of! If you had refrained from shooting this time, this mischance would not have befallen you."

Another time a certain lord Faikenberg, who was a soldier, was on a visit at Hudemühlen. He was a lively, jolly man, and he began to play tricks on Hinzelmann, and to mock and jeer him. Hinzelmann would not long put up with this, and he began to exhibit signs of great dissatisfaction. At last he said,—"Falkenberg, you are making very merry now at my expense, but wait till you come to Magdeburg, and there your cap will be burst in such a way that you will forget your jibes and your jeers." The nobleman was awed: he was persuaded that these words contained a hidden sense: he broke off the conversation with Hinzelmann, and shortly after departed. Not long after the siege of Magdeburg, under the Elector Maurice, commenced, at which this lord Falkenberg was present, under a German prince of high rank. The besieged made a gallant resistance, and night and day kept up a firing of double-harquebuses, and other kinds of artillery; and it happened that one day Falkenberg's chin was shot away by a ball from a falconet, and three days after he died of the wound, in great agony.

Any one whom the spirit could not endure he used to plague or punish for his vices. He accused the secretary at Hudemühlen of too much pride, took a great dislike to him on account of it, and night and day gave him every kind of annoyance. He once related with great glee how he had given the haughty secretary a sound box on the ear. When the secretary was asked about it, and whether the Spirit had been with him, he replied. "Ay, indeed, he has been with me but too often; this very night he tormented me in such a manner that I could not stand before him." He had a love affair with the chamber-maid; and one night as he was in high and confidential discourse with her, and they were sitting together in great joy, thinking that no one could see them but the four walls, the crafty spirit came and drove them asunder, and roughly tumbled the poor secretary out at the door, and then took up a broomstick and laid on him with it, that he made over head and neck for his chamber, and forgot his love altogether. Hinzelmann is said to have made some verses on the unfortunate lover, and to have often sung them for his amusement, and repeated them to travellers, laughing heartily at them.

One time some one at Hudemühlen was suddenly taken in the evening with a violent fit of the cholic, and a maid was despatched to the cellar to fetch some wine, in which the patient was to take his medicine. As the maid was sitting before the cask, and was just going to draw the wine, Hinzelmann was by her side, and said, "You will be pleased to recollect that, a few days ago, you scolded me and abused me; by way of punishment for it, you shall spend this night sitting in the cellar. As to the sick person, he is in no danger whatever; his pain will be all gone in half an hour, and the wine would rather injure him. So just stay sitting here till the cellar door is opened." The patient waited a long time, but no wine came; another maid was sent down, and she found the cellar door well secured on the outside with a good padlock, and the maid sitting within, who told her that Hinzelmann had fastened her up in that way. They wanted to open the cellar and let the maid out, but they could not find a key for the lock, though they searched with the greatest industry. Next morning the cellar was open, and the lock and key lying before the door. Just as the spirit said, all his pain left the sick man in the course of half an hour.

Hinzelmann had never shown himself to the master of the house at Hudemühlen, and whenever he begged of him that if he was shaped like a man, he would let himself be seen by him, he answered, "that the time was not yet come; that he should wait till it was agreeable to him." One night, as the master was lying awake in bed, he heard a rushing noise on one side of the chamber, and he conjectured that the spirit must be there. So he said "Hinzelmann, if you are there, answer me." "It is I," replied he; "what do you want?" As the room was quite light with the moonshine, it seemed to the master as if there was the shadow of a form like that of a child, perceptible in the place from which the sound proceeded. As he observed that the spirit was in a very friendly humour, he entered into conversation with him, and said, "Let me, for this once, see and feel you." But Hinzelmann would. not: "Will you reach me your hand, at least, that I may know whether you are flesh and bone like a man?" "No," said Hinzelmann; "I won't trust you; you are a knave; you might catch hold of me, and not let me go any more." After a long demur, however, and after he had promised, on his faith and honour, not to hold him, but to let him go again immediately, he said, "See, there is my hand." And as the master caught at it, it seemed to him as if he felt the fingers of the hand of a little child; but the spirit drew it back quickly. The master further desired that he would let him feel his face, to which he at last consented; and when he touched it, it seemed to him as if he had touched teeth, or a fleshless skeleton, and the face drew back instantaneously, so that he could not ascertain its exact shape; he only noticed that it, like the hand, was cold, and devoid of vital heat.

The cook, who was on terms of great intimacy with him, thought that she might venture to make a request of him, though another might not, and as she felt a strong desire to see Hinzelmann bodily, whom she heard talking every day, and whom she supplied with meat and drink, she prayed him earnestly to grant her that favour; but he would not, and said that this was not the right time, but that after some time, he would let himself be seen by any person. This refusal only stimulated her desire, and she pressed him more and more not to deny her request. He said she would repent of her curiosity if she would not give up her desire; and when all his representations were to no purpose, and she would not give over, he at last said to her, "Come to-morrow morning before sun-rise into the cellar, and carry in each hand a pail full of water, and your request shall be complied with." The maid inquired what the water was for: "That you will learn," answered he; "without it, the sight of me might be injurious to you."

Next morning the cook was ready at peep of dawn, took in each hand a pail of water, and went down to the cellar. She looked about her without seeing anything; but as she cast her eyes on the ground she perceived a tray, on which was lying a naked child apparently three years old, and two knives sticking crosswise in his heart, and his whole body streaming with blood. The maid was terrified at this sight to such a degree, that she lost her senses, and fell in a swoon on the ground. The spirit immediately took the water that she had brought with her, and poured it all over her head, by which means she came to herself again. She looked about for the tray, but all had vanished, and she only heard the voice of Hinzelmann, who said, "You see now how needful the water was; if it had not been at hand you had died here in the cellar. I hope your burning desire to see me is now pretty well cooled." He often afterwards illuded the cook with this trick, and told it to strangers with great glee and. laughter.

He frequently showed himself to innocent children when at play. The minister Feldmann recollected well, that when he was about fourteen or fifteen years old, and was not thinking particularly about him, he saw the Spirit in the form of a little boy going up the stairs very swiftly. When children were collected about Hudemühlen house, and were playing with one another, he used to get among them and play with them in the shape of a pretty little child, so that all the other children saw him plainly, and when they went home told their parents how, while they were engaged. in play, a strange child came to them and amused himself with them. This was confirmed by a maid, who went one time into a room in which four or six children were playing together, and among them she saw a strange little boy of a beautiful countenance, with curled yellow hair hanging down his shoulders, and. dressed in a red silk coat; and while she wanted to observe him more closely, he got out of the party, and disappeared. Hinzelmann let himself be seen also by a fool, named Claus, who was kept there, and used to pursue every sort of diversion with him. When the fool could not anywhere be found, and they asked him afterwards where he had been so long, he used to reply, "I was with the little wee man, and I was playing with him." If he was farther asked how big the little man was, he held his hand at a height about that of a child of four years. [b]

When the time came that the house-spirit was about to depart, he went to the master of the house and said to him, "See, I will make you a present; take care of it, and let it remind you of me." He then handed him a little *cross*—it is doubtful from the author's words whether of silk *(seide)* or strings *(saiten)*—very prettily plaited. It was the length of a finger, was hollow within, and jingled when it was shaken. Secondly, a *straw hat,* which he had made himself, and in which might be seen forms and figures very ingeniously made in the variously-coloured straw. Thirdly, a leathern *glove* set with pearls, which formed wonderful figures. He then subjoined this prophecy: "So long as these things remain unseparated in good preservation in your family, so long will your entire race flourish, and their good fortune continually increase; but if these presents are divided, lost, or wasted, your race will decrease and sink." And when he perceived that the master appeared to set no particular value on the present, he continued: "I fear that you do not much esteem these things, and will let them go out of your hands; I therefore counsel you to give them in charge to your sisters Anne and Catherine, who will take better care of them."

He accordingly gave the gifts to his sisters, who took them and kept them carefully, and never showed them to any but most particular friends. After their death they reverted to their brother, who took them to himself, and with him they remained so long as he lived. He showed them to the minister Feldmann, at his earnest request, during a confidential conversation. When he died, they came to his only daughter Adelaide, who was married to L. von H, along with the rest of the inheritance, and they remained for some time in her possession. The son of the minister Feldmann made several inquiries about what had afterwards become of the House-spirit's presents, and he learned that the straw-hat was given to the emperor Ferdinand II., who regarded it as something wonderful. The leathern glove was still in his time in the possession of a nobleman. It was short, and just exactly reached above the hand, and there was a snail worked with pearls on the part that came above the hand. What became of the little cross was never known.

The spirit departed of his own accord, after he had staid four years, from 1584 to 1588, at Hudemühlen. He said, before he went away, that he would return once more when the family would be declined, and that it would then flourish anew and increase in consequence. [c]

NOTES

[a] Heinze is the abbreviation of Heinrich (Henry). In the North of Germany the Kobold is also named Chimmeken and Wolterken, from Joachim and Walther.

[b] This is a usual measure of size for the Dwarfs, and even the angels, in the old German poetry. In Otnit it is said of Elberich: *nu bist in Kindes,maze des vierden jares alt;* and of Antilois in Ulrich's Alexander: *er war kleine und niht groz in der maze als din kint, wean si in vier jaren sint,* Grimm, Deut. Mythol, p. 418. We meet with it even in Italian poetry:
E sovra il dorso un nano si piccino
Che sembri di quattr'anni un fanciullino.
B. Tasso, Amadigi, C. c. st. 78.

[c] The feats of House-spirits, it is plain, may In general be ascribed to ventriloquism and to contrivances of servants and others.

Hödeken

Another Kobold or House-spirit took up his abode in the palace of the bishop of Hildesheim. He was named Hödeken or Hütchen, that is Hatekin or Little Hat, from his always wearing a little felt hat very much down upon his face. He was of a kind and obliging disposition, often told the bishop and others of what was to happen, and he took good care that the watchmen should not go to sleep on their post.

It was, however, dangerous to affront him. One of the scullions in the bishop's kitchen used to fling dirt on him and splash him 'with foul water. Hödeken complained to the head cook, who only laughed at him, and said, "Are you a spirit and afraid of a little boy?" "Since you won't punish the boy," replied Hödeken, "I will, in a few days, let you see how much afraid of him I am," and he went off in high dudgeon. But very soon after he got the boy asleep at the fire-side, and he strangled him, cut him up, and put him into the pot on the fire. When the cook abused him for what he had done, he squeezed toads all over the meat that was at the fire, and he soon after tumbled the cook from the bridge into the deep moat. At last people grew so much afraid of his setting fire to the town and palace, that the bishop had him exorcised and banished.

The following was one of Hödeken's principal exploits. There was a man in Hildesheim who had a light sort of wife, and one time when he was going on a journey he spoke to Hödeken and said, "My good fellow, just keep an eye on my wife while I am away, and see that all goes on right." Hödeken agreed to do so; and when the wife, after the departure of her husband, made her gallants come to her, and was going to make merry with them, Hödeken always threw himself in the middle and drove them away by assuming terrific forms; or, when any one had gone to bed, he invisibly flung him so roughly out on the floor as to crack his ribs. Thus they fared, one after another, as the light-o'-love dame introduced them into her chamber, so that no one ventured to come near her. At length, when the husband had returned home, the honest guardian of his honour presented himself before him full of joy, and said, "Your return is most grateful to me, that I may escape the trouble and disquiet that you had imposed upon me?" "Who are you, pray?" said the man. "I am Hödeken," replied he, "to whom, at your departure, you gave your wife in charge. To gratify you I have guarded her this time, and kept her from adultery, though with great and incessant toil. But I beg of you never more to commit her to my keeping; for I would sooner take charge of, and be accountable for, all the swine in Saxony than for one such woman, so many were the artifices and plots she devised to blink me."

King Goldemar

Another celebrated House-spirit was King Goldemar, who lived in great intimacy with Neveling von Hardenberg, on the Hardenstein at the Rühr, and often slept in the same bed with him. He played most beautifully on the harp, and he was in the habit of staking great sums of money at dice. He used to call Neveling brother-in-law, and often gave him warning of various things. He talked with all kinds of people, and used to make the clergy blush by discovering their secret transgressions. His hands were thin like those of a frog, cold and soft to the feel; he let himself be felt, but no one could see him. After remaining there for three years, he went away without offending any one. Some call him King Vollmar, and the chamber in which he lived is still said to be called Vollmar's Chamber. He insisted on having a place at the table for himself, and a stall in the stable for his horse; the food, the hay, and the oats were consumed, but of man or horse nothing more than the shadow ever was seen. When one time a curious person had strewed ashes and tares in his way to make him fall, that his foot-prints might be seen, he came behind him as be was lighting the fire and hewed him to pieces, which he put on the spit and roasted, and he began to boil the head and legs. As soon as the meat was ready it was brought to *Vollmar's* chamber, and people heard great cries of joy as it was consumed. After this there was no trace of King Voilmar; but over the door of his chamber was found written, that in future the house would be as unfortunate as it had hitherto been fortunate; the scattered property would not be brought together again till the time when three Hardenbergs of Hardenstein should be living at the same time. The spit and the roast meat were preserved for a long time; but they disappeared in the Lorrain war in 1651. The pot still remains built into the wall of the kitchen. [a]

NOTE

[a] Von Steinen, Weetfäl. Gesch. *ap.* Grimm, Deut. Mythol, p. 477

The Heinzelmänchen

It is not over fifty years since the Heinzelmänchen, as they are called, used to live and perform their exploits in Cologne. They were little naked mannikins, who used to do all sorts of work; bake bread, wash, and such like house-work. So it is said, but no one ever saw them.

In the time that the Heinzelmänchen were still there, there was in Cologne many a baker, who kept no man, for the little people used always to make over-night, as much black and white bread as the baker wanted for his shop. In many houses they used to wash and do all their work for the maids.

Now, about this time, there was an expert tailor to whom they appeared to have taken a great fancy, for when he married he found in his house, on the wedding-day, the finest victuals and the most beautiful vessels and utensils, which the little folk had stolen elsewhere and brought to their favourite. When, with time, his family increased, the little ones used to give the tailor's wife considerable aid in her household affairs; they washed for her, and on holidays and festival times they scoured the copper and tin, and the house from the garret to the cellar. If at any time the tailor had a press of work, he was sure to find it all ready done for him in the morning by the Heinzelmänchen. But curiosity began now to torment the tailor's wife, and she was dying to get one sight of the Heinzelmänchen, but do what she would she could never compass it. She one time strewed peas all down the stairs that they might fail and hurt themselves, and that so she might see them next morning. But this project missed, and since that time the Heinzelmänchen have totally disappeared, as has been everywhere the case, owing to the curiosity of people, which has at all times been the destruction of so much of what was beautiful in the world. The Heinzelmänchen, in consequence of this, went off all in a body out of the town with music playing, but people could only hear the music, for no one could see the mannikins themselves, who forthwith got into a boat and went away, whither no one knows. The good times, however, are said to have disappeared from Cologne along with the Heinzelmänchen. [a]

NOTE
[a] *Oral.* Cölns Vorzeit. Cöln. 1826.

NIXES

Kennt ihr der Nixen, munt're Schaar?
Von Auge schwarz und grün von Haar
Sie lauscht am Schilfgestade.
–MATTHISSON.

Know you the Nixes, gay and fair?
Their eyes are black, and green their hair—
They lurk in sedgy shores.

The Nixes, or Water-people, inhabit lakes and rivers. The man is like any other man, only he has green teeth. He also wears a green hat. The female Nixes appear like beautiful maidens. On fine sunny days they may be seen sitting on the banks, or on the branches of the trees, combing their long golden locks. When any person is shortly to be drowned, the Nixes may be previously seen dancing on the surface of the water. They inhabit a magnificent region below the water, whither they sometimes convey mortals. A girl from a village near Leipzig was one time at service in the house of a Nix. She said that everything there was very good; all she had to complain of was that she was obliged to eat her food without salt. The female Nixes frequently go to the market to buy meat: they are always dressed with extreme neatness, only a corner of their apron or some other part of their clothes is wet. The man has also occasionally gone to market. They are fond of carrying off women whom they make wives of, and often fetch an earthly midwife to assist at their labour. Among the many tales of the Nixes we select the following:—

The Peasant and the Waterman

A Water-man once lived on good terms with a peasant who dwelt not far from his lake. He often visited him, and at last begged that the peasant would visit him in his house under the water. The peasant consented, and went down with him. There was everything down under the water as in a stately palace on the land,—halls, chambers, and cabinets, with costly furniture of every description. The Water-man led his guest over the whole, and showed him everything that was in it. They came at length to a little chamber, where were standing several new pots turned upside down. The peasant asked what was in them. "They contain," was the reply, "the souls of drowned people, which I put under the pots and keep them close, so that they cannot get away." The peasant made no remark, and he came up again on the land. But for a long time the affair of the souls continued to give him great trouble, and be watched to find when the Water-man should be from home. When this occurred, as he had marked the right way down, he descended into the water-house, and, having made out the little chamber, he turned up all the pots one after another, and immediately the souls of the drowned people ascended out of the water, and recovered their liberty. [a]

NOTE

[a] This legend seems to be connected with the ancient idea of the water-deities taking the souls of drowned persons to themselves. In the Edda, this is done by the sea-goddess Ran.

The Water-Smith

There is a little lake in Westphalia called the Darmssen, from which the peasants in the adjacent village of Epe used to hear all through the night a sound as if of hammering upon an anvil. People who were awake used also to see something in the middle of the lake. They got one time into a boat and went to it, and there they found that it was a smith, who, with his body raised over the water, and a hammer in his hand, pointed to an anvil, and bid the people bring him something to forge. Prom that time forth they brought iron to him, and no people had such good plough-irons as those of Epe.

One time as a man from this village was getting reeds at the Darmssen, be found among them a little child that was rough all over his body. The smith cried out, "Don't take away my son!" but the man put the child on his back, and ran home with it. Since that time the smith has never more been seen or heard. The man reared the Roughy, and he became the cleverest and best lad in the place. But when he was twenty years old he said to the farmer, "Farmer, I must leave you. My father has called me!" "I am sorry for that," said the farmer. "Is there no way that you could stay with me?" "I will see about it," said the water-child. "Do you go to Braumske and fetch me a little sword; but you must give the seller whatever he asks for it, and not haggle about it." The farmer went to Braumske and bought the sword; but he haggled, and got something off the price. They now went together to the Darmssen, and the Roughy said, "Now mind. When I strike the water, if there comes up blood, I must go away; but if there comes milk, then I may stay with you." He struck the water, and there came neither milk nor blood. The Roughy was annoyed, and said, "You*have* been bargaining and haggling, and so there comes neither blood nor milk. Go off to Braumske and buy another sword." The farmer went and returned; but it was not till the third time that he bought a sword without haggling. When the Roughy struck the water with this it became as red as blood, and he threw himself into the lake, and never was seen more. [a]

NOTE

[a] Grimm, *ut sup.* p. 463.

The Working Waterman

At Seewenweiher, in the Black-Forest, a little Water-man *(Seemän-lein)* used to come and join the people, work the whole day long with them, and in the evening go back into the lakes. They used to set his breakfast and dinner apart for him. When, in apportioning the work, the rule of "Not too much and not too little" was infringed, he got angry, and knocked all the things about. Though his clothes were old and worn, he steadily refused to let the people get him new ones. But when at last they would do so, and one evening the lake-man was presented with a new coat, be said, "When one is paid off, one must go away. After this day I'll come no more to you." And, unmoved by the excuses of the people, he never let himself be seen again. [a]

NOTE
[a] Grimm, *ut sup.* p. 453.

The Nix-Labour

A midwife related that her mother was one night called up, and desired to make haste and come to the aid of a woman in labour. It was dark, but notwithstanding she got up and dressed herself, and went down, where she found a man waiting. She begged of him to stay till she should get a lantern, and she would go with him; but he was urgent, said he would show her the way without a lantern, and that there was no fear of her going astray.

He then bandaged her eyes, at which she was terrified, and was going to cry out; but he told her she was in no danger, and might go with him without any apprehension. They accordingly went away together, and the woman remarked that he struck the water with a rod, and that they went down deeper and deeper till they came to a room, in which there was no one but the lying-in woman.

Her guide now took the bandage off her eyes, led her up to the bed, and recommending her to his wife, went away. She then helped to bring the babe into the world, put the woman to bed, washed the babe, and did everything that was requisite.

The woman, grateful to the midwife, then secretly said to her: "I am a Christian woman as well as you; and I was carried off by a Water-man, who changed me. Whenever I bring a child into the world he always eats it on the third. day. Come on the third day to your pond, and you will see the water turned to blood. When my husband comes in now and offers you money, take no more from him than you usually get, or else he will twist your neck. Take good care!"

Just then the husband came in. He was in a great passion, and he looked all about; and when he saw that all had gone on properly he bestowed great praise on the midwife. He then threw a great heap of money on the table, and said, "Take as much as you will!" She, however, prudently answered, "I desire no more from you than from others, and that is a small sum. If you give me that I am content; if you think it too much, I ask nothing from you but to take me home again." "It is God," says he, "has directed you to say that." He paid her then the sum she mentioned, and conducted her home honestly. She was, however, afraid to go to the pond at the appointed day.

There are many other tales in Germany of midwives, and even ladies of rank, who have been called in to assist at Nix or Dwarf labours. The Ahnfrau von Ranzau, for example, and the Frau von Alvensleben—the Ladies Bountiful of Germany—were waked up in the night to attend the little women m their confinement. [a] There is the same danger in touching anything in the Dwarf as in the Nix abodes, but the Dwarfs usually bestow rings and other articles, which will cause the family to flourish. We have seen tales of the same kind in Scandinavia, and shall meet with them in many other countries.

NOTE

[a] A tale of this kind is to be seen in Luther's Table-talk, told by *die frau doctorin,* his wife. The scene of it was the river Mulda.

SWITZERLAND

Denn da hielten auch im lande
Noch die guten Zwerglein Hans;
Kleingestalt, doch hochbegabet,
Und so hülfreich liberaus!
—MÜLLER.

For then also in the country
The good Dwarflings still kept house;
Small in form, but highly gifted,
And so kind and generous!

WE NOW arrive at Switzerland, a country with which are usually
associated ideas of sublime and romantic scenery, simple manners,
and honest hearts. The character of the Swiss Dwarfs will be found
to correspond with these ideas. For, like the face of Nature, these
personifications of natural powers seem to become more gentle and
mild as they approach the sun and the south.

The Dwarfs, or little Hill- or Earth-men [a] of Switzerland, are
described as of a lively, joyous disposition, fond of strolling through
the valleys, and viewing and partaking in the labours of agriculture.
Kind and generous, they are represented as driving home stray
lambs, and leaving brush-wood and berries in the way of poor children. Their principal occupation is keeping cattle—not goats, sheep,
or cows, but the chamois, from whose milk they make excellent and
well-flavoured cheese. This cheese, when given by the Dwarfs to
any one, has the property of growing again when it has been cut or
bitten. But should the hungry owner be improvident enough to eat
up the whole of it and leave nothing from it to sprout from, he of

course has seen the end of his cheese.

The Kobolds are also to be met with in Switzerland. In the Vaudois, they call them Servants, [b] and believe that they live in remote dwellings and lonely shiels. [c] The most celebrated of them in those parts is Jean de la Boliéta, or, as he is called in German, Napf-Hans, *i. e.* Jack-of-the-Bowl, because it was the custom to lay for him every evening on the roof of the cow-house a bowl of fresh sweet cream, of which he was sure to give a good account. He used to lead the cows to feed in the most dangerous places, and yet none of them ever sustained the slightest injury. He always went along the same steep path on which no one ever saw even a single stone lying, though the whole side of the mountain was strewn as thickly as possible with boulders. It is stifi called Boliéta's Path. [d]

Rationalising theory has been at work with the Swiss Dwarfs also. It is supposed, that the early inhabitants of the Swiss mountains, when driven back by later tribes of immigrants, retired to the high lands and took refuge in the clefts and caverns of the mountains, whence they gradually showed themselves to the new settlers—approached them, assisted them, and were finally, as a species of Genii, raised to the region of the wonderful.

For our knowledge of the Dwarf Mythology of Switzerland, we are chiefly indebted to professor Wyss, of Bern, who has put some of the legends in a poetical dress, and given others in the notes to his Idylls as he styles them. [e] These legends were related by the peasants to Mr. Wyss or his friends, on their excursions through the mountains; and he declares that he has very rarely permitted himself to add to, or subtract from, the peasants' narrative. He adds, that the belief in these beings is strong in the minds of the people, not merely in the mountain districts, but also at the foot of Belp mountain, Belp, Gelterfingen, and other places about Bern. [f]

As a specimen of Mr. Wyss's manner of narrating these legends, we give here a faithful translation of his first Idyll [g]

NOTES

[a] In Swiss *Härdmandle*, pl. *Härdmändlene.*

[b] Wyss, Reise in das Berner Oberland, ii. 412. *Servants* is the term in the original.

[c] This Scottish word, signifying the summer cabin of the herdsmen on the mountains, exactly expresses the Seunhütten of the Swiss.

[d] Alpenrosen for 1824, *ap.* Grimm, Introd. to Irish Fairy Legends.

[e] Idyllen, Volkssagen, Legenden, und Erzählungen aus der Schweiz. Von .J. Rud Wyss, Prof. Bern, 1813.

[f] In Bilder und Sagen aus der Schweiz, von Dr. Rudolf. Müller. Glarua, 1842, may be found some legends of the Erdmännlein, but they are nearly all the same as those collected by Mr. Wyss. We give below those in which there is anything peculiar.

[g] The original is in German hexameters.

Gertrude and Rosy

GERTRUDE.
QUICK, daughter, quick! spin off what's on your rock.
'Tis Saturday night, and with the week you know
Our work must end; we shall the more enjoy
To-morrow's rest when all 's done out of hand. [a]
Quick, daughter, quick! spin off what 's on your rock. .
ROSY.
True, mother, but every minute sleep
Falls on my eyes as heavy as lead, and I
Must yawn do what I will; and then God knows
I can't help nodding though 'twere for my life;
Or ... oh! it might be of some use if you
Would once more, dearest mother, tell about
The wonderful, good-natured little Dwarfs,
What they here round the country used to do,
And how they showed their kindness to the hinds.
GERTRUDE.
See now! what industry!—your work itself
Should keep you waking. I have told you o'er
A thousand times the stories, and we lose,
If you grow wearied of them, store of joy
Reserved for winter-nights; besides, methinks,
The evening 's now too short for chat like this.
ROSY.
There 's only one thing I desire to hear
Again, and. sure, dear mother, never yet
Have you explained how 'twas the little men
Lived in the hills, and how, all through the year,
They sported round the country here, and gave
Marks of their kindness. For you 'll ne'er persuade
Me to believe that barely, one by one,
They wandered in the valleys, and appeared
Unto the people, and bestowed their gifts:
So, come now, tell at once, how 'twas the Dwarfs
Lived all together in society.

GERTRUDE.
'Tis plain, however, of itself, and well
Wise folks can see, that such an active race
Would never with their hands before them sit.
Ah! a right merry lively thing, and full
Of roguish tricks, the little Hill-man is,
And quickly too he gets into a rage,
If you behave not toward him mannerly,
And be not frank and delicate in your acts.
But, above all things, they delight to dwell,
Quiet and peaceful, in the secret clefts
Of hills and mountains, evermore concealed.
All through the winter, when with icy rind
The frost doth cover o'er the earth, the wise
And prudent little people keep them warm
By their fine fires, many a fathom down
Within the inmost rocks. Pure native gold,
And the rock-crystals shaped like towers, clear,
Transparent, gleam with colours thousandfold
Through the fair palace, and the Little-folk,
So happy and so gay, amuse themselves
Sometimes with singing—Oh, so sweet! 'twould charm
The heart of any one who heard it sound.
Sometimes with dancing, when they jump and spring
Like the young skipping kids in the Alp-grass.
Then when the spring is come, and in the fields
The flowers are blooming, with sweet May's approach,
They bolts and bars take from their doors and gates,
That early ere the hind or hunter stirs,
In the cool morning, they may sport and play;
Or ramble in the evening, when the moon
Lights up the plains. Seldom hath mortal man
Beheld them with his eyes; but should one chance
To see them, it betokens suffering
And a bad year, if bent in woe they glide
Through woods and thickets; but the sight proclaims
Joy and good luck, when social, in a ring,
On the green meads and fields, their hair adorned
With flowers, they shout and whirl their merry rounds.

Abundance then they joyously announce
For barn, for cellar, and for granary,
And a blest year to men, to herds, and game.
Thus they do constantly foreshow what will
Befall to-morrow and hereafter; now
Sighing, and still, by their lamenting tones,
A furious tempest; and again, with sweet
And smiling lips, and shouting, clear bright skies. [b]
Chief to the poor and good, they love to show
Kindness and favour, often bringing home
At night the straying lambs, and oftener still
In springtime nicely spreading, in the wood,
Brushwood, in noble bundles, in the way
Of needy children gone to fetch home fuel.
Many a good little girl, who well obeyed
Her mother,—or, mayhap, a little boy,—
Has, with surprise, found lying on the hills
Bright dazzling bowls of milk, and baskets too,
Nice little baskets, full of berries, left
By the kind hands of the wood-roaming Dwarfs.
Now be attentive while I tell you one
Out of a hundred and a hundred stories;
'Tis one, however, that concerns us more
Than all the rest, because it was my own
Great-great-grandfather that the thing befell,
In the old time, in years long since agone.
Where from the lofty rocks the boundary runs
Down to the vale, Barthel, of herdsmen first
In all the country round, was ploughing up
A spacious field, where he designed to try
The seed of corn; but with anxiety
His heart was filled, lest by any chance
His venture should miscarry, for his sheep
In the contagion he had lost, now poor
And without skill, he ventures on the plough.
Deliberate and still, at the plough-tail,
In furrows he cuts up the grassy soil,
While with the goad his little boy drives on
The panting ox. When, lo! along the tall

Rocky hill-side, a smoke ascends in clouds
Like snow-flakes, soaring from the summit up
Into the sky. At this the hungry boy
Began to think of food, for the poor child
Had tasted nothing all the live-long day
For lunch, and, looking up, he thus began:
"Ah! there the little Dwarf-folk are so gay
At their grand cooking, roasting, boiling now,
For a fine banquet, while with hunger I
Am dying. Had we here one little dish
Of the nice savoury food, were it but as
A sign that there 's a blessing on our work!"
'Twas thus the boy spake, and his father ploughed
Silently on, bent forwards o'er his work.
They turn the plough; when huzza! lo! behold
A miracle! there gleamed right from the midst
Of the dark furrow, toward them, a bright
Lustre, and there so charming! lay a plate
Heaped up with roast meat; by the plate, a loaf
Of bread upon the outspread table-cloth,
At the disposal of the honest pair.
Hurra! long live the friendly, generous Dwarfs!
Barthel had now enough—so had the boy—
And laughing gratefully and loud, they praise
And thank the givers; then, with strength restored,
They quick return unto their idle plough.
But when again their day's task they resume,
To break more of the field, encouraged now
To hope for a good crop, since the kind Dwarfs
Had given them the sign of luck they asked—
Hush! bread and plate, and crums, and knife and fork,
Were vanished clean; only—just for a sign
For ever of the truth—lay on the ridge
The white, nice-woven, pretty table-cloth.
ROSY.
O mother! mother! what? the glittering plate
And real? and the cloth with their own hands
Spun by the generous Dwarfs? No, I can ne'er
Believe it!—Was the thread then, real drawn

And. twisted thread, set in it evenly?
And was there too a flower, a pretty figure,
Nicely wrought in with warp and crossing woof?
Did there a handsome border go all round,
Enclosing all the figures?—Sure your great-
Great-grandfather, if really he was
The owner of the curious little cloth,
He would have left it carefully unto
His son and grandson for a legacy,
That, for a lasting witness of the meal
Given by the Dwarfs, it might to distant years,
The praise and wonder of our vale remain.
GERTRUDE.
Odds me! how wise the child is! what a loss
And pity 'tis that in old times the folk
Were not so thoughtful and so over-knowing!
Ah! our poor simple fathers should rise up
Out of their graves, and come to get advice
And comfort from the brooders that are now,—
As if they knew not what was right and fit!
Have but a little patience, girl, and spin
What's on your rock; to-morrow when 'tis day
I'll let you see the Dwarfs' flowered table-cloth,
Which, in the chest laid safe, inherited
From mother down to daughter, I have, long
Kept treasured under lock and key, for fear
Some little girl, like some one that you know,
Might out of curiosity, and not
Acquainted with its worth, set it astray.
ROSY.
Ah, that is kind, dear mother; and see now
How broad awake I am, and how so smart
I'm finishing my work since you relate
These pretty tales; but I will call you up
Out of your bed to-morrow in the morning
So early I Oh, I wish now it were day
Already, for I 'm sure I shall not get
One wink of sleep for thinking of the cloth. [c]

NOTES

[a] It is a notion in some parts of Germany, that if a girl leaves any flax or tow on her distaff unspun on Saturday night, none of what remains will make good thread. Grimm, Deut. Mythol. Anhang, p. lxxii.

[b] *Glanz* is the term employed in Switzerland.

[c] This legend was picked up by a friend of Mr. Wyss when on a topographical ramble in the neighbourhood of Bern. It was told to him by a peasant of Belp; "but," says Mr. Wyss, "if I recollect right, this man said it was a nice smoking-hot cake that was on the plate, and it was a servant, not the man's son, who was driving the plough. The circumstance of the table-cloth being handed down from mother to daughter," he adds, "is a fair addition which I have allowed myself."

The writer recollects to have heard this story, when a boy, from an old woman in Ireland; and he could probably point out the very field in the county of Kildare where it occurred. A man and a boy were ploughing: the boy, as they were about in the middle of their furrow, smelled roast beef, and wished for some. As they returned, it was lying on the grass before them. When they had eaten, the boy said "God bless me, and God bless the fairies!" The man did not give thanks, and he met with misfortunes very shortly after. —The same legend is also in Scotland.

The Chamois-Hunter

A The Chamois-hunter set out early one morning, and ascended the mountains. He had arrived at a great height, and was in view of some chamois, when, just as he was laying his bolt on his cross-bow, and was about to shoot, a terrible cry from a cleft of the rock interrupted his purpose. Turning round he saw a hideous Dwarf, with a battle-axe in his hand raised to slay him. "Why," cried he, in a rage, "hast thou so long been destroying my chamois, and leavest not with me my flock? But now thou shalt pay for it with thy blood.' The poor hunter turned pale at the stranger's words. In his terror he was near falling from the cliff.

At length, however, he recovered himself; and begged forgiveness of the Dwarf; pleaded his ignorance that the chamois belonged to him, declaring at the same time that he had no other means of support than what he derived from hunting. The Dwarf was pacified, laid down his axe, and said to him, "Tis well; never be seen here again, and I promise thee that every seventh day thou shalt find, early in the morning, a dead chamois hanging before thy cottage; but beware and keep from the others." The Dwarf then vanished, and the hunter returned thoughtfully home, little pleased with the prospect of the inactive live be was now to lead.

On the seventh morning he found, according to the Dwarf's promise, a fat chamois hanging in the branches of a tree before his cottage, of which he ate with great satisfaction. The next week it was the same, and so it continued for some months. But at last he grew weary of this idle life, and preferred, come what might, returning to the chase, and catching chamois for himself; to having his food provided for him without the remembrance of his toils to sweeten the repast. His determination made, he once more ascended the mountains. Almost the first object that met his view was a fine buck. The hunter levelled his bow and took aim at the prey; and as the Dwarf did not appear, he was just pulling the trigger, when the Dwarf stole behind him, took him by the ankle, and tumbled him down the precipice.

Others say the Dwarf gave the hunter a small cheese of chamois-milk, which would last him his whole life, but that he one day thoughtlessly ate the whole of it, or, as some will have it, a guest who was ignorant of the quality of it ate up the remainder. Poverty then drove him to return to the chamois-hunting, and he was thrown into a chasm by the Dwarf. [a]

NOTE

[a] The former account was obtained by a friend in Glarnerland. The latter was given to Mr. Wyss himself by a man of Zweylütschinen, very rich, says Mr. Wyss, in Dwarf lore, and who accompanied him to Lauterbrunnen. Schiller has founded his poem Der Alpenjäger on this legend.

The Dwarfs on the Tree

In the summer-time the troop of the Dwarfs came in great numbers down from the hills into the valley, and joined the men that were at work, either assisting them or merely looking on. They especially liked to be with the mowers in the hay-making season, seating themselves, greatly to their satisfaction, on the long thick branch of a maple-tree, among the dense foliage. But one time some mischief-loving people came by night and sawed the branch nearly through. The unsuspecting Dwarfs, as usual, sat down on it in the morning; the branch snapt in two, and the Dwarfs were thrown to the ground. When the people laughed at them they became greatly incensed, and cried out,

> O how is heaven so high
> And perfidy so great!
> Hero to-day and never more!
> and they never let themselves again be seen. [a]

It is also related that it was the custom of the Dwarfs to seat themselves on a large piece of rock, and thence to look on. the hay-makers when at work. But some mischievous people lighted a lire on the rock and made it quite hot, and then sweet off all the coals. In the morning the little people, coming to take their usual station, burned themselves in a lamentable manner. Full of anger, they cried out, "O wicked world! O wicked world!" called aloud for vengeance, and disappeared for ever.

NOTE

[a] Mr. Wyss heard this and the following tale in Haslithal and Gadmen.

Curiousity punished

In old times men lived in the valley, and around them, in the clefts and holes of the rocks, dwelt the Dwarfs. They were kind and friendly to the people, often performing hard and heavy work for them in the night; and when the country-people came early in the morning with their carts and tools, they saw, to their astonishment, that the work was already done, while the Dwarfs hid themselves in the bushes, and laughed aloud at the astonished rustics. Often, too, were the peasants incensed to find their corn, which was scarcely yet ripe, lying cut on the ground; but shortly after there was sure to come on such a hail-storm, that it became obvious that hardly a single stalk could have escaped destruction had it not been cut, and then, from the bottom of their hearts, they thanked the provident Dwarf-people. But at last mankind, through, their own folly, deprived themselves of the favour and kindness of the Dwarfs; they fled the country, and since that time no mortal eye has seen them. The cause of their departure was this:

A shepherd had a fine cherry-tree [a] that stood on the mountain. When in the summer the fruit had ripened, it happened that, three times running, the tree was-stript, and all tie fruit spread out on the benches and hurdles, where the shepherd himself used to spread it out to dry for the winter. The people of the village all said, "It could be none but the good-natured Dwarfs, who come by night tripping along with their feet covered with long mantles, as light as birds, and industriously perform for mankind their daily work. People have often watched them," continued the narrators, "but no one disturbs them; they are left to come and go as they please." This talk only excited the curiosity of the shepherd, and he longed to know why it was that the Dwarfs so carefully concealed their feet, and whether they were differently formed from those of men. Accordingly, next year, when the summer came, and the time when the Dwarfs secretly pulled the cherries, and brought them to the barn, the shepherd took a sack full of ashes, and strewed them about under the cherry-tree. Next morning, at break of day, he hastened to the place: the tree was plucked completely empty, and he saw the marks of several goose-feet impressed on the ashes. The shepherd then laughed and jested at having discovered the Dwarfs' secret. But soon after the Dwarfs broke and laid waste their houses, and fled down deeper in the mountain to their splendid secret palace, that had long lain empty to receive them. Vexed with mankind, they never more granted them their aid; and the imprudent shepherd who had betrayed them became sickly, and continued so to the end of his life. [b]

NOTES

[a] In several of the high valleys of Switzerland it is only a single cherry-tree which happens to be favourably situated that bears fruit. It bears abundantly and the fruit ripens about the month of August. *Wyss.*

[b] Compare the narrative in the Swiss dialect given by Grimm, Deut. Mythol. P. 419. The same peasant of Belp who related the first legend was Mr. Wyss's authority for this one. "The vanishing of the Bergänlein," says Mr Wyss, "appears to be a matter of importance to the popular faith. It is almost always ascribed to the fault of mankind—sometimes to their wickedness.

We may in these tales recognise the box of Pandora under a different form, but the ground is the same. Curiosity and wickedness are still the cause of superior beings withdrawing their favour from man.

"I have never anywhere else," says Mr Wyss, "heard of the goose-feet; but that all is not right with their feet is evident from the popular tradition giving long trailing mantles as the dress of the little people. Some will have it that their feet are regularly formed, but set on their legs the wrong way, so that the toes are behind and the heels before." Heywood in his Hierarchie of the Blessed Angels, p. 554, relates a story which would seem to refer to a similar belief.

The Rejected Gift

A dwarf came down one night from the chestnut woods on the side of the mountain over the village of Walchwyl, and enquired for the house of a midwife, whom he earnestly pressed to come out and go with him. She consented, and the Dwarf, bearing a light, led the way in silence to the woods. He stopped at last before a cleft in a rock, at which they entered, and the woman suddenly found herself in a magnificent hall. She was thence led through several rich apartments to the chamber of state, where the queen of the Dwarfs, for whom her services were required, was lying. She performed her office, and brought a fair young prince to the light. She was thanked and dismissed, and her former conductor appeared to lead her home. As he was taking leave of her, he filled her apron with something, bidding her on no account to look at it till she was in her own house. But the woman could not control her curiosity, and the moment the Dwarf disappeared, she partly opened the apron, and lo! there was nothing in it but some black coals. In a rage, she shook them out on the ground, but she kept two of them in her hands, as a proof of the shabby treatment she had met with from the Dwarfs. On reaching home, she threw them also down on the ground. Her husband cried out with joy and surprise, for they shone like carbuncles. She asserted that the Dwarf had put nothing but coals into her apron; but she ran out to call a neighbour, who knew more of such things than they did, and he on examining them pronounced them to be precious stones of great value. The woman immediately ran back to where she had shaken out the supposed coals, but they were all gone. [a]

NOTE

[a] Müller, Bilder und Sagen, p. 119; Coals are the usual form under which the Dwarfs conceal the precious metals. We also find this trait in Scandinavia. A smith who lived near Aarhuus in Jutland, as he was going to church, saw a Troll on the roadside very busy about two straws that had got across each other on a heap of coals, and which, do what he would, he could not remove from their position. He asked the smith to do it for him; but he who knew better things took up the coals with the cross straws on them, and carried them home in spite of the screams of the Troll, and when he reached his own house he found it was a large treasure he had got, over which the Troll had lost all power. Thiele, 1. 122.

The Wonderful Little Pouch

At noon one day a young peasant sat by the side of a wood, and, sighing, prayed to God to give him a morsel of food. A Dwarf suddenly emerged from the wood, and told him that his prayer should be fulfilled. He then gave him the pouch that he had on his side, with the assurance that he would always find in it wherewithal to satisfy his thirst and hunger, charging him at the same time not to consume it all and to share with any one who asked him for food. The Dwarf vanished, and the peasant put his hand into the pouch to make trial of it, and there he found a cake of new bread, a cheese, and a bottle of wine, on which he made a hearty meal. He then saw that the pouch swelled up as before, and looking in be found that it was again full of bread, cheese, and wine. He now felt sure of his food, and he lived on in an idle luxurious way, without doing any work. One day, as he was gorging himself there came up to him a feeble old man, who prayed him to give him a morsel to eat. He refused in a brutal, churlish tone, when instantly the bread and cheese broke, and scattered out of his hands, and pouch and all vanished. [a]

NOTE
[a] Müller, *ut sup.* p. 123.

Aid and Punishment

On the side of Mount Pilatus is a place named the Kastler-Alpe, now covered with stones and rubbish, but which once was verdant and fertile. The cause of the change was as follows.

The land there was formerly occupied by a farmer, a churlish, unfeeling man, who, though wealthy, let his only sister struggle with the greatest poverty in the valley beneath. The poor woman at length having fallen sick, and seeing no other resource, resolved to apply to her hardhearted brother for the means of employing a doctor. She sent her daughter to him; but all the prayers and tears of the poor girl failed to move him, and he told her he would, sooner than give her anything, see the Alpe covered with stones and rubbish. She departed, and as she went along a Dwarf suddenly appeared to her. She would have fled, but he gently detained her, and telling her he had heard all that had passed, gave her a parcel of herbs, which he assured her would cure her mother, and a little cheese, which he said would last them a long time.

On trial, the herbs quickly produced the promised effect; and when they went to cut the cheese they found the knife would not penetrate it, and no wonder, for it was pure gold. There also came a sudden storm on the mountain, and the Kastler-Alpe was reduced to its present eondition. [a]

NOTE
[a] Müller, *ut sup.* p. 126.

The Dwarf in search of Lodging

One night, during a tremendous storm of wind and rain, a Dwarf came travelling through a little village, and went from cottage to cottage, dripping with rain, knocking at the doors for admission. None, however, took pity on him, or would open the door to receive him: on the contrary, the inhabitants even mocked at his distress.

At the very end of the village there dwelt two honest poor people, a man and his wife. Tired and faint, the Dwarf crept on his staff up to their house, and tapped modestly three times at the little window. Immediately the old shepherd opened the door for him, and cheerfully offered him the little that the house afforded. The old woman produced some bread, milk, and cheese: the Dwarf sipped a few drops of the milk, and ate some crums of the bread and cheese. "I am not used," said he, laughing, "to eat such coarse food: but I thank you from my heart, and God reward you for it: now that I am rested, I will proceed on farther." "God forbid!" cried the good woman; "you surely don't think of going out in the night and in the storm! It were better for you to take a bed here, and set out in the daylight." But the Dwarf shook his head, and with a smile replied, "You little know what business I have to do this night on the top of the mountain. I have to provide for you too; and to-morrow you shall see that I am not ungrateful for the kindness you have shown to me." So saying, the Dwarf departed, and the worthy old couple went to rest.

But at break of day they were awaked by storm and tempest; the lightnings flashed along the red sky, and torrents of water poured down the hills and through the valley. A huge rock now tumbled from the top of the mountain, and rolled down toward the village, carrying along with it, in its course, trees, stones, and earth. Men and cattle, every thing in the village that had breath in it, were buried beneath it. The waves had now reached the cottage of the two old people, and in terror and dismay they stood out before their door. They then beheld approaching in the middle of the stream a large piece of rock, and on it, jumping merrily, the Dwarf, as if he was riding and steering it with a great trunk of a pine till he brought it before the house, where it stemmed the water and kept it from the cottage, so that both it and the good owners escaped. The Dwarf then swelled and grew higher and higher till he became a monstrous Giant, and vanished in the air, while the old people were praying to God and thanking him for their deiverance. [a]

NOTE

[a] This story is told of two places in the Highlands of Berning, of Ralligen, a little village on the lake of Thun, where there once stood a town called Roll; and again, of Schillingsdorf, a place in the valley of Grinderwald, formerly destroyed by a mountain slip.
The reader need scarcely be reminded of the stories of Lot and of Baucis and Philemon: see also Grimm's Kinder und Hausmärchen, iii. 153, for other parallels

Index

Paper books

VAMzzz Publishing is located in the very centre of old Amsterdam, in The Netherlands. Our publishing company creates high quality revised editions of five star occult, witchcraft, Gothic and esoteric classics, mostly written in the Fin de siècle-period and early 20th century.

As a publisher, we deeply respect the writer of any book we choose, so we join our forces (top level graphic design & thirty years of occult studies) to produce enchanting volumes which maximize the reading pleasure and inform, often with extra added information. In contrast to the current trend of digital screen addiction, we think, this variety of literature needs to be presented on paper. *No e-books, but real books!*

Apart from republications of valuable but forgotten books, we are also in the preparation of new publications on topics such as self-healing, magic, new astrology and more.

Previews of all books including a complete table of contents can be viewed on www.vamzzz.com. More books will be added to the list. *VAMzzz Publishing* strives to publish new volumes every month. Please visit our website regularly for the latest updates.

VAMzzz Publishing
P.O. Box 3340
1001 AC Amsterdam
The Netherlands
contactvamzzz@gmail.com
www.vamzzz.com

2

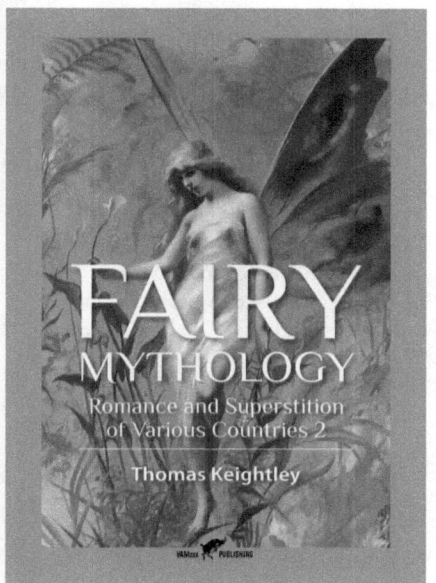

Recommended

Fairy Mythology
Romance and
Superstition of Various
Countries 2
by Thomas Keightley
404 pages, Paperback,
ISBN 9789492355102

The term "Fairy" covers all kinds of nature spirits and Elementals all over the world. Not just the tiny sugar sweet creatures hovering around flowers. Thomas Keightley collected an impressive amount of mostly European, and nowadays often "extinct" folklorist data on these invisible realm's inhabitants, and compiled these in *Fairy Mythology* (1870). In its revised edition, this massive work of over 800 pages, is republished in two volumes to meet modern reading standards. Volume 1 covers Scandinavia, Iceland, Feroer, the Orkneys, Shetland Islands, Rugen, Germany and Switserland. Volume 2 deals with Great Britain, the Scottish Highlands and Lowlands, England, Wales, the Isle of Man, Brittany, France, Greece, Italy, Spain, stories of the Finns and Slavonic people and some Jewish and African Fairy-lore. We encounter Fairies in many varieties, Pixies, Brownies, Leprechauns, Chancelings, the Boggard, Puck, the Phynodderee, Kobold, Urisk, Korrigen, the Korred, Tylwyth Teg and more. Just like volume 1, volume 2 displays a precious collection of ancient folklore directly based on the realm of the hidden Elemental nature.

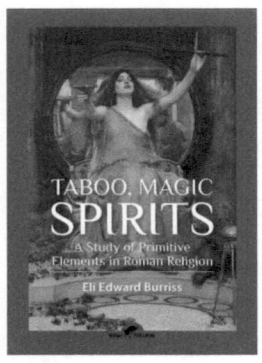

Taboo, Magic, Spirits
A study of primitive elements in Roman religion
by Eli Edward Burriss
200 pages, Paperback, ISBN 9789492355034

In Ancient Rome Mana was the term used for a mysterious, magical medium, which could be helpful or harmful (Taboo). Just like the Chinese qi, it could empower the positive and the negative. Contents: Mana, Magic and Animism – Positive and Negative Mana (Taboo) – Miscellaneous Taboos – Magic Acts: The General Principles – Removing Evils by - Magic Acts – Incantation and Prayer– Naturalism and Animism.

Chaldean Magic
It's Origin and Development
by François Lenormant
454 pages, Paperback, ISBN 9789492355027

The essentials of magic in Chaldea are presented inside a context of comparison or contrast to Egyptian, Median, Turanian, Finno-Tartarian and Akkadian magic, mythologies, religion and speech. Interesting is the Chaldean demonology, with its incubus, succubus, vampire, nightmare and many Elemental spirits, most of them coalesced with the primal powers of nature.

Unicorn
A mythological investigation
by Robert Brown Jr.
124 pages, Paperback, ISBN 9789492355072

Brown Jr. believes the unicorn to be a lunar symbol, and draws on mythology from a wide range of sources all over the world to build his case. The author discusses the heraldic use of the unicorn, relates the creature to ancient goddesses like Astarte, Hecate en the Gorgon Medusa, and provides the reader with lost esoteric Moon-lore.

Là-Bas
A Journey into the Self
by Joris-Karl Huysmans
378 pages, Paperback, ISBN 9789492355058

The plot of *Là-Bas* concerns the novelist Durtal, who is disgusted by the emptiness and vulgarity of the modern world. He seeks relief by turning to the study of the Middle Ages. Through his contacts in Paris, Durtal discovers that Satanism is not a thing of the past but alive and kicking in turn of the century France. The novel culminates with a description of a black mass.

Devil-worship in France
Or The Question of Lucifer
by Arthur Edward Waite
240 pages, Paperback, ISBN 9789492355065

In *Devil-Worship in France,* Waite attempts to discern what is genuine from what is fake in the evidence of 19th century Satanism. To get the answers he spends a great deal of time investigating the French Masonic echelon, debunking a "conspiracy of falsehood" and determining what should be understood by Satanism and what not. Huysmans' diabolical novel *Là-Bas* (1891) inspired Waite to write this sceptical analysis.

Testament of Solomon
A First Century AD Grimoire
76 pages, Paperback, ISBN 9789492355041

A first century AD grimoire, and therefore the oldest, and least known, of all grimoires (magical instruction books) in the occult tradition. The book describes health inflicting demons of zodiacal decans, summoned by King Solomon, and how he controlled them to use their forces to build his temple and more. Translated by F. C. Conybeare, appeared first in the *Jewish Quarterly Review* of October, 1898.

Amazons - *Two publications in one book* -
I. *The Amazons* by Guy Cadogan Rothery
II. *Religious Cults Associated With the Amazons*
    by Florence Mary Bennett
328 pages, Paperback, ISBN 9789492355089

Contents I: The Amazons of Antiquity – Amazons
in Far Asia – Modern Amazons of the Caucasus –
Amazons of Europe – Amazons of Africa – Amazons of
America – The Amazon Stones.
Contents II: The Amazons in Greek legend – The Great
Mother – Ephesian Artemis – Artemis Astrateia and
Apollo Amazonius – Ares.

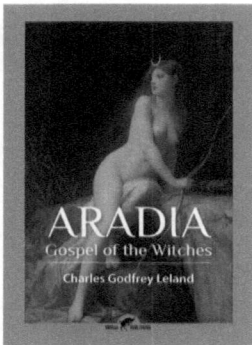

Aradia
Gospel of the Witches
by Charles Godfrey Leland
174 pages, Paperback, ISBN 9789492355010

This wonderful book describes the creation according to
Italian witch-lore. We also read about the witch-meeting
or sabbath (treguenda) and the book contains many
original magical recipes, like spells for love and good
fortune. Diana is further connected to the Moon and
the fairy world.

Etruscan Magic & Occult Remedies
(Two volumes in one book)
Charles Godfrey Leland
628 pages, Paperback, ISBN 9789492355003

Part One of the book gives us a complete and detailed
insight in the Etruscan and Roman rooted pantheon of
the Tuscan Streghe (witches). Part Two describes many
of their spells, incantations, sorcery and several lost
divination methods. Much information in this book,
Leland received first hand from the Tuscan witches
Maddalena and Marietta.

Ophiolatreia
Rites and Mysteries of Serpent Worship
Author: Hargrave Jennings
186 pages, Paperback, ISBN 9789492355126

An account of the rites and mysteries connected with the origin, rise and development of serpent worship in various parts of the world, enriched with interesting traditions, and a full description of the celebrated serpent mounds & temples, the whole forming an exposition of one of the phases of phallic, or sex worship.

Voodoos and Obeahs
Phases of West India Witchcraft
by Joseph J. Williams
374 pages, Paperback, ISBN 9789492355119

This work goes into great depth concerning the New World-African connection and is highly recommended if you want a deep understanding of the dramatic historical background of Haitian and Jamaican magic and witchcraft, and the profound influence of imperialism, slavery and racism on its development. Williams includes numerous quotations from rare documents and books on the topic.